THE PAINTED LADIES GU
TO VICTORIAN CALIFORNIA

Elizabeth Pomada
and
Michael Larsen

THE PAINTED LADIES™ GUIDE TO VICTORIAN CALIFORNIA

B & B's, Restaurants, Museums,
Groups & Suppliers

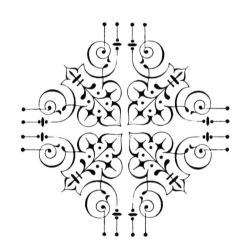

Dutton Studio Books
NEW YORK

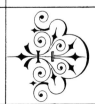

PHOTOGRAPH CREDITS

The photographs in this book were taken by Michael Larsen with the following exceptions:
The Red Victorian Bed & Breakfast Inn, Chateau Tivoli, The Sherman House, Spencer House, The Conservatory, The Miniature Mart, Jill Pilaroscia Architectural Colour, The Gingerbread Mansion, Linden Hall, Dillon's Antiques, Carroll Avenue, The Morey Mansion, Carson Mansion, and Heritage Square, Pasadena, by Douglas Keister;

The Archbishop's Mansion by Russell Abraham; Café Majestic by Café Majestic; Haas-Lilienthal House by Foundation for S.F. Heritage; Little/Raidl Design Studio by Roy Little; McGonaghy House by Kevin L. Levine; Falkirk Cultural Center by Elise Meyers; Lyford House by D. Morton; The Gables by owner; Sharpsteen Museum by owner; Hope-Merrill House by Robert Janover; Shaw House Inn by Bob von Normann; An Elegant Victorian by Doug Vieyra; Carter House by Patrick Cudahy; The Faulkner House by owner;

Crocker Art Museum by Crocker Art Museum; The Feather Bed by owner; Red Castle Inn, property of Mary Louise and Conley Weaver; Combellack-Blair House by A. McConnell; Winchester Mystery House by Winchester Mystery House; Victoriana by S. McNamans; Union Hotel by Steve Underwood; Workman Homestead by Julius Shulman; "Lucky" Baldwin's Queen Anne Cottage by L.A. Arboretum; Angels Attic by owner; The General Phineas Banning Residence Museum by Banning Foundation; Kimberley Crest House by Kimberley Foundation; Pinson & Ware by artists; Heritage Park Bed & Breakfast Inn by Heritage Park; Hotel del Coronado by Hotel del Coronado.

ACKNOWLEDGMENTS

Many thanks to the intrepid Victorian network and the many docents we've met, unsung heroes who help preserve the past to make our present understandable and our future hopeful. Thanks especially to the Victorian Alliance and Richard Zilman, to the Foundation for San Francisco's Architectural Heritage, Artistic License, and our "readers," colorist Jill Pilaroscia, Deborah Sakach of American Historic Inns, and Murray Burns of the Eastlake Inn. As always, we couldn't have done this book without the help and encouragement of Cyril I. Nelson, our intrepid editor, and of our families: Antonia, Ray, Carol, Rita, Alberta, Nahid, and Denny & Diana.

DUTTON STUDIO BOOKS/Published by the Penguin Group: Penguin Books USA Inc., 375 Hudson Street, New York, New York, 10014, U.S.A.; Penguin Books Ltd, 27 Wrights Lane, London W8 5TZ, England; Penguin Books Australia Ltd, Ringwood, Victoria, Australia; Penguin Books Canada Ltd, 2801 John Street, Markham, Ontario, Canada L3R 1B4; Penguin Books (N.Z.) Ltd, 182-190 Wairau Road, Auckland 10, New Zealand/Penguin Books Ltd, Registered Offices: Harmondsworth, Middlesex, England/First published by Dutton Studio Books, an imprint of Penguin Books USA Inc./ First printing, October, 1991/Copyright © Elizabeth Pomada and Michael Larsen, 1991/All rights reserved/Library of Congress Catalog Card Number: 91-75605./Printed and bound by Dai Nippon Printing Co., Ltd., Tokyo, Japan/Book designed by Marilyn Rey/Without limiting the rights under copyright reserved above, no part of this publication may be reproduced, stored in or introduced into a retrieval system, or transmitted, in any form, or by any means (electronic, mechanical, photocopying, recording, or otherwise), without the prior written permission of both the copyright owner and the publisher of the book./ISBN: 0-525-93363-8 (cloth); ISBN: 0-525-48594-5 (DP).
10 9 8 7 6 5 4 3 2 1 First Edition

CONTENTS

THE PAINTED LADIES GUIDE TO VICTORIAN CALIFORNIA

CRESCENT
CITY

•YREKA

•MT. SHASTA

ARCATA
EUREKA
FORTUNA
FERNDALE
•SCOTIA

WEAVERVILLE

•RED BLUFF

SUSANVILLE

WESTPORT
FORT BRAGG
MENDOCINO •WILLITS
LITTLE RIVER
ELK   UKIAH
GUALALA LAKE PLATT
HOPLAND
•CLOVERDALE
•GEYSERVILLE
MIDDLETOWN

•CHICO

QUINCY

•OROVILLE

MARYSVILLE   NEVADA
•YUBA CITY   CITY
GRASS CITY

TRUCKEE

WILLIAMS

NEWCASTLE AUBURN
ROSEVILLE • •GEORGETOWN
•WOODLAND •COLOMA
SACRAMENTO — •PLACERVILLE

SANTA ROSA
ST HELENA
GLEN ELLEN
•YOUNTVILLE
•NAPA YACAVILLE
PETALUMA SONOMA
OLEMA

BODEGA
BODEGA BAY
TOMALES

VALLEJO
•MARTINEZ
•BENICIA
•BERKELEY
•ALAMEDA
•OAKLAND
•SAN LEANDRO
•HAYWARD
FREMONT

SAN
FRANCISCO

HALF
MOON
BAY   RED
WOOD
CITY •PALO ALTO
•SAN JOSE
•SANTA CLARA
•LOS GATOS
BEN LOMOND
APTOS
SANTA CRUZ
CAPITOLA •WATSONVILLE
PACIFIC •SAN JUAN BATISTA
GROVE
MONTEREY

•LODI

AMADOR CITY
SUTTER CREEK
JACKSON
SAN ANDREAS
MURPHYS
ANGELS CAMP
COLUMBIA
•STOCKTON SONORA
JAMESTOWN TUOLUMNE

•MODESTO

•MARIPOSA
•FISH CAMP
OAKHURST

•BISHOP

•MADERA

FRESNO

•SELMA
•HANFORD VISALIA

•PORTERVILLE

•SALINAS

PASO ROBLES
•CAMBRIA
•TEMPLETON

•SAN LUIS OBISPO
•ARROYO GRANDE
•NIPOMO

•BAKERSFIELD

•LOS ALAMOS
•LOS OLIVOS
GOLETA
SANTA BARBARA
VENTURA SIMI VALLEY
CALABASAS •BURBANK
SANTA MONICA PASADENA
•ARCADIA
•MONROVIA
LOS
ANGELES •REDLANDS
WILMINGTON •RIVERSIDE •DESERT
HOT SPRINGS
•SANTA ANA
NEWPORT BEACH
•EL TORO

CATALINA
ISLAND

•JULIAN

SAN
DIEGO
•NATIONAL CITY

INTRODUCTION

The Painted Ladies Guide to Victorian California grew out of a listing of San Francisco Victoriana in the back of our last book, *The Painted Ladies Revisited*. As with the other Painted Ladies books, we have tried to make the book attractive enough to be a souvenir of a trip out West or a gift for the Victoriana buff back home.

With two major exceptions, *The Painted Ladies Guide to Victorian California* is the first inventory published of anything that might be of interest to people who like Victorian architecture. The guide is intended to be of value to people who live here as well as visitors to the state, who have only a limited time to see what the state has to offer.

Here are the two exceptions mentioned above. First, to do justice to the state's Victorian buildings would require more than one book on the architecture alone. We hope to give this magnificent legacy its due in future volumes. Many towns provide free maps of walking tours, and the books in the bibliography will guide you to most of what we've left out.

If an entry mentions a person or house included in one or more of the Painted Ladies books, the initials of the book appear at the end of the entry so that readers can refer to the book if they wish more information:

(PL)   *Painted Ladies*
(DPL) *Daughters of Painted Ladies*
(PLR) *The Painted Ladies Revisited*
(HTC) *How to Create a Painted Lady*

The second exception that we haven't covered is the world of California antiques, which, for the most part, we've left to the handy free guides available in most places.

The guide does try to be thorough in its listings of bed and breakfasts (B & B's), hotels, house museums, restaurants, preservation organizations, classes, tour groups, media, and suppliers of goods and services that would be helpful to homeowners.

To try to prevent the guide from becoming too dated too soon, it doesn't include exact prices. Instead, it uses a three-letter code:

(I)   Inexpensive
(M) Moderate
(E) Expensive

Five Tips

1. Many suppliers have catalogs. Again, the guide doesn't mention prices, so call if you wish to order one.

2. Most Victorians are not wheelchair-accessible. The guide indicates those that are.

3. Ladies: Avoid spike heels in Victorians. They may damage the floors.

4. Avoid smoking in Victorians. Regardless of how they feel about the questions of health and potential damage, owners of historic houses have to keep their Victorians smoke-free for insurance purposes.

5. Small businesses may close up unexpectedly or go out of business. Call before traveling far. This holds true especially for B & B's and for craftspeople, whom you should always call first because they are often out working and meet clients by appointment.

The Politics of Preservation

The Painted Ladies Guide to Victorian California is an economic, political, and preservation document. Government at all levels tends to be indifferent about preservation, if not downright hostile to it. What it does crave is economic development, and as J. Jackson Walter, president of the National Trust for Historic Preservation, has noted: "Historic preservation is the best form of economic development."

When you spend money in or on a Victorian, you are supporting preservation. California's Victorians generate hundreds of millions of dollars a year. This makes them an important factor in the state's economy. We hope that this guide will help Victorians earn the bureaucrats' respect, if not their love, so they will provide the laws and the funds needed to protect the state's architectural legacy.

Most of the people in the guide are entrepreneurs. One hopeful sign for the Victorians is the new generation of entrepreneurs across America who are creating livelihoods for themselves by bringing new life and interest to the Victorians.

Thinking Ahead

The guide hasn't rated entries, nor can it guarantee satisfaction from them. If you have any unusual experiences—joyful or difficult—because of any of the entries, please share them with us. They will help in preparing the next edition.

The guide is the longest of the Painted Ladies books and was the hardest to research. This kind of information has never been put together before. The bed-and-breakfast guides that have already been published helped with the B & B's, but B & B's go in and out of business faster than any guide can keep track of them.

The Old-House Journal Catalog, an invaluable aid to homeowners no matter where they live, helped with suppliers and craftspeople. But finding every craftsperson in the state who specializes in Victorians is a challenge we can only hope to come close to meeting. This is why we are very anxious to have your reaction to the guide, so we can make it as helpful to you as possible.

We would like the next edition of the guide to be as complete as possible, so if there's anything you would like to see in the next edition, or if you find anything that we left out or you discover something new, please call 415-673-0939, or write to 1029 Jones St., San Francisco, CA 94109. Please send information and photographs if they're available.

If you are the first person to send us information about a new entry (and you don't own it!), we will acknowledge your contribution in the next edition and send you a free copy. Many thanks in advance for your help.

California has a lifetime's worth of natural beauty, great architecture of all kinds, and fun things to do. Since this guide can't be exhaustive about everything that the state has to offer, use it in conjunction with general guides. You might find Elizabeth's book *Places to Go with Children in Northern California* helpful. In most cases, what kids enjoy, you will too.

We were surprised and delighted to discover the depth and richness of California's Victorian resources, and we're already looking forward to a bigger and better second edition.

The ABC's of B & B's

Having seen almost every Victorian bed-and-breakfast in the state, we would like to offer some observations and advice that will help you understand and make the most of the experience.

Staying at a B & B is a chance to escape the problems of everyday life and indulge in the fantasy of living in the past. But a B & B is an expression of the owner's taste, vision, budget, creativity, and attention to detail, so B & B's vary as much as the people who own them. That's why morning fare can vary from a simple continental breakfast to a full-scale feast.

Bed-and-breakfast owners sometimes do something special like piloting hot-air balloons or making wine or jam, doing needlepoint, or collecting dolls. Hobbies such as these can make your stay memorable.

We sometimes wonder if all human motivation doesn't boil down to love or money. Successful B & B's are usually created with both. They are labors of love that require significant investments of money as well as energy.

Because they are labors of love, the people that own them are dedicated, hardworking, and a pleasure to know. In fact, during the fourteen years that we've been working on the Painted Ladies books, we've found that people who own, enjoy, and work with Victorians are a very likable group of people.

Two of the couples we met in the Gold Country who own B & B's are refugees from Los Angeles, and they are delighted with the new lives they have created in old houses. Doing what you love must be good for you.

Minding Your B's & Q's

Here is some advice about staying at B & B's:

People: Staying at a B & B involves meeting people. Since it is usually someone's home, the first person you meet is the owner, who will tell you about the inn, attend to your needs, and give you good advice about the best way to spend time in the area.

Indeed, how the owner welcomes you is an essential factor in how much you enjoy your stay. Guests may not fare as well at the hands of paid staff people, who may not be as caring or knowledgeable as an owner, for whom running an inn is not just a job but a way of life.

Staying at a B & B is an excellent way to make friends with people from different places with similar interests. As you will see from the guestbooks visitors sign, people from all over the world stay at B & B's. Breakfast, afternoon tea, even sharing a bathroom presents an opportunity to meet people. This is good news if you're a gregarious extrovert. If you prefer privacy, plan your stay accordingly.

Decor: Most B & B's are decorated in a country-Victorian style rather than the High Victorian style found in some of the San Francisco bed-and-breakfasts. At the same time, staying at B & B's will inspire decorating ideas for your home.

Pets: Many B & B's have a cat or dog. We've indicated pets when we found them. If you're allergic to animals, ask about them when you call to reserve a room.

Feathers: Many B & B's have feather comforters and pillows. Sensuous if you like them, Sneeze City if you're allergic to them. Check when you reserve.

Children: Although B & B's cannot legally deny admittance to children, they're usually not welcome because of the potential noise and the potential damage to irreplaceable antiques. B & B's that welcome children are indicated.

Here today: It usually takes five years for a B & B to start earning money. New B & B owners who aren't prepared for the wait don't always make it from the red to the black. So don't turn up on somebody's doorstep without calling first.

Here tomorrow: During peak season, busy B & B's may require that you stay more than one night.

Compared to the homogenized simplicity of a motel or the impersonal anonymity of a hotel, staying at a B & B is the next best thing to living in one. It is truly a home away from home.

SAN FRANCISCO

"Careful now, we're dealing here with a myth.
This city is a point upon a map of fog, Lemuria in a
sea unknown. Like us, it doesn't quite exist."
                    —Ambrose Bierce

Welcome to the Victorian capital of the United States! San Francisco has more to offer fans of Victoriana than any other city in America.

For visitors, there are museums, B & B's, restaurants, and tours. For visitors and residents, there are classes, auction houses, organizations, painters, color consultants, craftspeople, and other suppliers of goods and services that help to maintain the city's major attraction: the greatest collection of redwood Victorians in the world.

By 1906, almost 50,000 Victorians had been built in San Francisco. The 13,437 Victorians that have survived "progress" offer a feast for the eyes no matter what your taste in color or architecture.

San Francisco's Victorians come in all sizes, from cottages to mansions, and in an amazing mélange of styles and substyles including Italianate, Gothic Revival, Queen Anne, Queen Anne cottages, Queen Anne row houses, Queen Anne Eclectic, Queen Anne French Revival, Colonial Queen Anne, Stick, Stick cottages, San Francisco Stick, Stick/Eastlake, Stick/ Italianate villas, Colonial Revival, Classic Revival, Elizabethan or Old English, and French neo-Baroque.

Add to these the thousands of handsome Edwardians in town, and you have a treasure trove of gorgeous architecture that will repay with pleasure the time you devote to it.

San Francisco is a city of neighborhoods, and it's in the neighborhoods outside downtown that you will discover the city's Victorian legacy. Drive or walk around Pacific Heights, the Western Addition, Haight Ashbury, Eureka and Noe Valleys, the Mission District, and Potrero Hill.

Painted Ladies: San Francisco's Resplendent Victorians and *The Painted Ladies Revisited: San Francisco's Resplendent Victorians Inside and Out* are laid out so that you can tour the neighborhoods that they're in. If you use the books as a basis for discovering the Victorians and digress where your eyes lead you, you'll do fine.

For more information about Victorian architecture in San Francisco, read *Here Today: San Francisco's Architectural Heritage*, text by Roger Olmsted and T. H. Watkins, photographs by Morley Baer and others; and *Victoria's Legacy* by Judith Lynch Waldhorn and Sally B. Woodbridge, drawings by Wendy Wheeler. Both, alas, are out of print. Also look for *A Gift to the Street*, photographs by Carol Olwell, commentary by Judith Lynch Waldhorn.

Few pleasures in life are greater than roaming around San Francisco on a sunny day discovering the city's fabulous collection of Victorians. We envy you if you will be seeing them for the first time.

Bed-and-Breakfast Inns

Alamo Square Inn 719 Scott St. at Fulton, 94117; 415-922-2055 (M/E). Eliza Baum built her own Queen Anne/Classic Revival home in 1895, and Wayne Corn and Klause May restored it, joining it to the Craftsman/ Classical home next door to create a welcoming inn. The inn is located on Alamo Square diagonally across the street from the famous Westerfeld Mansion.

Shiny oak floors and wood paneling, a stately staircase with a stained-glass skylight, fireplaces, and homey yet authentic touches add to the comfort of the rooms, which range from cozy singles to pleasant

The Archbishop's Mansion, San Francisco

suites. The parlors blend Victorian and Oriental appointments to create an inviting setting for afternoon tea and sherry. Continental breakfast is served in the solarium connecting the two buildings. An innovative catering staff is on hand for weddings and meetings.

The Archbishop's Mansion 1000 Fulton St., 94117; 415-563-7872/800-543-5820 (M/E). Built in 1904 for Archbishop Patrick Riordan, this Second Empire mansion is one of the grandest of San Francisco's historic land-mark homes. After the earthquake, the mansion served as a refugee center, and its vault housed the city's gold bars and important papers. Jonathan Shannon and Jeffrey Ross have designed each room individually, mixing fine antiques with reproductions, Oriental rugs, rich tapes-tries, hand-painted ceilings, and unique treasures to give the Mansion a comfortable luxuriousness.

Since Fulton Street slopes downhill to the Opera House six blocks away, each of the fifteen rooms has been designed to reflect the spirit of a nineteenth-century opera, from the cozy La Bohème room to the imposing Don Giovanni suite. Our favorite is the Carmen suite with its tempting bath in front of the fireplace (most rooms have fireplaces) and the libretto handy for reading in the W.C. behind the antique screen.

All the amenities one could ask for are here, including an elevator and limousine service. Breakfast is served in baskets brought to the room. Afternoon wine is served in the front parlor under the glorious ribboned ceiling created by stencil artist Larry Boyce. Parties held in the central hallway are serenaded with Noël Coward's 1904 Bechstein grand piano. Meetings and receptions may be arranged. (PLR)

Art Center Bed & Breakfast 1902 Filbert St. at Laguna, 94123; 415-567-1526 (M). This cute little blue, adobe tan, and white Stick cottage was built to resemble the Louisiana home the owner had left during the Gold Rush, next to what was Washer Woman's Cove, a freshwater lagoon at the foot of Laguna Street. Today, George and Helvi Wamsley combine their art gallery and

Chateau Tivoli, San Francisco

workshop with four country-fresh guest apartments with stocked kitchens and fireplaces. The "I Left My Heart in San Francisco" Suite has a Jacuzzi and a fireplace. Children are welcome, and there's a little garden.

The Bed-and-Breakfast Inn 2 and 4 Charlton Ct., 94123; 415-921-9784 (M/E). Located on a quiet mews off chic Union Street, this was one of San Francisco's first B & B's, and it is still a small, cozy, romantic hideaway. The simple Italianate structures, painted four shades of green, white, and black, house ten cheerful rooms ranging from tiny "pension rooms" with sinks and shared baths to The Mayfair, a penthouse apartment with a kitchen, two baths, a loft bedroom, and huge living space. Each room is stocked with fruit and mineral water, and fortune cookies are to be found on your pillow at night. The library and garden are perfect for unwinding.

Chateau Tivoli 1057 Steiner St., 94115; 415-776-5462/800-228-1647 (M/E). One of San Francisco's newest B & B's is America's most glorious Painted Lady. Owners Rodney Karr and Willard Gersbach supervised contractor Russell Epstein on the total restoration and in selecting the twenty-two colors of paint for the exterior. Fifteen thousand dollars' worth of gold leaf was used to embellish the Chateau. In 1989, the California Heritage Council named Chateau Tivoli the best restoration of a Victorian house in California.

The majestic Chateauesque/Queen Anne was built in 1892 for Oregon lumber baron Daniel B. Jackson by architect William Armitage. In 1898, it was bought by Mrs. Ernestine Kreling, owner of the Tivoli Opera House, who made her home a social center. In 1929, a Yiddish school took over, making it the Yiddish cultural center of the Bay Area until 1961. During the sixties, it became a center for hippies and a New Age group who allowed the place to fall into complete ruin.

Wedding receptions and conferences are held on the lavishly decorated first floor.

The five spacious rooms and two suites are graced with flowers and fruit and beautified with Bradbury & Bradbury wallpaper. Continental breakfast and afternoon libations are offered; masseuse and limousine services are available. (PLR)

Inn on Castro 321 Castro St. off Market, 94114; 415-861-0321 (M). Eclecticism reigns in this B & B in the heart of the Castro district. There are contemporary furnishings, paintings, and exotic plants throughout the five rooms, all with private bath. Oriental paper umbrellas cover the ceiling of one room. Another is decorated with an aviary of hand-painted birds. The exterior blues, grays, turquoises, and pinks seen in *Painted Ladies Revisited* give this B & B curb appeal.

The Inn San Francsico 943 South Van Ness Ave., 94110; 415-641-0188 (M/E). Painted in mauve, plum, rose, cream, teal, and a splash of gold leaf, this 1872 Italianate was the home of Mr. and Mrs. John English and their seven children. The English family raised polo ponies on the surrounding grounds. Architect Deborah Daily and her brother, Joel, bought the house in 1977, and spent two years restoring the stuccoed façade with San Francisco Renaissance. Jill Pilaro-

The Inn San Francisco, San Francisco

scia added the finishing touch with her gold leaf–enriched design. The discovery of an existing residential hotel license led to the idea of establishing a bed-and-breakfast.

Red velvet curtains, the original fretwork, thick fringed shades, silk-lined walls, stained glass, marble mantels, and shiny brass and glass create a soigné decor.

Victorian comforts such as heavy, quieting draperies and flickering candles blend with contemporary conveniences like the hot tub in the solarium of the most romantic suite as well as amenities such as the television, telephones, and small refrigerators. A bountiful breakfast buffet is served in the elaborate double front parlors or in the flower-filled garden. The gazebo under the fig tree in the back garden shelters a hot tub. Guests may also enjoy the panoramic view of San Francisco from the rooftop sun deck. There are twenty-two rooms, most with bath, some with a spa or fireplace.

Jackson Court 2198 Jackson St. at Buchanan, 94115; 415-929-7670 (M). This baronial 1901 brownstone in a quiet Pacific Heights neighborhood, built by the Callahan family, who lived there until 1951, exemplifies San Francisco's "do-your-own-thing" tradition. Sculpted into a grand fireplace, which commands the main parlor, are the faces of the original master and mistress of the house. They gaze at you above two cherubs who represent the East and West winds gently blowing harmony across the hearth. The turn-of-the-century ambience throughout the seven capacious rooms and three suites attracts overnighters and time-share owners who also appreciate the two fully stocked kitchens and knowledgeable concierge service.

The Langtry 637 Steiner St., 94117; 415-863-0538 (M/E). This restored towering 1894 Queen Anne B & B has been designed by women with women in mind. Each of the four rooms, from cozy to voluminous, with or without bath, is named after a well-known woman: Virginia Woolf, Natalie Barney, Mary McLeod Bethune, and Eleanor Roosevelt. The Victoria Woodhull Suite is three top-floor rooms sleeping four, with a breakfast nook in the turret overlooking the city.

A soufflé breakfast is served in your room or in the large kitchen. Afternoon tea and wine are communal, and there's always a crystal decanter on your nightstand for nightcaps. You can relax in the hot tub on the starlit wooden deck. The owners are members of the Bay Area Women's Network. Limousine service from the airport, catered dinners, parties, meetings, and secretarial service can be arranged. Male guests are welcome.

The Majestic 1500 Sutter St. at Gough, 94109; 415-441-1100/800-869-8966 (M/E). Quiet, impeccable, old-world manners reign in this imposing five-story 1902 structure, one of the city's oldest hotels. French Empire and English antiques elicit memories of a genteel, elegant home and evoke the ambience of a golden era. Canopy beds and armoires make the fifty-one rooms and nine suites comfortable. Visual delights abound, from marble fireplaces to a nineteenth-century Napoleon III ormolu bronze clock with Neoclassical winged figures in the lobby parlor to yellow Regency monkey murals in the elevator.

When you walk into the opulent marble and verdigris lobby, you understand why the Majestic has been awarded a Certificate of Recognition for Architectural Preservation and Restoration by the California Heritage Council. Valet parking, downtown limousine service, concierge service, and well-equipped meeting rooms are available, along with valet and room service. The hotel and restaurant (please see below) are wheelchair-accessible.

The Mansions Hotel 2220 Sacramento St., 94115; 415-929-9444 (M/E). The Mansions Hotel is two side-by-side historic mansions. The stone Queen Anne built in 1887 by Senator Charles Chambers is a registered historic landmark. Queen Victoria would appreciate the spirit of play in this outrageous, irreverent extravaganza. Claudia, the resident ghost, plays the parlor piano.

Owner Bob Pritikin plays the saw in the Victorian cabaret theater. And a wild sense of humor prevails over this maddeningly eclectic collection of fine and funny treasures, with Beniamino Bufano sculpture vying for attention with stuffed toys.

Along with the nineteen small to grand rooms, all with private bath, and all strangely endearing, there's a billiard room and a wishing well. Full breakfast is served, with tongue in cheek, in the country kitchen or in bed. Meeting and dining rooms can accommodate banquets, conferences, and special occasions.

The Monte Cristo B & B 600 Presidio, 94115; 415-931-1875 (M). This 1875 saloon and hotel was also a bordello, a refuge after the 1906 earthquake, and a speakeasy. Each of the fifteen rooms has a special touch, such as a 250-year-old wedding bed or a sunken tiled tub. The house is furnished in American antiques.

Nob Hill Inn 1000 Pine St. at Taylor, 94109; 415-673-6080 (M/E). Built just after the 1906 earthquake and fire, this small gracious hotel, done in the subdued manner of a London town house, is in walking distance of Union Square, the financial district, and Chinatown. Twenty-one rooms, including suites and apartments with kitchens, are romantically decorated with original tile-faced fireplaces and fine silks. Guests will appreciate the fresh flowers and chocolates. Croissants, fresh juice, and coffee are served for breakfast, bedside on Victorian wicker trays or in the drawing room. Bob Buckter created the polychrome color scheme.

Nolan House 1071 Page St., 94117; 415-863-0384 (M). Guests in this quiet 1889 cream, pale gray, gray-blue, and black Queen Anne/Eastlake home in the Haight Ashbury district enjoy six cheerful rooms, all with feather beds and private baths. The four original bedrooms, done up in French Victorian antiques and period decor with fine woods and chandeliers, have their original marble fireplaces. Children are

welcome. A full American breakfast is served and off-street parking is available.

The Queen Anne 1590 Sutter St. at Octavia, 94109; 415-441-2828 (M). Built in 1890 as Miss Mary Lake's School for Girls, The Queen Anne is a comfortable Victorian-style guesthouse. The forty-nine rooms and suites are individually decorated with English and American antiques, wood-burning fireplaces, bay windows, and authentic Victoriana. Continental breakfast is served in the rooms; tea and sherry are served on silver trays each afternoon in the parlor. Guests may opt for elevators rather than mounting the restored grand staircase. Some rooms are equipped for the handicapped. The Queen Anne's three meeting rooms can accommodate from 10 to 150 people.

The Red Victorian Bed & Breakfast Inn 1665 Haight St., 94117; 415-864-1978 (M/E). The sixties are alive and well in "the Haight." Owner and artist-in-residence Sami Sunchild feels that her "American Beauty Rose" Victorian celebrates the Flower-Power history of the area, so if you missed the Summer of Love the first time around, here's a second chance. Originally built in 1904 as a country-resort hotel, the Red Victorian boasts a collection of fifteen unique rooms that evoke nostalgic memories.

Choose from the arboreal Conservatory, the peaceful Japanese Tea Garden, the dazzling Flower Child Room, and the Peacock Suite with a moon window looking from the bathtub in the bedroom to the sitting room with its Indian awning, turn-of-the-century electric fireplace, and Persian temple lamp. The rooms that share baths have wonderful hand-painted ceramic sinks. Even the baths are imaginative creations. Sami's transformational poem-paintings line the walls. Guests from all over the world relax in the Meditation Room, along with the cat and dog.

Continental breakfast, afternoon tea, and inspirational videos are always available in the Global Village Marketplace, Peace Bazaar, and EcoCenter on the ground floor.

The Red Victorian Bed & Breakfast Inn, San Francisco

Painted Ladies fans will appreciate Bob Buckter's five reds, two roses, two greens, two violets, gray, silver, eggshell, turquoise, and two golds on the vibrant award-winning exterior. Check for robin's-egg blue in the egg-and-dart molding.

San Remo Hotel 2237 Mason St., 94133; 415-776-8688 (I/M). A. P. Giannini, founder of the Bank of America, built this hotel, a three-story Italianate, the month after the 1906 earthquake for the merchants and fishermen on the Wharf. Thomas and Robert Field have renovated and restored it, retaining the Victorian working-class flavor that makes it popular with budget-minded travelers today.

There are sixty-two small but sweet antiques-decorated rooms, with the "residential" rooms rented by the week smaller and more spare than the "tourist" rooms.

Most rooms have sinks. The multiple-bath facilities sparkle with Victorian tile floors, clawfooted tubs, and brass pull-chain toilets with oak tanks and brass fixtures and accessories. Bathrooms are cleaned every hour! Guests appreciate the San Francisciana on the walls, the abundant greenery and skylights, the self-service snack bar, baskets of muffins, the laundry facilities, and the general camaraderie.

Views of Coit Tower, and Telegraph, Nob, and Russian Hills seen through leaded-glass windows make this small inn attractive, as does its proximity to Fisherman's Wharf and North Beach. The romantic rooftop penthouse, with views of Coit Tower and the city, and a small private bath, is a Best Buy.

The New San Remo Restaurant downstairs serves hearty Italian fare in a Victorian setting.

The Sherman House, San Francisco

service. An intimate dining room serves meals. Receptions and seminars may be arranged. A limousine can whisk you from the airport to a home that once welcomed Luisa Tetrazzini, Victor Herbert, David Belasco, and Lotta Crabtree. (See below for restaurant information.)

Spencer House 1080 Haight St. at Baker, 94117; 415-626-9205 (M/E). Designed for John Spencer in 1887, this Queen Anne Painted Lady, noted for its rare eight-sided Palladian tower and splendid interior woodwork, has been turned into an elegant, comfortable European-style bed-and-breakfast by Jack and Barbara Chambers. Candlelight breakfasts are served in the formal dining room, which boasts the original Lincrusta wall covering, a built-in buffet with arches that echo the Palladian entryway, and combination gas and electric chandeliers and sconces.

Barbara collects Napoleonic art and memorabilia that is blended with the carefully chosen and restored antiques purchased here and in England and used throughout the inn. As with most English manors, there are dogs in residence. The

The Sherman House 2160 Green St., 94123; 415-563-3600/800-424-5777 (E). An intimate luxury hotel, part of the prestigious Relais & Chateaux group, has been created a block from Union Street in the frosted-white 1876 Mansard mansion built for Leander Sherman, founder of the Sherman Clay Music Company. Manou Mobedshahi, the owner, spent four years restoring the mansion with well-known interior designer William Gaylord.

Each of the fourteen rooms and suites is individually designed and meticulously furnished in French Second Empire, Biedermeier, or English Jacobean style. Tapestried canopies on the feather beds are balanced with modern amenities such as wet bars, whirlpool tubs in black-granite bathrooms, and hidden stereo and TV systems. Some suites have two fireplaces. One suite in the carriage house has two private gardens and a gazebo.

Personal and professional services abound, including twenty-four-hour room

Spencer House, San Francisco

restored parquet floors demand a "no spike heels" request, always a good idea on old floors. (PL, PLR)

Stanyan Park Hotel 750 Stanyan St. at Waller, 94117; 415-751-1000 (M). The oldest existing hotel on the border of Golden Gate Park, the Stanyan Park was built in 1904 and has always been a hotel. Now listed on the National Register of Historic Places, this Queen Anne is painted in three shades of adobe rose-taupe. The hotel offers thirty redone rooms and six large suites, light and airy with English and American Victorian furnishings. Continental breakfast and afternoon tea and cookies are served. The suites are suitable for small receptions and meetings. Four of the suites, with two bedrooms, living room, dining room, and full kitchen, are a Best Buy for families.

Union Street Inn 2229 Union St., 94123; 415-346-0424 (M/E). Located on one of the City's most popular shopping streets, this inn combines the charm and elegance of a nineteenth-century Edwardian home (1902) with the friendly, personal attention of a European-style pensione. A golden retriever guards the five colorful rooms. The carriage house, separated from the inn by an old-fashioned English garden, has a refrigerator and a Jacuzzi. Guests will enjoy lingering over coffee in the garden, with its holly tree, lilacs, roses, and camellias. The innkeeper will arrange for cars, theater tickets, and tours.

Victorian Inn on the Park 301 Lyon St. at Fell, 94117; 415-931-1830 (M/E). This imposing landmark Queen Anne built in 1897, in Queen Victoria's Diamond Jubilee Year, bedecked in pale gray, blue, and white, faces the panhandle of Golden Gate Park. The elaborate architectural detail, fireplaces, and fine wood floors and paneling were designed by architect William Curlett and have been lovingly restored. A view of the city beckons from the balustraded porch of the open belvedere in the Belvedere Suite, which also has two fireplaces. The twelve rooms, all with private bath, are graced with

mahogany paneling and Bradbury & Bradbury wallpapers. Fresh-baked pastries and fruit platters are served in the oak-paneled dining room. Small meeting facilities are available.

The Washington Square Inn 1660 Stockton St. at Filbert, 94133; 415-981-4220/800-388-0220 (M/E). Overlooking Washington Square, this small, comfortable hotel in North Beach is in walking distance of Fisherman's Wharf and Chinatown. The fifteen rooms, with shared and private baths, sitting areas, and lovely views, are cheerfully decorated in Laura Ashley country style. Continental breakfast, afternoon tea, and wine are included.

Restaurants

Big Four Huntington Hotel, 1075 California St. at Taylor, 94108; 415-771-1140 (M). Named after the nineteenth-century railroad titans Huntington, Crocker, Stanford, and Hopkins, the Big Four restaurant serves excellent California cuisine. Decorated by designer Tony Hale with green leather banquettes, etched glass, and shiny brass, the Big Four is reminiscent of an elegant men's club. The restaurant is a perfect showcase for an extensive collection of Victorian California photographs and memorabilia. You can dine well, and learn about San Francisco history at the same time, at breakfast, lunch, and dinner, seven days a week.

Café Majestic Hotel Majestic, 1500 Sutter St. at Gough, 94109; 415-776-6400 (M). Owner Tom Marshall serves innovative California and contemporary cuisine sparked by Victorian recipes and themes for breakfast, lunch, and dinner in a lovely re-creation of the original Victorian dining room. Fluted columns, potted palms, and pianists who play jazz and classical pieces add to the ambience. The Christmas menu is a replica of one served at the Majestic at the turn of the century, and many holiday dishes are authentic.

The adjacent bar, walled by an antique

collection of rare butterflies and centered around a nineteenth-century French mahogany bar, creates the ambience of a private Victorian club.

Garden Court Sheraton Palace, Market St. at New Montgomery, 94105; 415-392-8600 (M). The Garden Court is an authentic Victorian palm garden, surrounded by palatial columns and illuminated by a sparkling stained-glass skylight. Enrico Caruso was here when the 1906 earthquake interrupted his breakfast of oysters. He fled, never to return. Recently painstakingly restored, the Garden Court is the centerpiece for the historic hotel, a national registered landmark, and is one of the most important Victorian rooms in America.

At its gala reopening, columnist Herb Caen wrote, "All is as it was, only better, and celebrates the meticulous artistry of the Bay Area's craftsmen. My god, we have a lot of talented people around here! And how wonderful to see what they can accomplish, given the time and money." Allen Dragge of Reflection Studios cleaned and repaired 70,000 pieces of glass in the 8,000-square-foot ceiling, which dates back to 1907 and has its own seismic bracing system.

Guests may enjoy breakfast, lunch, dinner, and brunch (to the sounds of live musicians). Or they may simply relax, have a cup of coffee, and watch the passing throng, as one could a century ago. The menu blends a turn-of-the-century feeling with contemporary cuisine.

The New San Remo Restaurant 2237 Mason St., 94133; 415-673-9090 (M). Housed in the San Remo Hotel, a handsome Victorian beautifully appointed with etched glass and flowers, antique fans, and a tin ceiling, the spacious, brightly lit dining room is a turn-of-the-century time capsule. The menu offers authentic Northern Italian cuisine and includes special lunches and five-course dinners at family-style prices. The cocktail lounge has a magnificent mahogany bar that once graced the old Red Garter on Broadway.

The Sherman House 2160 Green St., 94123;

415-563-3600 (E). The intimate, lavishly furnished dining room of one of San Francisco's internationally acclaimed small hotels is also open to the public for breakfast, musical Sunday brunches, lunch, and dinner by reservation. Tea and aperitifs are served in a Second Empire salon or in the solarium.

Places to Visit

The Columbarium 1 Loraine Ct. off Anza St., west of Stanyan, 94118; 415-221-1838/ 1611. Tour Saturday, 10 A.M. to 1 P.M., and by appointment. Designed by B.J.S. Cahill in 1898 and one of the great architectural masterpieces of the city, this Roman Baroque, Neoclassic structure is a symbol of the American Renaissance, with its ceiling mosaics, marble-inlaid floor, and superb stained-glass windows (one could be by John La Farge).

Victorians sought to regard death without fear or morbid feelings, and the light and airy interior of the Columbarium reflects that view as it is furnished like a Victorian parlor. Special slide lectures on the art and architecture of death and Victorian funeral customs, urns, and mourning outfits may be arranged. The nineteenth-century polychrome exterior was designed by Bob Buckter. Once the building has been completely restored by the Neptune Society, the three-acre park will be restored for meditation. (PLR)

The Conservatory John F. Kennedy Dr., Golden Gate Park, 94118; 415-666-7017. Daily, 9 A.M. to 6 P.M., April through October; until 5 P.M. in winter. Fee. Rental available. California's first municipal greenhouse, the oldest building in Golden Gate Park, was designed from prefabricated glass sections shipped around Cape Horn in 1875, to look like the Victoria and Albert Celebration Hall in London. This enormous glass structure, with mostly white leading and with a band of jeweled stained glass at the crest, took four years to construct, and was rebuilt after a fire in 1883. The exhibit of planted and potted plants changes with the seasons.

Café Majestic, San Francisco

Just past the Park Presidio overpass on a small lake, you can gaze at the Portals of the Past, all that remains of a Nob Hill mansion after the 1906 earthquake.

Haas-Lilienthal House 2007 Franklin St. 94109; 415-441-3004. Wednesday, 12 to 4 P.M.; Sunday, 11 A.M. to 4:30 P.M. Fee. Merchant William Haas built this magnificent redwood Queen Anne in 1886, and it is still kept as it was for the Haas-Lilienthal family. It's home for the Foundation for San Francisco's Architectural Heritage, and is open to a public wishing to see a handsomely furnished Victorian mansion. The Lincrusta-lined dining room is notable. The upstairs playroom is a treat for youngsters. Conser-

Garden Court, Sheraton Palace, San Francisco

The Conservatory, San Francisco

Haas-Lilienthal House, San Francisco

vation programs are offered, and the house is available for rentals. There are neighborhood weekend walks on Sundays at 12:30 P.M.

Museum of the City of San Francisco 2801 Leavenworth St., The Cannery, 11 A.M. to 4 P.M. Wednesday through Sunday, and by appointment. Free. Archivist Gladys Hansen has assembled a stellar collection of San Francisciana.

The Octagon 2645 Gough St. at Union, 94109; 415-441-7512. Noon to 3 P.M. on the second and fourth Thursday and the second Sunday of each month except January. Donation. Groups by appointment. The National Society of the Colonial Dames saved this 1861 Octagon, built by William C. and Harriet S. McElroy. One of two remaining octagons in San Francisco, it was moved from across the street in 1953. (The other is on Green St. between Jones and

Leavenworth.) A century ago, octagons were believed to be both healthful and lucky. This model was built with a cupola, bracketed cornice, and quoins accentuating the angled walls. The collections represent decorative arts of the Colonial and Federal periods.

San Francisco History Room and Archives San Francisco Public Library Main Branch, Civic Center, Third Floor, Larkin St. at McAllister, 94102; 415-558-3949. Thursday and Saturday; 10 A.M. to 6 P.M.; Tuesday and Friday; 12 to 6 P.M.: Wednesday, 1 to 6 P.M. Free.

Society of California Pioneers Pioneer Hall, 456 McAllister St., 94102; 415-861-5278. Open 10 A.M. to 4 P.M. weekdays. Closed holidays and August. Free. Groups by appointment. The society maintains a museum of nineteenth-century California paintings. It also houses a Children's History Gallery, Gold Rush artifacts, and costume displays.

Drive-bys

Phelps Place Historic District Oak St. west of Divisidero. The oldest frame dwelling in San Francisco, built for Abner Phelps in 1850, is in a small park space off Oak Street. Conflicting reports have the house either built by John Middleton & Sons, realtors, of lumber brought around Cape Horn from Maine, or purchased in New Orleans and shipped around the Horn in sections to ease the homesickness of Phelps's bride, the former Augusta Roussell of New Orleans. It does look like a two-story Louisiana cottage. Facing it on the right, at 1153 Oak Street, is the Mish House, a San Francisco landmark built in 1897 for $1,700 for Mrs. Sarah Mish, a dressmaker. It was renovated in 1976 by the Preservation Group, which has moved and refurbished several other homes on the block to create the "District," and was one of the original *Painted Ladies*.

Stern Grove Trocadero Clubhouse 19th Ave. and Sloat Blvd. (Park and Recreation Department: 415-666-7200.) A gem of a small Stick/Eastlake cottage in yellow with white and blue trim is now available for small parties and gatherings.

Vedanta Temple Webster St. at Filbert. This mystical gray and red 1890s Queen Anne mansion is a triumph of balconies, gingerbread, and Moorish embellishments.

Historic and Preservation Groups

Alamo Square Neighborhood Association P.O. Box 15372, 94115; 415-863-0538.

American Decorative Arts Forum c/o M. H. de Young Memorial Museum, Golden Gate Park, 94118. Monthly lectures and receptions on the decorative arts at the de Young or in private homes. Trips. Newsletter.

Art Deco Society of California 100 Bush St., #511, 94104; 415-553-DECO. Dedicated to education and preservation through social and entertainment events. A resource for information on the era. Newsletter.

California Historical Society 2090 Jackson St., 94109; 415-567-1848. The art and history collection is awaiting placement in a new location as of this writing. Information may be obtained at the CHS Research Library and Archives, which may be visited by appointment.

The Foundation for San Francisco's Architectural Heritage 2007 Franklin St., 94109; 415-441-3000. Located in the Haas-Lilienthal house, the foundation is a publicly supported, nonprofit organization formed as a private counterpart to the city's Landmarks Preservation Advisory Board. Conservation programs are offered, along with meetings, lectures, tours (415-441-3004), rehabilitation information, and a newsletter. One goal is to educate the public to assist in the intelligent reuse of San Francisco's urban and architectural heritage.

Landmarks Preservation Advisory Board of San Francisco's Planning Department c/o San Francisco Planning Dept., 450 McCallister St., 94102; 415-558-6345.

PADS (Planning Association for Divisidero Street) 710 Broderick St., 94117; 415-565-3733.

Planning Association for the Richmond District 414 Clement St., #5, 94118. Neighborhood environmental organization for the Richmond district.

San Francisco History Association and Museum 311 Hoffman St., 94114; 415-552-4543. The group puts on history exhibits in San Francisco and around the state. There are regular meetings with swap periods, guest speakers, and a quarterly newsletter.

San Francisco Historical Society P.O. Box 569, 94101; 415-567-2725. Explore the City's past, present, and future through lectures, films, excursions, and special events.

Victorian Alliance 824 Grove St., 94117; 415-824-2666. A clearinghouse for people interested in restoring Victorian homes, and preservation and architecture. Monthly meetings, newsletters, Fall house tour.

WANA (Western Addition Neighborhood Association) 1948 Sutter St., 94115.

Tours and Classes

City Guides Tours—Friends of the San Francisco Public Library Main Library, Civic Center, Larkin St. at McAllister, 94102; 415-557-4266. One-and-one-half-hour walks with volunteer guides who enjoy the city and its history.

Cable Car Seminars & Tours 1111 Hamilton Ave., Palo Alto, 94301; 415-328-5898. Although the office is located outside the city, most of the tours given are in San Francisco, and many are conducted from motorized cable cars.

Helen's Walk Tour P.O. Box 9164, Berkeley, 94709; 415-524-4544. Group rates. Helen Rendon offers Victorian house tours, revealing the city's charms from a native's point of view.

Native Tours P.O. Box 31183, 94131; 415-282-8757. Group rates. James Rittel offers an intimate look at the history and architecture of the city.

Day Studio-Workshop, Inc. 1504 Bryant St., 94103; 415-626-9300. Comprehensive, practical instruction for the do-it-yourselfer on the art of painted finishes for interior walls, floors, furniture, and architectural trim. Marbleizing, wood graining, trompe l'oeil, stenciling, wall glazing, gilding, and color workshops. Brochures.

San Francisco on Foot Max C. Kirkeberg, S.F. State University. 415-469-2049/282-6022.

San Francisco Tour Guide Guild P.O. Box 6752, 94101-6752; 415-753-8600.

UC Extension has evening classes on design and architecture. Call 415-642-4111 for information and a catalog.

Emporiums

"As a rule, the most expensive character of locks, knobs, and other builder's hardware is that which is sold for the smallest sums; especially does the rule apply to door furnishings...as there is nothing which gives house-keepers so much annoyance as to have the locks and fastenings getting out of order."
    —E. C. Hussey, *Home Building*, 1875

Bell'Occhio 8 Brady St., 94103; 415-864-4048. Antique ribbons, flowers, and decorative flourishes.

Bloomers 2975 Washington, 94115; 415-563-3266. This innovative florist also stocks a wide, inviting array of ribbons, tassels, and fabric ornaments.

Cradle of the Sun 3848 24th St., 94114; 415-821-7667, 1546 Polk St., 94109; 415-567-9091. Beveled, etched, and antique stained glass windows. Custom orders, repairs, tools, supplies, and classes.

Creative Paint & Wallpaper Inc. 999 Geary St. at Polk, 94109; 415-441-8850. Manager Wyman Chin can tell you all you need to know to purchase and use the right paints and wall coverings, inside and out, for your home.

Dunn-Edwards Paints & Wallcoverings 540 9th St., 94103; 415-252-9980. Daly City listing: 415-992-9660. Computer color-matching facilities.

Stern Grove Trocadero Clubhouse, San Francisco

Kelly-Moore Paint Co. 364 Divisidero St. at Oak, 94117; 415-552-1606, 3414 Army St. at Valencia, 94110; 415-826-3440.

San Francisco Victorian Gift and Memorabilia Catalog 3420 Market St., Suite 11, 94114; 415-826-0493. Russell Epstein. Books, photos, lithographs, paintings, jewelry, stained glass, plaster, and cards available by mail.

The Secret Garden Store 64 South Park, 94107; 415-974-6868. Distinctive garden art, fountains, furniture, and accessories for the garden. By appointment.

The Sylvester Mansion Antiques 1556 Revere St. (Bayview district), 94124; 415-822-3074. Linda Blacketer opens her antiques-filled classic Italianate home on the third Saturday of each month, 12 to 5 P.M., or by appointment. (PLR)

The Twigs, Inc. 5700 3rd St., 94124; 415-822-1626. Upholstery fabrics and hand-screened

wallpapers in eighteenth- and nineteenth-century French, German, American, Belgian, Italian, Swiss, and English designs available to designers, architects, historical societies, museums, and historic restorers (no retail).

Victorian Interiors 575 Hayes St., 94102; 415-431-7191. Tuesday through Saturday, 11:30 A.M.–7 P.M., and by appointment. Victorian Interiors is a restoration service and antique shop specializing in the re-creation of period interiors, vintage 1870–1920. Antiques, collectibles, refinishing, reupholstery, thirty-five different lines including W. R. Norman tin ceilings, carpets and lace curtains from J. R. Burrows, Classic Ceilings, Anaglypta and Lincrusta, Arstyl flexible moldings, Nomastyle moldings, niches, and rosettes, wallpapers, and silk picture hangers.

The Brillon Collection, over fourteen hundred patterns of antique wallpapers dating from 1850 to 1915, is Victorian Interiors' pride and joy. Reproduced by Victorian Collectibles Ltd., this is one of the largest, most varied collections of American papers discovered to date. The ceilings, hand-painted on canvas, are portable. Any of the designs can be flocked to order. Detachable corner blocks and border bands and complete rolls in Arts & Crafts patterns, florals, and stripes are available.

The Victorian Shoppe Pier 39, P2, 94133; 415-781-4770. Debbie Patrick has transformed her passion for drawing Victorians into a store bursting with Victorian houses in every shape and size: ceramics, jewelry, watercolor and pen and ink drawings, needlepoint, notepaper, and silk screens.

Auctioneers

Butterfield & Butterfield 220 San Bruno Ave., 94103; 415-861-7500. Free appraisals Monday, 9 A.M. to 12 P.M. The oldest West Coast full-service auction house offers the complete range of auction services including selling estate and museum pieces. Brochures on how to buy and sell at an auction as well as historical research and museum services are also available.

Butterfield West, formerly known as Utah Street Auctions, at 164 Utah St., offers moderately priced household furnishings and decorative arts. Auctions are held Monday and Tuesday, twice a month. For preview information, call 415-861-7500, ext. 308. Mailing list.

Christie's 3516 Sacramento St., 94123; 415-346-6633.

La Salle 1525 Union St., 94123; 415-931-9200.

Suppliers and Craftsmen

"The great use of life is to spend it on something that will outlast it." —William James

Artistic License 1925 'A' Fillmore St., 94115; 415-922-2854. Artistic License is a group of artisans known for the highest standards of period architectural and decorative art restoration. The group acts as a forum for the exchange of information, experiences, and skills among its members, as well as a public resource to educate and promote the highest standards for architectural and decorative art restoration. Anyone can become an Associate Member. Members among the following list of craftspeople are noted by (AL).

David B. Adams 2412 18th St., 94110; 415-621-1618. Painted finishes.

Architectural Resources Group Pier 9, The Embarcadero, 94111; 415-421-1680. Architectural and urban-planning services related to historic preservation, downtown revitalization, restoration, and rehabilitation. Literature.

Cynthia Baron 229 Jersey St., 94114; 415-282-4486. Collective Antiques, 212 Utah St., 94114; 415-621-3800. An interior-design consultant who specializes in antiques treasure hunts, textiles, paisleys from Scotland, Victorian embroideries, and design for both period and contemporary homes. (PLR)

Barton Construction Co. 415-641-0646. Steve Barton. Stonework, slab, concrete, and marble fabrication.

Bay Area Ornamental Iron Works 1314 Fitzgerald Ave., 94124; 415-822-7844. Ornamental wrought iron for decoration and protection, in stock and custom work.

Bay City Paint Company 2279 Market St., 94114; 415-431-4914. Specialty paints and brushes, START refinishing supplies for furniture and interior wood finishing, Japan colors, caseins, aniline dye stains, glaze coat, and wood-graining tools. Gold, silver, composition leaf and leafing supplies, bronze powders, lacquer sticks, Ripolin high-pigment French enamels. Literature.

Beronio Lumber Co. 2525 Marin St., 94124; 415-824-4300. Classic wood columns, flooring, panels, trim.

Anne B. Bloomfield 2229 Webster St., 94115; 415-922-1063. Architectural historian, preservation surveys, National Register nominations, architectural restoration research, house histories.

Michael Bondi Metal Design (AL) 1818 Shorey, Oakland, 94607; 510-763-1327. Contemporary and classical styles in iron, copper, brass, bronze, and aluminum. Functional solutions for architectural and interior design.

Helen Bouthell Wallcovering 415-254-3155. Wall-covering installations.

Larry Boyce Stencil Artist (AL) 415-563-5384. (PLR)

Bradbury & Bradbury Fine Art Wallpaper 1925 'A' Fillmore St., 94115; 415-922-2989. By appointment. Created by Bruce Bradbury (AL) in the tradition of the Arts & Crafts movement, this small company sells Victorian- and early-twentieth-century-style handprinted wallpapers and borders by mail order. Housed in a Victorian flat, the in-house design service under director Paul Duchscherer (AL) offers individualized help in preparing room schemes. Sample room installations, with B & B's signature ornamental ceilings, may be viewed first-hand, along with the full range of their collection, by appointment. (DPL, PLR)

Peter Bridgman (AL) 415-653-9590. Wall-covering installations. Papers, vinyls, foils, fabric.

Don Bucker, Painter 1369 29th Ave., 94122; 415-664-9354.

Caldwell Building Wreckers 195 Bayshore Blvd., 94124; 415-550-6777. Robert Caldwell. Recycled lumber and building materials bought and sold.

California Institute for the Restoration and Conservation Arts Circa Atelier, 3556 Sacramento St., 94118; 415-931-0444. "Bounty hunter for art and antiques," Gillian Windsor-Morgan specializes in furniture restoration. She gilds mirrors; rebuilds, gilds, and "fauxs" columns, refinishes doors; and carves finials.

Carey & Co. Architecture 300 Brannan, Suite 402, 94107; 415-957-0100. Alice Ross Carey, AIA, Principal (AL). Architectural services in the areas of restoration, rehabilitation and adaptive reuse of historically significant structures. In addition, the firm provides material conservation, National Register nominations, investment tax credit, and façade easement assistance.

Thomas Church Landscapes 415-863-4009. Grace Hall, landscape architecture.

Clearheart 106 Coleridge, 94110; 415-647-1388. Skeeter Jones. Victorian restoration and architectural woodworking of millwork and façades.

Cirecast 380 7th St., 94103; 415-863-8319. Restoration-hardware specialists. Custom hardware manufacturer. Locating, designing, and reproducing authentic builder's hardware, from doorknobs to drawer pulls, using the lost-wax method, with flexible or metal molds, in gold, silver, silicon, bronze, or aluminum. Catalog available.

Classic Remodeling Corp. 2241 Quesada Ave., 94124; 415-641-1380. John Smithyman.

Jerry Coe 415-527-2950. Architectural and sculptural metalsmith.

David Condon (AL) Kiln Works 415-763-5464. Architectural sculpture.

Dr. Marjorie Dobkin 295 Union St., 94133; 415-391-0686. Cultural Resource Studies.

Paul D'Orleans 272 Anderson St., 94110; 415-641-7768. Faux finishes, interior and exterior painting.

Allen Dragge (AL) Reflection Studios 1418 62nd St., Emeryville, 94608; 510-652-4884. Leaded glass. Restored the glass ceiling of the Sheraton Palace Garden Court.

Paul Duchscherer (AL). 415-922-2989. Architectural- and decorative-arts historian, teacher, and designer. (PLR)

Hank Dunlop 3996 23rd St., 94114; 415-285-4633. Historical research, restoration, consulting, lecturing.

David L. Dunning 4647 17th St., 94117; 415-564-7415. The Electric Paint Co. Architectural Imaging and Graphic Services by computer.

Echuguren and Co. 150 Powell St., #303, 94102; 415-982-0701. Slate-roof, marble, and granite remodeling.

Paul Ellis 477 Duboce St., 94117; 415-626-5646. Costumer.

Evans & Brown Co. 3450 3rd St., Unit 1D, 94124; 415-648-9430. Mark Evans and Charley Brown. Creative faux finishes.

Fox Marble and Granite 1400 Minnesota St., 94107; 415-647-5160. Alex Blair. Interior and exterior installation. Counters, doors, walls, fireplaces, mantels.

Franklin Design 2026 California St., 94109; 415-922-3400. Interior design by Bert Franklin. Craig Beckstead, vice president. (PLR)

Anton Feutsch (AL) 510-526-6354. Wood carver, sculptor.

Gingerbread 2269 Chestnut St., Suite 209, 94123; 415-673-4116. Kit Haskell, artist.

Creates line drawings of houses on note-cards, mugs, T-shirts, wooden panels, screens, and as pen-and-ink drawings.

Guilroy Cornice Works 801 Army St., 94124; 415-621-0561. Sheet metal.

Haas Wood & Ivory Works 64 Clementina St., 94105; 415-421-8273. Ornamentation. Custom molding, wood turning. Balusters, newels, columns.

Hardy Architects 443 15th Ave., #5, 94118; 415-221-4293. Thomas Rex Hardy, AIA, has an extensive background in alteration work. He was the project architect for restoration of Stern Grove's Stick/Eastlake Trocadero Clubhouse, now used for small parties and gatherings, and also for the restoration of the Garden Court at the Sheraton Palace.

Herald Street & Benjamin (AL) 1219 Folsom St., 94103; 415-431-7735. Kate Herald, J. Benjamin Seklir, Ron Albers. Quality finishing of furniture, cabinetry, woodwork, interior and exterior on-site work.

Hoppe Imports 2055 Bryant St., 94110; 415-641-1557. Statuary, antiques, and furniture.

Horse-drawn Carriages Pier 41, Fisherman's Wharf, 94133; 415-398-0857.

John Isola (AL) Illustrious Lighting, 290 San Bruno Ave., 94103; 415-255-2272. Period-lighting specialist.

Kaatz Contractors, Inc. 292 Ocean Ave., 94112; 415-566-9629. Rich McCullough. Marble maintenance and metal refinishing since 1924.

Lorna Kollmeyer 415-661-8211. Ornamental plaster.

Erik Kramvik (AL) 415-922-5219/333-4932. Design and fine woodworking.

B. C. Landenberger 2707 Judah St., 94122-1433; 415-664-8015. Brett Landenberger and Scott Waterman. Decorative and fine arts, decorative paper designs, decorative paste papers for frames and walls. Decorative paint, stenciling, gilding, and wall coverings.

Andreas Lehmann (AL) 415-465-7158. Cut glass to order.

Little/Raidl Design Studios 49 Hartford St., 94114; 415-552-3557. "Custom Art Glass in the Tiffany Manner." Roy Little and Jim Raidl use glass as paint, with light, texture, and sun-dappled effects on interior and exterior windows, glass screens, and arches of vines with sculpted edges that fit into tall doorways. (PLR)

Mandy Livingston 415-530-4766. Decorative artist combining artistic skills and craftsmanship. Fantasy finishes, trompe l'oeil, custom designing. Furniture a specialty.

Lowpensky Moldings 900 Palou Ave., 94124; 415-822-7422. Custom millwork, Victorian molding, re-sawing, and surfacing.

Patrick McGrew Associates, Architects 41 Sutter St., Suite 500, 94104; 415-981-3060. An architect with a keen interest in preservation and identification of landmark structures.

Ami Magill 415-550-8719. Faux finishes.

Carlo Marchiori 357 Frederick, 94117; 415-564-6671. Trompe l'oeil murals, Grand Master paintings, Pompeian rooms. (PLR)

Shelley Masters 4037 23rd St., 94114; 415-695-7844. Painted exterior and interior finishes, faux iron, texturing. Verdigris, columns. Teaches faux finishes.

Kathryn Mathewson Associates Garden Design/Builders 64 South Park, 94107; 415-974-6868. Kathryn Mathewson was the first woman recipient of the 1990 National Landscape Association Superior Award for Landscape Design. From cottage gardens to master plans for complexes such as Skywalker Ranch, Mathewson allows the garden to develop into an integral essential element of daily life.

Mayta & Jensen General Contracting & Remolding 1790 Yosemite Ave., 94124-2964; 415-822-2200. Interior finishes, architectural millwork, maintenance, and new construction.

Little/Raidl Design Studio, San Francisco

Miller Designs 450 Shotwell St., 94110; 415-821-3380. Don Miller. Furniture and upholstery restoration.

The Miniature Mart 1807 Octavia St., 94109; 415-563-8745. By appointment only. Ellen and John Blauer "appreciate the LITTLE things in life," collecting and creating extraordinary handmade miniature furnishings and model rooms. (PLR)

David John Modell (AL) 415-239-0585. Architectural restoration design.

Joni Monnich (AL) Lilyguild. 415-724-4405. Decorative finishes. Creative staining of Lincrusta, etc.

Ocean Sash & Door 3154 17th Street, 94110; 415-863-1256. Custom and stock wood doors, windows and frames, greenhouses, arches and curves.

Page & Turnbull, Inc. 364 Bush St., 94104; 415-362-5154. Charles Page and Jay Turnbull, specialists in historic architectural preservation and restoration, have a staff of architects, planners, historians, and conservators. Page helped found the Foundation for San Francisco's Architectural Heritage.

Painting & Decorating Contractors' Association, Inc. 635 Potrero Ave., Suite A, 94110; 415-550-6886.

Sreco Papic 478 Utah St., 94110; 415-431-0314. Restoration of interior and exterior furniture.

George Payne 415-861-8086. Plaster restoration and ornamentation.

John Ploss 1232 Haight St., 94117; 415-626-8790. Architecture and planning.

Rainbow and Painting Decorating Co. 1452 Broadway, 94109; 415-885-6690. Painters.

Gail Redman (AL) 415-431-1595. Fine wood turning.

Restoration Associates 326 Ritch St., 94107; 415-974-5555. Seth Curlin, restoration architect and contractor.

Restoration Period, Inc. 3 Dorman Ave., 94124; 415-285-0949. John Carney and Eduardo Diestra. Refinishing of fine furniture. Restoration and conservation of period furniture, art, and sculpture. Hand-rubbed finishes. French polish; lacquer; faux; Art Deco. Museum conservator on staff. Recommendations at home by appointment.

Restoration Services 2652 Harrison, 94110; 415-282-4559. Bryan K. Singleton. Wood restoration.

Return to Splendor 415-530-1051. Mark Egeland. Wallpaper installation, graining, and marbleizing.

George Zaffle, San Francisco

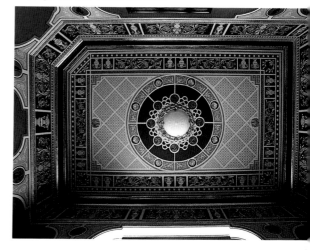

The Miniature Mart, San Francisco

Patrick J. Ruane, Inc. 181 South Park, 94107; 415-546-7600. Plastering, stucco, replacements, and repair. Worked on the Sheraton Palace Hotel plaster medallions and friezes.

Stephen Rynerson (AL) 415-428-1102. Period and architectural design. (PLR)

San Francisco Restoration 1379 Harrison St., 94103; 415-861-4877. James Mannix specializes in high-end restoration of old homes and commercial buildings.

San Francisco Victoriana 2070 Newcomb St. at Selby, 94124; 415-648-0313. Fax: 415-648-2812. Store hours: Monday through Friday, 7:30 A.M. to 4 P.M., Saturday 9 A.M. to 1 P.M. Catalog available. Architectural molding, castings, and embossed wall coverings. Has the largest variety of stock wood moldings in Northern California, reproductions of originals made from 1840 to 1940, with samples available. Stain grades and custom matching services for large or small quantities. Cast ceiling centerpieces, cornices, brackets, shields, festoons, egg and dart, etc., thirty-five stocked ceiling centerpiece designs.

Rick Schaefer 415-863-2048. Wood ornament, moldings.

John Seecamp 415-824-3493. Staining, wood finishing and graining, faux finishes.

Signature Studios P.O. Box 4214-59, 94142; 415-221-5093. A. D. Norton and Patricia O'Neil create and restore architectural stained glass, and etched and blasted glass.

Jill Pilaroscia Architectural Colour, San Francisco

Gerald M. Smith Jr. Antiques & Art Restorations 758-A Fell St., 94117; 415-255-1334. Restoration of antiques, fine furniture, and art. Rewiring lamps, metal polishing and repair, glass, ceramic, and fabric repair, staining and custom refinishing, faux finishes, wood and veneer repairs.

Sotirkos Designs 455 Irwin St., #401, 94107; 415-552-6820. Woodwork.

Specialty Glass & Marble Co. 241 Quint St., 94124. Showroom: Henry Adams St. at Kansas, #207, 94103; 415-821-2929. Terry Markarian. Mirror and glass fabrication, beveling and edge finishing, sandblasting and resilvering, as well as marble and granite work. Custom residential and commercial work.

Steven F. Stevens Stained Glass Studio 1258 Pacific St., 94109; 415-885-5236. Traditional and contemporary design, repairs and restoration. (PLR)

Thierry Vidal 415-931-5334. Furniture restoration, wood graining.

Tree Lovers' Floors, Inc. 415-252-5702. Creation and restoration of fine wood floors.

Victorian Interiors 575 Hayes St., 94102; 415-431-7191. See previous listing.

Vranizan Design/Build 7 Coleridge St., 94110; 415-821-0431. Robert Vranizan, Pres. General contracting, custom remodeling, Victorian restoration.

Phil Waen (AL) 415-849-1842. Classic illumination, lighting.

Nat Weinstein 489 27th St., 94131; 415-641-5528. Graining, marbleizing, antique and hardwood finishing.

Paul Winans (AL) Winans Construction. 415-653-7288. Residential remodeling and new construction, restoration of historic structures.

Bob Winebarger (AL) 415-527-8397. Furniture maker.

Winfield Design Associates 2690 Harrison St., 94110; 415-647-6787. Wall coverings.

George Zaffle (AL) Zaffle Painting Studio. 415-621-7653. Stencil design, specialty painting. (PLR)

Donna Zigmund 1907 Mason St., 94133; 415-771-8281. Interior faux finishes—glazing, gilding, marbleizing, painting, and restoration.

Painters and Color Consultants

Joseph Adamo P.O. Box 411362, 94141; 415-821-3372. Color design, painting. (DPL, HTC, PLR)

Bob Buckter (AL) 3877 20th St., 94114; 415-922-7444. America's best-known color consultant. Literature. (PL, DPL, HTC, PLR)

Classic Shades Painting Co. 187 Coleridge St., #2, 94110; 415-647-6224. Danny Beltran.

Color Quest 1793-A McAllister St., 94115; 415-921-1121. Paul Vincent Kensinger. Interior and exterior painting, restoration, color consultation, and faux finishes. (PLR)

Concepts in Color 1618 Castro St., 94114; 415-647-7070. Aryae Levy.

Robert Dufort (AL) Magic Brush, Inc. 1500-B Davidson Ave., 94124; 415-641-8622. Color, painting, and restoration. Noted for the restoration and painting of the Westerfeld Mansion. (DPL, HTC, PLR)

Russell Epstein 3420 Market St., #11, 94114; 415-826-0493. Painting and restoration. (PLR)

Butch Kardum Painting & Color Design 210 San Jose Ave., 94110; 415-824-1623. The founding father of the Colorist movement. (PL, PLR)

Mirage Inc. 415-828-9284. Bill Weber, Tony Klaas. Created the North Beach mural at Columbus and Broadway. (PLR)

Pago Painting 415-753-6064. Brian Molony,

Victorian specialist. Painting, restoration, reconstruction, color design. (PLR)

Peacock Painting Co. 505 Chenery St., 94131; 415-584-1816. Ron McCambridge. (PLR)

Jill Pilaroscia Architectural Colour (AL) 220 Eureka St., 94114; 415-861-8086. Architectural services including consulting, research, lectures and seminars, and restoration design. Product color, materials and finishes selection, and mail-away color program. Literature. (HTC, PLR)

Precision Painters 690 Arkansas, 94107; 415-626-3131. Exterior decoration.

S.F. Colors & Restoration 415-331-8252. Esther Canaletich. Painting, carpentry, and restoration.

S. F. Renaissance Color Design 415-921-5197. Tony Canaletich. (PL, PLR)

Strokes Fine Painters 415-824-8376. Dar Greenberg. Interior and exterior painting and restoration.

Women Painters of S.F. 415-337-0397. Painters.

THE EAST BAY

*"And if I has but one penny in the world,
thou shouldst have it to buy gingerbread."*
—William Shakespeare

Berkeley and Oakland are the two best-known towns in the East Bay. Thanks to the presence of the University of California, Berkeley is one of the biggest little towns in America. Its bookstores, restaurants, and cultural attractions are the envy of cities far larger.

Oakland, however, has more to offer lovers of Victoriana. In fact, one of the most ambitious restoration projects in California has been slowly taking shape in downtown Oakland in the area around Thirteenth Street and Martin Luther King, Jr., Highway.

Alameda, fortunate enough to stay out of the way of "progress," has one of the finest and most beautifully painted collections of Victorians in the country.

And as if this weren't enough, the East Bay also has the finest collection of house museums in the state. Take that, San Francisco!

For the purposes of this guide, the East Bay consists of Alameda and Contra Costa counties, and two towns across the Carquinez Strait, Vallejo and Benicia.

OAKLAND

Restaurants

T.J.'s Gingerbread House 741 Fifth St., 94067; 510-444-7373. Lunch, tea, and dinner, Tuesday through Saturday (M/E). Hansel and Gretel's wicked witch would be envious of this Gothic cottage restaurant which looks good enough to eat. Upstairs is a fantasy land of dolls overlooking hearty Cajun/Creole dishes that you choose when you reserve your table.

The shop downstairs sells a world of gingerbread: cookies, dolls, T-shirts, soap, tea, even bubble bath. And there's a neo-gazebo for parties. T.J.'s fantasy-come-true is located near Oakland's Bret Harte Boardwalk, a block of colorful Italianate and Stick cottages turned into stores, offices, and restaurants.

Places to Visit

Camron-Stanford House 1418 Lakeside Dr., 94612; 510-836-1976. Tours on Wednesday, 11 A.M. to 4 P.M.; Sunday, 1 to 5 P.M.. Donation. First Sunday of the month free. Groups by reservation. Tea and tour, weddings and receptions by arrangement.

This crested white, black, and ecru Italianate is the last Victorian mansion on Oakland's Lake Merritt. After serving as a home to five of the families who helped build San Francisco and Oakland, the house became the Oakland Museum for more than sixty years, until 1967, when the new Oakland Museum was built. The mansion was saved from demolition by the Camron-Stanford House Preservation Association, a citizens' volunteer organization that rents the building for $1 a year from the city. Volunteers put together special exhibits and offer research resources and school and community outreach programs.

Upstairs, velvet mantel covers, elegant gasoliers, shining alabaster statues and fine paintings, including one of Franklina Gray Bartlett as a fourteen-month-old bacchante, have been re-created following newspaper stories and letters by Franklina before and after her marriage. The newspaper story of her wedding was titled "A Wedding in the High Life."

There is also a bust of David "Golden-Spike" Hewes, done in Carrara marble during his nineteen-month Grand Tour of Europe, which was his honeymoon with his second wife, Franklina's mother. They took

Camron-Stanford House, Oakland

Franklina with them. The Camron-Stanford House is listed on the National Register.

Dunsmuir House and Gardens 2960 Peralta Oaks Ct., 94605; 510-562-0328. Tours 12 to 4 P.M., Sunday and Wednesday, April through September. Groups, teas, lunches, dinners, and receptions by reservation. Fee. Off Hwy. 580 at the Foothill MacArthur exit. This thirty-seven-room masterpiece of Colonial Revival architecture is a gem of Victorian taste and Gilded Age opulence. It was built in 1899 as a gift from Alexander Dunsmuir to his beloved Josephine. But he died forty-one days after their marriage, and she pined away and joined him fifteen months later.

Wood paneling, parquet floors, a Tiffany-style domed skylight topping the central staircase, and ten fireplaces have been restored to their original splendor. The forty acres of hills and gardens include a carriage house, milk barn, potting shed, pool, and outbuildings that now house gift shops. Rumor has it that John McLaren, creator of

Camron-Stanford House, Oakland

Golden Gate Park, helped plan the Dunsmuir House gardens. Special events such as Christmas and Mother's Day celebrations, and carriage rides and sing-alongs on the horse-drawn trolley have visitors coming back for more.

Oakland Museum 1000 Oak St., 94607; 510-273-3401. For recorded information: 510-834-2413. Wednesday through Saturday, 10 A.M. to 5 P.M.; Sunday, 12 to 7 P.M., except holidays. Free. California art, history, and natural history are beautifully displayed on three floors. The 1890s shiny red fire pump engine and the Victorian collection are special, from the samples of gingerbread moldings to velvet-dressed models on their way to the opera in their shiny carriages.

Preservation Park Blocks of commercial Victorian buildings and a collection of vintage Victorians that have been saved, moved, restored, and turned into commercial and office buildings in downtown Oakland at Thirteenth Street and Martin Luther King, Jr., Hwy. may be the West Coast's largest restoration project.

Groups, Artisans, and Suppliers

California Preservation Foundation 1615 Broadway, Suite 705, 94612; 510-763-0972. A statewide nonprofit organization promoting historic preservation. Its officers offer advice on the politics, economics, and governmental structure of preservation in California. The organization helps interested individuals and committed local groups to see and explain the values of historic, architectural, and cultural resources to the larger community; publicizes tax benefits and building reuse potential; and assists private citizens and public officials who want to create and use preservation tools and techniques in local planning. Information sharing and networking, workshops and newsletter, publications. A list of engineers who are experienced in upgrading homes against earthquake damage is available.

City Miner Salvage 5920 San Pablo Ave., 94608; 510-653-4540. Recycling of quality used building materials.

East Bay Regional Park District Public Affairs Dept., 11500 Skyline Blvd., 94619-2443; 510-531-9300. Newsletter listing of special events at house museums.

Karl Kardel & Co. 415-261-4149. Exterior painting and color design.

Doug Keister 5826 Fremont St., 94608; 510-658-5766. Photographer of the Painted Ladies books and calendars. Industrial and architectural photography.

Oakland Heritage Alliance 1418 Lakeside Dr., P.O. Box 12425, 94604; 510-763-8218. Architectural and historic preservation society. Walking tours, lectures, newsletter, and special events.

Oakland Landmarks Commission Oakland City Hall, 14th St. at Washington, 94606; 510-273-3611.

Piedmont Historical Society 358 Hillside Ave., 94611.

RicArt Painting and Decorating Co. P.O. Box 1801, Pleasanton, 94566; 510-463-1283. Rick E. Arteaga worked on Oakland's Preservation Park.

Today and Tomorrow 2554 West St., 94612; 510-834-5557. Alfonzia Aquia, colorist.

BERKELEY

BAHA Architectural & Historical Survey Berkeley City Hall, 2180 Milvia St., 94707.

Berkeley Architectural Heritage Association P.O. Box 7066, Landscape Station, 94707.

Berkeley Architectural Salvage 2741 10th St., 94710; 510-849-2025. Monday through Saturday, 10 A.M. to 5 P.M. Alan Goodman offers brass plumbing and chandeliers, corbels, columns and gingerbread, windows, doors and hardware, and marble parts and fixtures for the restoration of Victorians and other old buildings. Catalog.

Berkeley Historical Society P.O. Box 1190, 94701; 132-B Grant St., 94703; 510-524-9880. Monday through Friday, 9 A.M. to 12 P.M. Celebrates Berkeley's people and their history in photographs and memorabilia exhibits in the Old City Hall at 2134 Martin Luther King Way. Members are offered a newsletter, oral history and research files, and programs.

Classic Illumination, Inc. 2743 9th St., 94710; 510-849-1842. Antique, reproduction, and custom-designed period lighting fixtures including standing lamps, wall sconces, chandeliers, torchieres, and shades of all kinds. Catalog.

Lacis 2982 Adeline St., 94703; 415-843-7178. Specializing in lace, lacemaking, costumes, and Victoriana. New and period lace curtains, lace accessories, antique needlework tools, period costume patterns, and books. Catalog.

Monsen Plating & Silversmiths 3370 Adeline St., 94703; 510-655-0890. Historic Architectural Elements.

Ohmega Salvage 2407 San Pablo Ave., 94702; 510-843-7368. Steve Drobinsky buys and sells doors, windows, stained glass, pedestal sinks, clawfoot tubs, architectural elements, lighting fixtures, brass, wrought iron, marble and specialty items, Victorian hardware, mantels, glass blocks, mirrors, and old stoves. A catalog of reproduction plumbing and hardware is available.

The Owner Builder Center 2530 San Pablo Ave., 94702; 510-848-6860. A nonprofit school that offers hands-on workshops for homeowners in skills such as painting, landscape design, wallpaper hanging, finish carpentry, ceramic tile installation, design, and on-site construction. Construction and remodeling consulting.

Restoration Hardware 3496 Blackhawk Plaza Circle, Space D-1, Danville, 94506; 510-736-0255.

Sunrise Specialty 5540 Doyle St., 94606; 510-845-4751. Tuesday through Saturday, 10 A.M. to 6 P.M. Antique-style fixtures and faucets made with original materials, including solid oak, vitreous china, and solid brass, from a towel bar to a complete bath. Prices from 15 cents for an angle stop and flange to $2,500 for a 5'8" clawfoot tub with oak rim and brass-plated legs. Catalog.

Urban Ore 6th & Gilman and 2nd & Gilman Sts., 94703; 510-526-7080. Architectural salvage.

ALAMEDA

Garrett Mansion: A Bed-and-Breakfast Inn 900 Union St., 94501; 510-521-4779 (M). This classic Colonial Revival residence, painted in two blues, cream, and ochre, was built in 1893 for industrialist W. T. Garrett and used, for fifty years, as a boardinghouse. The coffered ceiling and inset oak panels with egg-and-dart-pattern beading and the heavily embossed Lincrusta-Walton stained to match have been polished and waxed in the massive restoration the new owners have given to the house.

An orchestra balcony overlooks the entryway. Upstairs, guests retire to six fresh, comfortable rooms, three with shared bath. Breakfast may be taken in the room, in the oak-lined dining room, or the upstairs guest sitting room, where a jigsaw puzzle awaits to challenge visitors. Window seats beckon for cozy reading, and the beach is four blocks away.

Alameda Historical Museum 2324 Alameda Ave., 94501-4541; 510-521-1233. Wednesday through Friday, 1:30 to 4 P.M.; Saturday, 11:30 A.M. to 4 P.M.; Sunday, 1:30 to 4 P.M. Free. The official repository of objects relating to the history of the city, the museum contains collections of vintage clothing worn by Alameda citizens, household furnishings and implements, toys, model trains, bicycles, a cinema-arts room, and art. The museum's pride and joy is quite modern, however.

Alameda Historical Museum, Alameda

"Paint an Alameda House" is a hands-on exhibit of color design for older houses, featuring computerized images of sixteen of Alameda's beautiful homes—an electronic coloring book that teaches as it amuses.

Alameda Victorian Preservation Society P.O. Box 1677, 94501; 510-523-AVPS. Victorian grand charity ball, picnic, historic projects, meetings, newsletter.

Gaslight Emporium 1708 Lincoln Ave., 94501; 510-522-1900. Tuesday through Saturday, 11 A.M. to 6:30 P.M. Tom and Tommie (Thomasina Ann) Veirs make fine hand-dipped old-fashioned chocolates and chocolate roses, and sell them, along with handmade Victorian candy boxes, clothing, jewelry, dolls, ornaments, lace, tassels, cameos, and collectibles. They also give classes in making Victorian Christmas ornaments and decorations.

At Gaslight Interiors (510-865-4125), Tommie also offers interior design, authentic re-creations, and historic restoration, including nineteenth-century wall, window, and ceiling treatments, furniture searches, needlework, and artifact restoration.

Idle Designs 510-521-5783. Stephen Idle, color consultant.

Ruiz Antiques 2333 Clement Avenue, 94501; 510-769-6082. Historic architectural elements.

SAN LEANDRO

Best House Bed 'n' Breakfast Inn 1315 Clarke St., 94577; 510-351-0911 (M). Originally the town house for popular San Leandro civic leader Joseph Dumont, this 1880 Stick property was sold to pioneer Daniel Best, the man who invented the caterpillar tractor. The five sunny rooms, decorated with a clever mix of period items, boast brass or canopy beds and peaceful views. Rolling lawns, an arbor, a gazebo, and a bubbling waterwheel attract guests and those attending weddings and meetings.

WALNUT CREEK

The Mansion at Lakewood 1056 Hacienda Dr., 94598; 510-946-9075 (E). Ralph Waldo

Gaslight Emporium, Alameda

McGonaghy House, Hayward

Emerson once wrote that "hospitality consists in a little fire, a little food, and an immense quiet." Behind the gates of this three-acre estate, the twentieth-century traveler will find exactly that. The Mansion is a sprawling light and dark gray and white Gothic home, once an 1861 estate and the center of twenty thousand acres given to the Pacheco family as a land grant.

The seven rooms, each with its own distinctive amenities, bath, and decor, combine romance, history, and modern luxury. The Estate Suite's padded walls surround you in quiet. There's an extraordinary antique brass bed, and a sitting area, fireplace, private terrace, and Jacuzzi tub for two. Guests have the use of two parlors, an immense library-music room, and an elegant dining room with a glass window for viewing the visiting deer. Weddings and conferences are easily arranged. The plush bunnies, ceramic bunnies, and bunny collectibles add a welcome touch of whimsy.

Shadelands Ranch Historical Museum 2660 Ygnacio Valley Rd., 94598; 510-935-7871. Wednesday, 11:30 A.M. to 4 P.M.; Sunday, 1 to 4 P.M. Groups by appointment. Fee. Hiram Penniman came to California to find gold and found it in the land itself. He made his fortune in fruit and celebrated by building this grand Classical Revival house in 1902. The Walnut Creek Historical Society, headquartered here, has restored the house, completely outfitting the eight rooms with Mr. Penniman's furniture, which reflects the Oriental influence popular at the turn of the century. The history room has maps, photo books, oral histories, films, and files of the area. The house, listed on the National Register, is surrounded by fruit- and walnut-farming equipment. Part of the orchards remain in back of the house.

HAYWARD

Hayward Area Historical Society Museum 22701 Main St., 94541; 510-581-0223. Monday through Friday, 11 A.M. to 4 P.M.; Saturday, 12 to 4 P.M. Fee. Adventure into the past in this delightful museum shop and collection. A nineteenth-century piano, photos of all the mayors, Victoriana, Graflex studio photographers' cameras, a nineteenth-century fire pumper, and maps, photographs, toys, clothes, and cherished memories can be found in this treasure trove.

McConaghy House 18701 Hesperian Blvd., 94541; 510-581-0223. Thursday through Sunday, 1 to 4 P.M. Fee. The twelve furnished rooms in this substantial 1866 Queen Anne, painted white with three blues and black sashes, show how a prosperous farming home looked. The whole house is decorated for holidays. In summer, there's a rose garden party on the grounds and in the old tank house, which is now a little theater.

At Easter, one hundred yards of ribbons deck the house. And even Prince Albert would enjoy Christmas at the McConaghy house. The tree and the house are decorated with handmade Christmas decorations such as stars, hearts, pretzels, pine cones, and red tissue roses made from low-cost materials that would have been available to the Victorian homemaker. The child's room has its own Christmas cheer. Visitors delight in the "walking Christmas Tree," and the gift boutique.

Meek Estate Hampton Rd. at Boston Rd., 94541; 510-581-0223/881-6715. By appointment. This elegant Italianate villa, built in 1869, has been undergoing a complete restoration, so call before visiting.

LAFAYETTE

Lafayette Historical Society P.O. Box 133, 94549.

FREMONT

Lord Bradley's Inn 43344 Mission Blvd., 94539; 510-490-0520 (I/M). The Solon Washington Hotel, built in the 1870s next to Mission San Jose, has become the keystone for this welcoming bed-and-breakfast with a British flavor, English Victorian interior, and new turreted outbuildings in cream with blue-gray and dark peach. Keith Medeiros painted the boards before putting them on the building.

Each of the eight bedrooms, all with bath, is named after a member of the Medeiros family, and each has an individual motif, such as antique valentines or Charles Dickens's story prints. Lord Bradley's is a family affair: the oldest son does all the stained glass in the house, another son hand-carves amusing one-of-a-kind furniture, a daughter does the sewing. The common rooms are filled with books. Breakfast is served in the common room, or on the patio, with hummingbirds providing the floor show.

Ardenwood Farm George W. Patterson House, Ardenwood Regional Park, 34600 Ardenwood Blvd. at Hwy. 84, 94555; 510-796-0663/796-0199. Administration: East Bay Regional Park District, 11500 Skyline Blvd., 94619; 510-531-9300. Thursday through Sunday, 10 A.M. to 4 P.M. April through November and some holidays. Fee. House tours by appointment and on a first-come, first-served basis. Call 510-791-4196. Rain may close park.

George Patterson, a '49er who found gold in farmland, married Clara, added on a ruffled white Queen Anne in 1889 to the 1857 farmhouse, and named it after a high school production of Shakespeare's *As You Like It*. Patterson progeny lived here until 1969. Volunteers in Victorian dress proudly show off their painstaking restoration of the house with its woods, fine carpets and wallpapers, and family mementos.

Appropriately costumed helpers attend to the Victorian flower garden, with its jasmine, asters, and heartsease, put fresh flowers throughout the Patterson House, demonstrate the social graces of the Victorian era, and show off farming and crafts skills such as lacemaking and barrel making. Buggy and wagon tours are very popular, especially with wedding parties, and there are horsecars, stages, and the Deer Park train to amuse younger visitors. Farm-grown produce is sold near the front-gate gift shop. Weddings, programs, picnics, and group tours by arrangement.

Volunteer opportunities are available in restoration, farming, gardening, tours, historic crafts, or farmyard demonstration. The 205-acre farm is a look into the Bay Area's farming past. Its motto:

> May learning, science, useful art,
> Adorn thy life, improve thy heart,
> May kind affection, love so dear,
> Hereafter bless, and guide you here.

Historical Niles, Antique Center of Fremont Maps and Guides from Niles Merchant Association, 510-792-8023. Niles was established in the 1850s as a junction point of the Southern Pacific Railroad from the coast to San Jose and southern coast points. Vallejo's Mills, first in the county, were run by long flume from Alameda Creek, and the largest nursery in California was here. In 1912, Essanay Studios was at the height of its moviemaking fame, with stars Bronco Billy, Charlie Chaplin, Wallace Beery, and Ben Turpin. Almost three dozen antique stores, including Victorian specialists Les Belles Antiques (37549 Niles Blvd., 94536; 510-794-4773), are a real draw. The annual summer flea market attracts one hundred thousand antiques seekers from all over the West.

James Shinn House 1251 Peralta Ave., 94538; 510-794-0554/791-4340. First Wednesday and third Sunday of the month, 1 to 3 P.M. Donation. Groups by appointment. This Victorian farmhouse was built in 1876 on a three-hundred-acre ranch in the Niles District by James Shinn, who established one of the first nurseries in the state and imported rare trees from all over the world. Some of the trees are still on the grounds, a four-and-a-half-acre park. The redwood house is furnished authentically as a prosperous ranch.

ALBANY

Bed & Breakfast International 1181-B Solano Ave., 94706. Office: 510-525-4569. Reservations: 800-872-4500. Private homestays in homes, guesthouses, on houseboats, and in Victorian inns. Stay in Victorian homes all over California from San Diego to Mt. Shasta.

PT. RICHMOND

East Brother Light Station 117 Park Pt., 94801; 510-233-2385 (E). The ultimate Victorian hideaway can be found on an island in the middle of San Pablo Strait, the waterway connecting San Francisco Bay and San Pablo Bay. The gingerbread-laden, scalloped-patterned, shingled beige, white, and chocolate lighthouse is reached only by boat and a high vertical ladder.

Built in 1873, East Brother was manned until 1969, when the light was automated, but the foghorn still blasts away when it's foggy. Volunteers have restored and preserved East Brother as a living museum for the perpetual use and benefit of the public. It is listed on the National Register.

Guests are picked up at a San Pablo dock Thursday to Sunday and reach the island in time for afternoon potables, a welcoming talk, and a stroll around the small island. A delicious five-course dinner with wine, and breakfast the next morning are included in the price. Each of the four period decorated rooms has a water view, but our favorite is the San Francisco Room upstairs near the parlor. Games and reading materials in the parlor make for a relaxing evening. The next morning, after breakfast and a deafening sample of the foghorn, you're returned to the real world.

MARTINEZ

John Muir National Historic Site 4202 Alhambra Ave. off John Muir Pkwy., 94553; 510-228-8860. Self-guided tours, Wednesday through Sunday, 10 A.M. to 4:30 P.M. Guided tours and environmental living programs by reservation. Donation. "I hold dearly cherished memories about [the house] and find garden grounds full of trees and bushes and flowers that my wife and

Ardenwood Farm, Fremont

father-in-law and I planted—fine things from every land…"—John Muir

John Muir's father-in-law built this imposing Italianate towered villa in 1882, and Muir lived here from 1890 until 1914. Today, it's one of the best-presented Victorian houses in the state, with its closets still filled with clothing, a suitcase on the bed ready for travel, Muir's glasses and pencils on the desk in his "scribble den," and pictures of his friends President Theodore Roosevelt and naturalist John Burroughs on the walls. You can even go up to the attic and ring the ranch bell in the belltower.

Muir's inspiring words are spread around the house. In the back parlor near the grand piano, read "All things move in music and write it." In the hall: "No American wilderness that I know of is so dangerous as a city house with all the modern improvements. One should go to the woods for safety, if nothing else…" And "How grand would be a home in a hollow Sequoia!"

The John Muir Memorial Association, P.O. Box 2433, 94553, opens the house for Muir's birthday celebration, bagpipes and all.

Martinez Museum 1005 Escobar St., P.O. Box 14, 94553; 510-228-8160. Tuesday and Thursday, 11:30 A.M. to 3 P.M.; first and third Sunday of each month, 1 to 4 P.M. Guided tours. Research library. Dr. J. S. Moore's 1890 Victorian cottage and dental office

houses a collection of local and county memorabilia. The Martinez Historical Society also housed here provides maps and profiles of the historic downtown area and the antique shops from Marina Vista to Main along Ferry Street.

BENICIA

This historic town, a major antiques center, was founded in 1847 by Dr. Robert Baylor Semple and Thomas O. Larkin on land owned by General Mariano Vallejo and named for his wife, Benicia. It was once the capital of California. A Visitor's Guide and walking maps of the antiques and historical house districts are available from the Benicia Main Street Program, the Benicia Antique Group, and the Chamber of Commerce, 831 First St., 95410 (707-745-2120). P.O. Box 185. Hours: Monday through Friday, 8:30 A.M. to 5 P.M., Saturday and Sunday, 11 A.M. to 3 P.M. Antiques events are held throughout the year.

The Captain Walsh House 235 East L St., 94510; 707-747-5653 (M). The only Gothic Revival house in Benicia, the Frisbie-Walsh House has been completely restored by architect Reed Robbins and her husband, Steve. Andrew Jackson Downing designed the house, a prefab from Boston shipped around Cape Horn in 1849, and it is identical

East Brother Light Station, Pt. Richmond

John Muir National Historic Site, Martinez

cheer in the rustic bar, and twelve large turn-of-the-century rooms with brass beds, interesting antiques, some tongue-in-cheek decor, and Jacuzzi tubs. Purists will request Victoriana or Four Poster rather than Louis Le Mad or Mei Ling.

After dining behind the etched-glass windows in the dining room on fresh local oysters, pan-fried sturgeon with cucumber-mint and corn relishes, or grilled king salmon with raspberry and kiwi-ginger sauces on mixed-pepper rice pasta, you may find yourself loath to drive home. A great idea: the Union Hotel offers any last-minute unoccupied room at a reduced rate as part of its "dine and don't drive" program.

Places to See, Artisans, and Suppliers

Benicia Historical Society, Inc. P.O. Box 773, 94510. Meetings, newsletter.

Benicia Tours 707-745-9508. By reservation. Danica Ziegler, local history buff, talks and walks you through Benicia's historical district.

Bradbury & Bradbury Wallpapers P.O. Box 155-C, 94510; 707-746-1900. Tours by

Dillon's Antiques, Benicia

to Lachryma Montis, the historic Vallejo home in Sonoma. Both houses were shipped on the same boat. Vallejo's daughter, Epifina de Guadalupe Vallejo Frisbie, lived here, and Captain Walsh bought it in 1852.

The Benicia Historic Society fought hard to save the house from improper reuse. Today, it's painted in chapel gray with white trim and green sashes. There are four ingenious guestrooms, each with bath and fireplace. Epifina would be pleased with the room named after her. The Harvest Room has grape-leaf stencils on the walls and original grape-leaf molding on the ceiling. The Library Room has a vaulted ceiling and reading loft. A Murphy bed appears out of one of the bookcases. Another hidden bed comes out of the paneling in the parlor.

A breakfast buffet is served on the porch or breakfast patio. Meetings, parties, and weddings may be arranged. And there's a harp in the parlor for recitals. The large outside dog has its own Gothic doghouse. The Captain Walsh House is across the street from City Hall, the city pool, and tennis courts.

Union Hotel 401 First St., 94510; 707-746-0100 (M). The town's oldest three-story structure, dating back to 1882, was once a famed bordello. It now offers good California cooking in the dining room, good

appointment. Specializing in hand-printed Victorian and early twentieth-century wallpapers and borders, Bruce Bradbury (AL) and company sell worldwide by mail order. They also offer a design service to help with individual planning needs. Arranged into coordinated "roomsets" for walls and ceilings, the Victorian collection may be viewed in their catalog. Samples available. Videotape shows history of and how to wallpaper. (DPL, PLR)

Dillon's Antiques 121 E. J St., 94510; 707-745-2815. Tuesday through Sunday, 10 A.M. to 5 P.M. James and Mary Jean Dillon painted their home like the cover house of *Painted Ladies*, in yellow, with blue and white trim. The barn in back holds furniture, clocks, and collectibles. James Dillon also repairs old clocks. Theirs is one of the almost three dozen antiques and crafts stores in Benicia. (DPL)

Across the street, St. Paul's Episcopal Church (First and J), built in 1859 as the first Episcopal cathedral in Northern California, is a pink and white Gothic charmer on the outside, grandly carved and brightly painted on the inside.

Fischer-Hanlon House 135 West G St., 94510; 707-745-3385. Saturday and Sunday, 12 to 4 P.M. and by reservation for weddings, receptions, and meetings.

This handsome Federal home has a Victorian interior. Built in 1849 and reconstructed in 1856, the three Hanlon schoolteacher sisters lived here together for more than seventy years.

Little People Shop 333 1st St., 94510; 707-745-9411. Miniatures and dollhouse specialists.

Paul's Design Studio and Woodshop 320 Gull Pt., 94510; 707-745-8453. Paul Harford creates fireplace mantels, bookcases, and mirror accents, with architectural emphasis on woodworking.

Elizabeth Pigeon 707-745-8817. Architect specializing in preservation and restoration.

Preservation Painting 366 Military E., 94510; 707-745-6513. Mike Brown does exterior and interior painting, signs, and faux finishes.

Vintage Carriage Tours Start from 1st and D Sts.; 707-745-0408. Wednesday through Sunday afternoons in season. Call for brochure and reservations

VALLEJO

Vallejo Architectural Heritage District Vallejo Chamber of Commerce, 2 Florida St., 94590; 707-644-5551. Guides for the almost two dozen pre-1900 homes built in architectural styles popular before the turn of the century.

MARIN COUNTY

*"Nothing is so dangerous as being too modern.
One is apt to grow old-fashioned quite suddenly."*
—Oscar Wilde

Wealth, creative people, natural beauty—Marin County has it all. As soon as you cross the Golden Gate Bridge, the naked hills of the Golden Gate National Recreation Area and the rainbow on the entrance to the tunnel at the top of the Waldo Grade symbolize your arrival in a unique part of the world. After you drive around the county's populated areas off Route 101 and explore Marin's quiet, gorgeous coast, you will understand why some of San Francisco's top Victorian artists live here.

Lodging

SAUSALITO

Casa Madrona Hotel & Restaurant 801 Bridgeway, 94965; 415-332-0502 (M/E). The old and new casas in this completely rebuilt hotel provide "a nineteenth-century reminder of a less hurried time." After taking the elevator from Bridgeway, climb up two sets of stairs through the garden to the top of the hill and you reach the original 1885 Stick residence of businessman William Grout Barrett. The twelve rooms, all with bath, retain the original moldings, banisters, and mantels. Some are truly Victorian in feeling and furnishings, and some have bay views and private verandas. The Belle Vista Suite even has a tub for two in the living room.

The new section of Casa Madrona is a series of individually themed New England–style cottages and suites with views, fireplaces, and modern amenities such as minibars. The outdoor spa, available by reservation, can be very romantic. One favorite, the Artist's Loft, provides easel, paints, and brushes in a Parisian artist's atelier, with a sweeping view of the bay. Fresh-baked pastries make the continental breakfast a delight.

Casa Madrona's award-winning restaurant serves excellent American cuisine at lunch, dinner, and Sunday brunch.

The Sausalito Hotel 16 El Portal, 94965; 415-332-4155 (M/E). Up the stairs of this 1915 Mission Revival hotel is an authentic Victorian hotel with a racy past. Rumors of a bordello in the twenties and prohibition liquor abound. The fifteen rooms, with private and shared baths, are all named for Queen Victoria's relatives. Some of the rooms—even the inexpensive Lady Hastings and Princess Beatrice—have bay views. Carefully chosen nineteenth-century antiques and period lamps dress up each room. Most notable is the Marquess of Queensbury suite, with its fireplace, and General Ulysses S. Grant's grand Renaissance Revival bedroom suite. An ample continental breakfast and free parking are included in the price. The hotel is steps away from the ferry landing.

OLEMA

Olema Inn 1876 10000 Sir Francis Drake Blvd., 94950; 415-663-9559 (M). The Olema Inn opened on the Fourth of July, 1876, as a gathering place for loggers, ranchers, and farmers who frequented the once rowdy town of Olema. Faithfully restored in 1988, the inn offers six spare, country-Victorian rooms with private modern baths. Its location at the junction of Highway 1 and Sir Francis Drake Boulevard make it a con-

Tomales Inn, Tomales

venient place to stay while exploring Point Reyes National Seashore. Continental breakfast is served in the restaurant downstairs.

The Olema Inn Restaurant serves dinner Friday through Monday, emphasizing fresh local produce.

Bear Valley Inn B & B 88 Bear Valley Rd., 94950; 415-663-1777 (M). There are three comfortable rooms in this two-story 1899 Victorian ranch house near Point Reyes National Seashore. The house was originally built for the foreman of the Shafter Estate, a large turn-of-the-century ranch. A retired airline stewardess and her husband who once managed a small restaurant and had some remodeling experience, are turning their white-and-blue trimmed house into a relaxed, down-home spot.

BOLINAS

Blue Heron Inn 11 Wharf Rd., P.O. Box 309,

94924; 415-868-1102 (M). Bolinas was once Marin's largest town, with seven hotels, eleven taverns, and eleven sawmills—and you got there whenever the low tide opened the lagoon mudflats. Today's residents remove the turn-off sign on Route 1 to help maintain their privacy. The only inn is composed of two airy rooms behind a cute little café in a small blue and white Victorian cottage on the main street—with a neon sign for "Open." Both country-style rooms have a clawfoot tub in the bathroom, and a full breakfast is served in the café.

TOMALES

Tomales Inn: A Victorian Retreat 25 Valley St., P.O. Box 376, 94971; 707-878-9992 (M). This sprawling Victorian, painted creamy white, slate blue, and wine, nestles five peaceful rooms under the eaves, two with private bath. Paintings by the last owner, Byron Randall, brighten up the inviting parlor, and sculptures hide in the flowery garden. An expanded continental breakfast is served in the dining room. The inn is a lovely setting for weddings, conferences, and retreats.

Inns of Pt. Reyes P.O. Box 145, Inverness, 94937; 415-663-1420. A referral service.

Falkirk Cultural Center, San Rafael

Lyford House, Tiburon

Lodging Switchboard of Coastal Marin P.O. Box 644, Pt. Reyes Sta., 94956; 415-663-9445. A referral service.

Restaurants

Lark Creek Inn 234 Magnolia Ave., Larkspur, 94939; 415-924-7766. Lunch Monday through Friday, brunch on weekends; dinner daily. Award-winning nouvelle-American chef Bradley Ogden and co-proprietor Michael Dellar transformed the Lark Creek Inn with a cheery yellow and white facelift, and brought the redwood forest inside through their imaginative use of windows, skylights, white walls, polished plank floors, and tables. The Yankee pot roast and dumplings, fried egg sandwiches, brownie sundaes, and peach shortcakes are favorites.

Goods and Services

Better Construction 272 Shoreline Hwy. #1, Mill Valley, 94941; 415-383-2161. Kelly Carlin and Patrick Burke. Interior remodels and exterior rehabilitation.

Clark Chelsey Painting 415-381-1772.

Croworks 415-454-6809. Croworks is a family-owned company of artisans skilled in the Victorian traditions of decorative painted finishes. Faux bois techniques transform wood surfaces—from walls to fireplaces—into marble. Jewel-like decorative touches applied to fine furniture create patterns of tortoise shell, inlaid ivory and shagreen. Croworks also designs murals and painted floors.

Door/Ways Al Garvey. 281 Scenic Road, Fairfax, 94930; 415-453-5275. Custom-made doors, sculptured wood environments.

William Eichenberger 580 Irwin St., San Rafael, 94901; 415-457-1190. Furniture maker; period, modern, shoji, cabinetry.

Feathered Serpent Press 1565 Vendola Dr., San Rafael, 94903; 415-499-8751. Feathered Serpent produces limited edition books in the nineteenth-century tradition of William Morris and the fine presses of the Arts & Crafts movement. This award-winning firm uses antique presses, hand-set Victorian typefaces, fine paper, and traditional binding methods. Commissions of special books.

Bruce Nelson Local Color Painting Co. (AL) 990 Green Hill Rd., Mill Valley, 94941; 415-389-8018. Award-winning painting and restoration of historic, commercial, and residential properties.

Ruby Newman P.O. Box 303, Fairfax, 94930; 415-457-1303. Painter, ceramicist, tile maker. Decorative and fine art finishes. Restoration of wooden painted collectibles, specializing in nineteenth-century carousel art and architecture.

Pagliacco Turning and Milling P.O. Box 225, Woodacre, 94973; 415-488-4333. Architectural wood-turning service. California redwood balusters, newel posts, railings, columns, and capital. Catalog.

PATINAe 264 Manor Drive, Mill Valley, 94941; 415-383-8113. Christy Cizek, decorative finishes. (HTC)

Roger Scharmer 415-383-4070. Garden specialist. Teaches at the University of California at Berkeley.

Shades of the Past P.O. Box 206, Fairfax, 94978; 415-459-6999. Tracy Holcomb re-creates turn-of-the-century silk and velvet lampshades with Italian glass-beaded fringe and offers a line of ornate reproduction brass bases. An artist, designer, and artisan, she works with residential and commercial clients to create unique lighting for specific decorative needs. Brochure available.

Yesterday's Rose 572 Las Colinda Rd., San Rafael, 94903; 415-474-2119. Nursery specializing in vintage herbs and flowers.

Places to Visit

The China Cabin Belvedere-Tiburon Landmarks Society, P.O. Box 134, Belvedere-Tiburon, 94920; 415-435-2251. Tours Wednesday and Sunday afternoons. Available for receptions. The social saloon of the SS *China*, built in New York City by William Webb, the greatest American shipbuilder of the mid-nineteenth century, was a casualty of shipbuilding progress, and turned into a weekend cottage. Beverly Bastian led the members of the Belvedere-Tiburon Landmarks Society in restoring the saloon to its original glory. This took eight years and $600,000, plus $400,000 worth of volunteer labor. Today, decorative patterns fashioned in wood, plaster, and compo are gilded with twenty-two-karat gold leaf. On the polished floor, an inlaid compass rose marks the position of the main mast, and indentations in the walnut-inlaid border of the white-oak floor mark where the grand double staircase descended to the dining salon and first-class cabins. Elaborate columns grace fluted walnut pilasters.

Church of Old St. Hilary's in the Wildflowers Alemany and Esperanza Sts., Tiburon, 94920; 415-435-1853. Sunday through Wednesday, 1 to 4 P.M., April through September, and by appointment. Donation. Weeds and flowers that grow on these grounds, some nowhere else in the world, are exhibited in this Gothic treasure.

Falkirk Cultural Center 1408 Mission Ave., San Rafael, 94901; 415-485-3328. Tuesday, Wednesday, Friday, 10 A.M. to 6 P.M.; Thursday, 10 A.M. to 9 P.M.; Saturday, 10 A.M. to 1 P.M. Group tours and rentals by arrangement. Donation. Magnificent oaks and magnolias frame the seventeen-room mansion designed by Clinton Day in 1888, now on the register of National Historic Places. The picturesque roofline, with gables and chimneys, shaped bays, and decorative details, create an excellent example of the Queen Anne–style country home. Set on eleven acres of park, with reflecting pool and a historic greenhouse, it now serves as a contemporary art center for the city.

Lyford House Richardson Bay Audubon Center, 376 Greenwood Beach Rd., Tiburon, 94920; 415-388-2525. Sunday, 1 to 4 P.M., October through May, and by appointment. Donation. This yellow and white Stick villa with a mansard roof was built by dairy farmer Benjamin Lyford and his wife, Hilarita Reed, at Strawberry Point. It was floated across Richardson Bay in 1957, restored, and refurnished. The former dining room is a gallery for changing natural history and wildlife exhibits.

Marin County Historical Society Museum 1125 B St., Boyd Park, San Rafael, 94903; 415-454-8538. Wednesday through Sunday, 1 to 4 P.M. Free. (Closed for earthquake repairs; call before visiting.) Ira W. Cook built this Gothic Revival cottage with ornate bargeboards as a guesthouse in 1879. His granddaughter Louise donated it and its wonderful gardens to San Rafael in 1905. Designed to "stir the imagination and bring back panoramas of the past," this overstuffed museum displays original Mexican land grants and pioneer mementos such as Lillie Coit's shoes and wedding regalia.

Groups

Belvedere-Tiburon Landmarks Society 1600 Juanita Lane, P.O. Box 134, Belvedere-Tiburon, 94920; 415-435-1853. The society owns and maintains China Cabin and Old St. Hilary's and offers publications, tours, concerts, exhibits, archives, a reference library, and a collector's shop. Its purpose is the acquisition and preservation of property of historical significance to California's heritage.

Marin County Historical Society 125 B St., San Rafael, 94901; 415-454-8538.

San Anselmo Historical Commission San Anselmo Public Library, 110 Tunstead Ave., San Anselmo, 94960.

San Rafael Cultural Commission Dollar House, 1408 Mission St., San Rafael, 94901.

Sausalito Historical Society Sausalito Public Library, 420 Litho St., Sausalito, 94965; 415-289-4117.

THE WINE COUNTRY
Sonoma, Napa, and Lake Counties

An Innkeeper's Credo:
"Office Hours: Open Most days around 9 or 10.
Occasionally as early as 7, but Some Days as late as 12 or 1.
We close about 5:30 or 6, Occasionally around 4 or 5,
*   but sometimes as late as 11 or 12.*
Some Days or afternoons we aren't there at all, and lately,
*   I've been here just about All the Time,*
Except When I'm Someplace Else,
*   But I Should be Here Then, Too."*

There are few areas in the world that instantly evoke both tranquillity and excitement. California's Wine Country, one of the world's most valued wine regions, is one place that Californians head for in search of peace, beauty, and the underlying promise of haute cuisine, chic spas, and elegant getaway spots.

Even though wine is a billion-dollar industry, the area has striated hillsides rather than smokestacks. The laboratories are in modern and historic buildings. Many of these historic buildings are open to visitors, who arrive by car and bicycle to taste and to appreciate tradition.

On the outskirts of the town of Sonoma, you can visit Buena Vista winery, founded in 1857 by Count Agoston Haraszthy, the father of winemaking in California, at 18000 Old Winery Rd., 707-938-1266.

Beaulieu Vineyards, founded in 1900 by Georges de Latour, is at 11960 St. Helena Hwy., in Rutherford; 707-963-2411.

The Beringer Rhine House is the center of the oldest continuously operated winery in Napa Valley, established in 1876 by Jacob and Frederick Beringer. Here you can see wine vats in limestone hills tunneled by Chinese laborers and learn about California and winemaking history.

The Christian Brothers modern facilities and Greystone Cellars, built in 1889 of locally quarried stone, doubles as a museum: 100 S. St. Helena Hwy., Hwy. 29, St. Helena; 707-963-4480.

PETALUMA

Petaluma, America's egg basket, is a 130-year-old river town built on what was once General Mariano Vallejo's ranch. Petaluma has also been called "Little San Francisco" because of its fine stock of Victorian homes and iron-front buildings. Antique stores abound.

Victorian Christmas in Petaluma is special, with Santa Claus arriving in a paddle-wheel steamboat and then heading a holiday horse-and-carriage procession. The riverfront is alive with packetboats and schooners; gaslamps glow, garlands of greenery festoon the cast-iron buildings, and carolers wander the streets. There is also a midsummer River Festival.

For information on the Victorian Christmas and for driving and walking tours, there are three contacts: the Petaluma Chamber of Commerce, 215 Howard St., 707-762-2785; the Petaluma Historical Museum, 4th and B Sts., 707-778-4398; or the Petaluma Visitor Center at 116 E. Lakeville off Hwy. 101, 707-762-2785. Petaluma was a Main Street Project, and you may take a Parlor Holiday Tour by calling 707-762-9348.

"Victorian Homes of the A Street Historic District" encompasses six blocks, from Keller to Liberty to A, B, and Sixth streets, and from Greek Revival to Queen Anne styles, representing Petaluma's past history. For tours, call Ross Parkerson, 707-762-2706. The Centennial Block, an iron-front building built in 1876, once housed a music hall where Mark Twain appeared.

Bed-and-Breakfast Inns

Cavanagh Inn 10 Keller St., 94952; 707-765-4657 (I/M). Gray, white, and burgundy highlight this Craftsman cottage next door to the main house, a 1903 Neoclassic Georgian Revival Victorian. There are three country-style rooms in the wood-paneled cottage, and four Victorian-style rooms in the main house. An outdoor deck is surrounded by English gardens. A jar full of homemade cookies, fresh apple cider or lemonade, and a stocked refrigerator are on hand. Fresh Petaluma eggs are always served in the full breakfast.

The 7th Street Inn 525 7th St. at I, 94952; 707-769-0480 (M). Blue-gray, white, navy blue, and a touch of pink embellish this stately 1892 Queen Anne home. Morris Fredericks, a contractor from Germany who served on the first city council, built this house and lived out his life here with his wife, Theodora, and six children. The maid's room is now a suite with a sun porch. The water tower in back has been transformed into a romantic guestroom with a skylight sleeping loft and fireplace. A new carriage house was added in 1989 for another comfortable room. Guests can loll on the sun deck before sharing a bountiful breakfast.

Restaurants

Alfred's 17 Keller St., 94952; 707-778-7287. Lunch Tuesday through Saturday; dinner daily except Monday (M/E). A historic Gothic church, painted in two shades of pinky-beige, houses Petaluma's favorite Italian steakhouse.

McNear's Saloon & Dining House 23 Petaluma Blvd. N., 94952; 707-765-2121. Country cooking daily, 11:30 A.M. to 1 A.M. Historic murals and sports memorabilia decorate the walls of the beautifully restored iron-front building, a detail of which appeared in *Daughters of Painted Ladies*. Fresh barbecued Tomales Bay Oysters are served in front of the restaurant at 5 P.M., on Fridays and Saturdays. Inside, there are pocket billiards, darts, foosball (honest), and shuffleboard, as well as a Kids' Happy Hour, Sunday champagne brunch, live music, and dancing.

The Old River Inn 222 Weller St., 94952; 707-765-0111. Lunch Monday through Friday; brunch on weekends; dinner daily. (M). You can walk across the river from the Great Petaluma Mill shopping complex to a pretty blue-gray and white Queen Anne for elegant dining on the river in a Victorian setting. There's outdoor patio seating for the continental cuisine, and banquet facilities are available.

Places to Visit

Petaluma Historic Library and Museum 4th and B Sts., 94952; 707-778-4398. Thursday through Monday, 1 to 4 P.M. Free. Changing exhibits from the 1850s display Petaluma's history. The stained glass alone makes the museum worth a visit.

Craftspeople and Tours

Barquero Ceramics 1710 Capistrano Dr., 94954; 707-763-8820. Marilyn Barquero, ceramicist, creator of handmade "Painted Ladies" cookie jars. Wholesale and retail.

The Brassman 707-762-9044. Dan Reed. Antique lights.

Bright Lights 707-664-6043. Allen Van Etten. Victorian and deco lighting fixtures.

Construction/Remodeling/Repairs 415-459-1369/707-778-8407. Mike Bicheler and Joel Radford.

Custom Architectural Pieces 707-762-6811. Kurt Bainum. Turn-of-the-century doors and windows copied, repaired, or replaced. One-of-a-kind reproductions.

Debi's Designs 416 G St., 94952; 707-763-9219. Debi Riddle. Tiffany-style lamps, leaded windows, restorations, sandblasted etching.

EMP's Graphic Eye 430 Petaluma Blvd., N. Petaluma 94952; 707-763-4450. Bill Empey and Sharon Whyms. Etched- and beveled-glass custom orders.

Heads Up/Sonoma Woodworks 133 Copeland St., 94952; 707-762-5548. Oak bathroom and kitchen accessories, including mirrors, medicine cabinets, and pull-chain toilets. Brochure.

Historic Homes of Petaluma. House tours and guides; 707-765-6685.

Millwork Marin 1771 Bodega Ave., 94952; 707-762-7358. Jim Eastburn. Manufacturer and distributor of architectural millwork.

O'Brien Painting 707-763-2857. Don O'Brien.

Stroke & Coat Painting 707-938-2843. (DPL)

James Webb 327 Howard St., 94952; 707-762-3444. Lost-art restorations. Architectural design, restoration, interior and exterior color planning, antique plaster medallions, brackets, doors, windows, and moldings.

BODEGA

Schoolhouse Inn 17110 Bodega Lane, P.O. Box 136, 94922; 707-876-3257 (M). This white-towered Italianate edged in forest green is the schoolhouse used in the Hitchcock movie *The Birds*. Since it really was a schoolhouse from 1873 until 1961, guests will find original slate chalkboards and school desks blending well with the nineteenth-century furnishings in the four rooms, each with private bath. Breakfast is served in the large open parlor upstairs, which is also used for parties, workshops, and local theatrical presentations. Today, the birds are well behaved.

BODEGA BAY

Bay Hill Mansion Bed & Breakfast 3919 Bay Hill Road, P.O. Box 567, 94923; 707-875-3577/800-526-5927 (M/E). An imposing gray and white shingled Neo Queen Anne, Bay Hill Mansion is high on a hill on the north end of town, with panoramic views of the bay and the Pacific Ocean. Although only the Honeymooners' Hideaway, which is right off the lobby, has its own bath, all five rooms come with fluffy bathrobes. Wedding and group specials.

OCCIDENTAL

Heart's Desire Inn 3657 Church Street, P.O. Box 857, 95465; 707-874-1311 (M/E). Nestled against a hillside of berries and fruit trees is a two-story 1860s Victorian farmhouse with hearts built into the brick chimneys. Renovation has given the eight rooms, all with private bath, a European air, with polished fir wood floors, fresh flowers, down comforters and pillows, and antique pine furnishings.

The Honeymoon Suite has a fireplace, four-poster bed, and a private deck. The Garden Room, which is wheelchair-accessible, enjoys the lulling sounds of the fountain in the courtyard. Jake the Cat presides over the breakfast buffet, which includes locally made preserves and honey.

GUERNEVILLE

Santa Nella House Pocket Creek Canyon, 12130 Hwy. 116, 95446; 707-869-9488 (M). A Wedgwood blue and white 1870s Italianate nestled in the redwoods is just a short walk away from the Russian River and Korbel Champagne Cellars (when the summer bridge is in). Home of the builder of the Santa Nella Winery, the house was the site of one of the first sawmills in the area and a stagecoach stop. The wraparound veranda, gazebo, and bucolic setting invite you to relax. Or enjoy the old pool table on the sun deck, a hot tub, and a whirlpool. Three of the four rooms have fireplaces and private

Schoolhouse Inn, Bodega

bath. Each is decorated in a different style, with a welcoming Victorian feeling.

SEBASTOPOL

The Gravenstein Inn 3160 Hicks Rd., 95472; 707-829-0493 (M). Moses C. Hicks built this yellow and white Greek Revival/Victorian home in 1872, and it is now a national historic landmark beautifully restored by new owners. Two of the four rooms have private baths, and guests arrive to find wine and cookies and "old" radios with vintage programs on tape.

The Victorian Room is graced by family portraits and a private porch overlooking the swimming pool and horseshoe pits. There are meeting rooms for business functions. Vacationers can cuddle up with a book in the well-stocked library, have a barbecue on the outdoor pit, play games, and play on the 1873 square Chickering piano in the parlor. You can also pick your own Gravenstein apples.

Suppliers and Groups

Carriage Charter 3325 Hwy. 116 N., 95472; 707-823-7083. A touring coach, stagecoach, Victoria and pair calèche, brougham, and a Concord stagecoach and surrey are avail-

able hourly or daily for drives on wine-country farm roads. All these authentic horse-drawn vehicles are available for Victorian travel and entertainment at any Northern California location.

Gregg Lowery 303 Pleasant Hill Rd., 95472; 707-829-5342. Landscape gardener. Vintage gardens a specialty.

Ray's Trading Co. 3570 Gravenstein Hwy. S., 95472; 707-829-9726. Ray Burrows. Antiques and salvage. Doors, windows, sinks, tubs, hardware, and "a good source of missing links."

Remember Yesterday 930 Gravenstein Hwy. S., 95472; 707-829-9111. Kerosene, gas, and early electric lighting. Lamps, parts, shades, repairs.

School Bell Antiques 3555 Gravenstein Hwy. S., 95472; 707-833-2878. Daily, 10 A.M. to 5 P.M. A dealer collective (twenty-four members) in a historic Victorian schoolhouse.

Western Sonoma County Historical Society P.O. Box 816, 95473. A nonprofit organization that depends on memberships, grants, and contributions to support its efforts to protect and preserve Sonoma's local heritage through house tours, preservations awards, archives, and an Apple Blossom Festival. The WSCHS also runs Luther Burbank Gold Ridge Experiment Farm and is in the process of organizing the new West County Museum in the restored/renovated Santa Rosa–Petaluma railroad depot.

SANTA ROSA

The Gables 4257 Petaluma Hill Rd., 95404; 707-585-7777 (I/M). Fifteen gables crown the unusual keyhole-shaped windows of this High Victorian Gothic Revival historical landmark home, built in 1877 by gold-mining farmer William Roberts.

The five rooms are wonderfully Victorian and comfortable, with clawfoot tubs in the private baths, goose-down comforters, fresh flowers, and good books. The little

The Gables, Santa Rosa

Pygmalion House 331 Orange St., 95401; 707-526-3407 (I/M). Three grays, white, and blue illuminate this 1880s towered Queen Anne. It's named Pygmalion to honor its transformation from an old dilapidated house to a grand lady in 1983. Each of the five colorful rooms has its own private bath, and the high ceilings, extensive window coverings, and continental touches will add to the comfort level. Evening snacks are offered in the parlor. A bountiful breakfast featuring the innkeeper's homemade plum jam is served in the country kitchen.

Places to Visit

Luther Burbank Home and Gardens Santa Rosa at Sonoma Ave., P.O. Box 1678, 95402; 707-524-5445. Wednesday through Sunday, April through Mid-October, 10 A.M. to 3:30 P.M. Docent-led tours of house and greenhouse every half hour—fee. Memorial

cottage next to Taylor Creek, where the honeymooning Roberts family first lived, is now a romantic hideaway with a kitchenette, wood stove, and sleeping loft with a sleigh bed. Guests can wander on three and a half acres, pet the outdoor cats, or loll on the sun deck. Located on the eastern outskirts of town, the Gables is halfway between Glen Ellen and Healdsburg. By the time this book is published, the exterior will be made up with creams, roses, burgundy, and a touch of green.

Melitta Station Inn 5850 Melita Rd., 95405; 707-538-7712 (M). "Melita" means "poppy" in Miwok, and when the Santa Rosa mapmaker incorporated the town of Melitta into the city, an *L* was dropped from the name. Once a stagecoach stop, this turn-of-the-century railroad station has been transformed into a six-room bed-and-breakfast furnished with antiques and American folk art. Stenciled railings and moldings lead guests to the sitting room with its rough-beam cathedral ceiling, old Welsh sideboard, and French doors opening to a balcony overlooking the garden. Guests may have their buffet breakfast on the balcony or in front of the wood-burning stove. Evening refreshments are also available.

Camellia Inn, Healdsburg

Gardens open daily year-round—free. Group tours and community outreach programs by reservation. The eminent horticulturist lived in this little cottage from 1884 to 1906; his widow, Elizabeth, lived here from his death in 1926 until hers in 1977. Most of the furnishings are original, including Burbank's desk in the music room, the tile-bordered fireplace in the parlor, the Burbank family china in the kitchen, and Elizabeth's antique copper collection in the dining room. The former carriage house is now a museum featuring displays of his life and work and a gift shop.

The Luther Burbank Home and Gardens hosts an annual holiday open house and gift sale the first weekend in December.

Associations

Sonoma County Historical Society P.O. Box 1873, 95402, 707-527-2461, or c/o John Schubert, P.O. Box 2037, Guerneville, 94556; 707-869-3764.

Sonoma County Museum 425 7th St., 95401; 707-579-1500. Wednesday through Sunday, 11 A.M. to 4 P.M. Historical museum foundation. Meetings, newsletter, volunteer opportunities. Changing art and history exhibits. Gift shop.

WINDSOR

Country Meadow Inn 113560 Old Redwood Hwy., 95492; 707-431-1276 (M). This elegant shingled redwood 1890s Queen Anne, painted blue, burgundy, and dark brown, is perched atop a lushly landscaped knoll surrounded by rolling hills, vineyards, and a meadow. Serenity and love of the land is the theme here, with chickens raised for eggs, vegetables for the frittatas, and fresh flowers for the rooms.

Each of the five rooms has its own bath, and in time, each will have a fireplace. The Southern Suite has a double whirlpool tub. Bicycles, badminton, picnics, and a pool are available. The fig, apricot, pineapple-guava, and peach trees provide fruit for

midnight snacks and for the fresh breakfast jam. The innkeeper has a really easy recipe for strawberry sauce: boil a cup of water, add cornstarch that has been mixed with cold water, add berries, and keep cooking until you like the consistency.

HEALDSBURG

Camellia Inn 211 North St., 95448; 707-433-8182 (I/M). This elegant, aptly named 1869 Italianate town house, framed by pine trees, is painted in three shades of salmon pink and white, outside and in. Built by Ransom Powell and then bought by Dr. J. W. Seawall in 1892, the house was the town's first hospital. Seawall's friend, Luther Burbank, provided many of the thirty different varieties of camellias gracing the grounds.

The English Minton tiles by Morer around the fireplace in the second parlor quote the Seven Ages of Man from *As You Like It*. The nine rooms are named after camellia varieties in the garden, including Moon Glow and Demitasse. Some rooms have gas fireplaces and double Jacuzzi tubs. All but two have private baths. Canopy beds, fine linens and coverlets, Bradbury & Bradbury wallpaper, views of the gardens and mountains, a terrace, and a villa-styled swimming pool that echoes the fish pond in front will make your stay most enjoyable. A buffet breakfast is served in the main dining room. Occasionally, owner Ray Lewand gives tours of his prizewinning home winery.

Grape Leaf Inn 539 Johnson St., 95448; 707-433-8140 (M/E). Lavender, grape, and gold tones shine on this Painted Lady. The heart of this 1900 Queen Anne is still Victorian, with lace tablecloths, fireplaces, and family portraits. But ingenious construction by proprietor Terry Sweet has added skylights and dormer windows, giving space, light, and charm to the seven rooms named for grape varietals, all with private baths, five with whirlpool tubs, and two with showers. Even the bubble bath is purple.

One of the family members was told in

school that one should never use purple paint on a house, so the family did, with great success. The lovely rooms are also in tones of lavender, rose, and blue. Fat purple roses and purple daisies grow in the landscaped gardens. Full country breakfasts and local wines and cheeses are complimentary, as are the wine tastings under the trees.

Haydon House B & B Inn 321 Haydon St., 95448; 707-433-5228 (M). This Colonial Revival mansion painted in two blues and white hides a deliciously detailed brand-new Victorian Gothic cottage in three blues and white. The main house used to be a convent, so the few rooms without private baths have washbasins. All six are cheerfully decorated in Laura Ashley country-Victorian style, with lace, lithographs, and love seats. The cottage rooms boast four-poster queen-size beds and double whirlpool tubs.

Healdsburg Inn on the Plaza 116 Matheson St., P.O. Box 1196, 95448; 707-433-6991 (E). The second floor of the landmark 1900 Wells Fargo building on the Plaza has been converted into a comfortable nine-room hotel. With fanciful names like Moonbeams, Sonnets, Skydance, and Minuet, the rooms are furnished with American antiques, and lots of style in sunrise/sunset colors. Light wells are used to provide light for interior spaces, and one of the most dramatic rooms, in what was once a photography studio, features a twenty-foot slanted skylight.

Each room has a private bath with a clawfoot tub, scented soaps, bubble bath, and rubber duckie. Guests gather in the TV lounge, the roof garden, or the solarium for a full breakfast—champagne brunch on weekends—and evening tea. The house cat doesn't bother the chirping lovebirds in the solarium. The gracious, knowledgeable manager also presides over the art gallery on the ground floor.

Two wonderful shops and a bakery share the block on the charming Plaza, in a town filled with interesting shops, antique stores, and Victorians.

Madrona Manor Hotel and Restaurant 1001 Westside Rd., 95448; 707-433-4231/800-258-4003 (M/E). The baronial 1881 Mansard summer home of wealthy San Franciscan John Paxton is now one of the premier hotels and dining rooms in the wine country. The splendid cornices and spindlework, especially on the Carpenter Gothic carriage house, are picked out in two beige tones with blue-gray and burgundy details.

John and Carol Muir have restored the mansion, carriage house, and meadow wood complex, once the kitchens, and built a secluded garden suite, creating eighteen rooms and two suites, all with full baths, gloriously wallpapered and filled with fine rosewood, antique furniture, and Oriental carpets. Some of the American Victorian Renaissance furniture is original to the house, including the carved rosewood piano in the music room. A jigsaw puzzle in progress awaits you in the lobby drawing room, as does the pool behind the citrus grove.

The European buffet breakfast includes meats, cheeses, soft-boiled eggs, Madrona Manor toast, and fresh hot churros. Madrona Manor is listed in the National Register of Historic Places and offers facilities for weddings and seminars. The Muirs will be happy to tell you about the one hundred wineries within a radius of twenty miles. This is a family-run inn, with son Mark heading the maintenance crew and son Todd serving as executive chef.

Madrona Manor Restaurant 1001 Westside Rd., 95448; 707-433-4231 (M/E). Dinner nightly 6 to 9 P.M., prix fixe or à la carte; Sunday brunch. California Culinary Academy graduate Chef Todd Muir composes menus that celebrate the area's fresh produce and seafood. For example, a late summer Tribute to Figs included a Fresh Corn Timbale combining corn, figs and goat cheese, fresh sea bass with purple potatoes in a creamy leek-tarragon sauce, four varieties of tomatoes in a salad with opal basil, special lamb with fig chutney, and passion fruit in crème brulée, sorbet, and sabayon.

Grape Leaf Inn, Healdsburg

The manor's brick oven, smokehouse, orchard, and herb and vegetable gardens help provide the ingredients for Todd's creations. Much of the menu meets A.H.A. guidelines with zest. Pastry chef Maureen Morehouse creates chocolate magic and works wonders with fresh fruit.

The Raford House B & B 10630 Wohler Rd., 95448; 707-887-9573 (M/E). In the 1880s, Raford W. Peterson built the Raford House as a residence for his family and ranch hands. Then it was surrounded by four hundred acres of hops. Today, the white, cream, and wine-painted house overlooks vineyards and orchards. There are seven antiques-furnished rooms and six baths.

Groups

Tile Heritage Foundation P.O. Box 1850, 95448; 707-431-8453 (TILE). This nonprofit nationwide organization is designed for the research and preservation of ceramic surfaces. Information about the care, repair, maintenance, and availability of all types of tile, both antique and contemporary, is available through its growing network of industry people, designers, architects, historians, collectors, and restoration experts. Tile Heritage Library and Research Facility is available for use by appointment.

Madrona Manor Hotel and Restaurant, Healdsburg

Hope-Merrill House, Geyserville

Hope-Merrill House, Geyserville

Suppliers

Horse-drawn Vineyard Tours 15851 Chalk Hill Rd., 95448; 707-433-2422. Five Oak Farm, Alexander Valley. Wine-tasting excursions with lunch. Evening vineyard tours and dinner by reservation.

The Remodeler P.O. Box 1717, 95448; 707-433-7324. Rick Ryan. Restoration and rebuilding.

GEYSERVILLE

Hope-Bosworth House and Hope-Merrill House Bed & Breakfast Inns 21238 and 21253 Geyserville Ave., P.O. Box 42, 95441; 707-857-3356 (M). Rosalie and Bob Hope have restored two fine Victorians diagonally across the street from each other. Each has its own style, but both share the swimming pool, vineyard, lattice gazebo, and grape and kiwi arbors. The Hopes are generous, gregarious hosts.

The Hope-Bosworth House is a charming blue, white, and wine Queen Anne "pattern-book house" built entirely of heart redwood by George M. Bosworth in 1904. After the 1906 earthquake, when the chimneys fell off along with the wall plaster, the Bosworths repaired the house and stayed on until the mid-1960s. Only two of the many palms that surrounded it remain today, but the white picket fence is still covered with roses popular when the house was built. Wicker, chintz, bird's-eye maple furnishings, original oak-grained woodwork, and antique light fixtures enhance the period furnishings in the five rooms.

The Hope-Merrill House, a stunning 1870 Stick/Eastlake Victorian, received the 1989 Great American Home Award, First

Hope-Bosworth House, Geyserville

Prize, from the National Trust for Historic Preservation in recognition of its outstanding residential rehabilitation. "From wallpaper to bathroom fixtures, Bob and Rosalie Hope have lavished a love of historical detail on their Alexander Valley wine country bed-and-breakfast inn. Guests feel right at home in the Hopes' Victorian bed and breakfast." The *New York Times* called it "a treasure trove for lovers of Victoriana."

Whirlpool baths, showers for two, the original Lincrusta-Walton wainscoting in the downstairs entrance and upstairs hallway, original quarter-sawn oak graining on the doors and woodwork, fine furnishings, and multiple fireplaces add to the ambience. The house is a showcase of early Bradbury & Bradbury wallpapers, many designed especially for the house, such as the lily design chosen to go with Mrs. Hope's cranberry china on which breakfast is served. Rosalie is known for her innovative breakfast recipes. The Pac-a-Picnic lunch basket features fresh Sonoma County foods and a bottle of "Bob's Best Batch" private label award-winning wine. Berkeley color consultant Karl Kardel designed the sable brown, vanilla, and burnt sienna color scheme. A Victorian garden awaits out back.

CLOVERDALE

Ye Olde' Shelford House 29955 River Rd., 95425; 707-894-5956 (M). Eurastus M. Shelford built his Stick home in 1885 on land which was once Rancho Musalacon. Al and Ina Sauder have completely restored the yellow and light- and dark-rose house and rebuilt the carriage house, using family heirlooms to fashion six light and airy country-comfortable bedrooms, four with bath. The shared bath upstairs has a sitdown shower and an arboretum with a skylight. Windows, skylights, and window seats enhance your enjoyment of the surrounding vineyards.

There are bicycles—even a bicycle built for two—for adventuring. Afterward, relax in the pool or hot tub under the stars. A country breakfast starts the day, and beverages and a filled cookie jar are always at the ready. Ina dressed the Victorian dolls that greet you throughout the house.

Ye Olde' Shelford House owns and operates a turn-of-the-century surrey pulled by Brandy, a strawberry roan/Belgian draft horse, and Case, a quarter horse. Morning and afternoon tours of the Cloverdale back roads include a picnic lunch and tastings at the Pat Paulsen Winery. By reservation: 707-894-5956.

Abrams House Inn 314 No. Main St., 95423; 707-894-2412 (I/M). A touch of orange accents this yellow and white 1870 Stick home near the center of town. The largest of the spare, country Victorian rooms has a four-poster bed, a private bath, and a private porch. Guests share the sitting room, two parlors, a dining room, a back porch, and the garden. The innkeepers offer a full breakfast and evening refreshments. Bicycles are on hand for exploring.

Vintage Towers 302 N. Main St., 95425; 707-894-4535 (M). The three towers—round, square, and octagonal—on this grand 1900 Queen Anne Mansion were added in 1913 by architect Brainard Jones. Now dressed in blues, with white and red accents, the house is listed on the National Register. Visitors can see the blueprints for the additions in the hallway. Fine wood paneling and built-in closets were added at the same time, and everything is now shipshape.

The present owners, a designer for Paramount Studios and the ex–pastry chef from the noted Citrus restaurant in Los Angeles, have brought their own taste and treasures to Vintage Towers. Old travel posters, classic radios, artwork, and rare pottery add special touches to the seven rooms, most with baths.

Full breakfasts, refreshments in the evening, bicycles (one tandem), player pianos, a gazebo in the rose garden, and swings on the forty-foot porch may be enjoyed by all.

Places to Visit

Cloverdale Historical Society Museum 215 No. Cloverdale Blvd., 95425; 707-894-2067. Monday through Friday, 10 A.M. to 3 P.M., and by appointment. Donation. A walking-tour map of Cloverdale is available here. A charming collection of Victoriana resides in this 1875 red, white, and blue brick cottage laced with gingerbread. Butter churns, miniatures, an organ, and the doll collection on the antique bed look right at home. Pioneer Isaac Shaw once owned this house and the Victorian garden surrounding it. The picket fence in front is restored to match the original. On the other side of the garden is the Cloverdale coffee and ice-cream store, the oldest commercial building in town.

HOPLAND

Thatcher Inn Hwy. 101, 95449; 707-744-1890 (M/E). This well-appointed Victorian country inn, a Queen Anne in tan, brown, and green, in what is called "the Gateway to Mendocino County," was established in 1890. After a welcome in the main lobby or by the fire in the Fireside Library, guests head for the twenty individually furnished rooms, all with bath, on the second and third floors.

Full breakfasts in the dining room can start a day of strolling among the gift shops, art studios, antique stores, and tasting rooms that are within walking distance. A visit to the first-rate Hopland Brewery may also be of interest. Special-events package plans for group meetings, weddings, banquets, and weekday and weekend escapes are available.

The Thatcher Inn Grand Dining Room, a large Victorian dining hall, offers California-continental cuisine and fine wines in a classic atmosphere. Breakfast, lunch, and dinner are offered seven days a week.

KENWOOD

Wine Country Wagons P.O. Box 1069, 95452; 707-833-2724. Daily by reservation. Horse-drawn wagon tours and gourmet picnics with Sonoma County products.

GLEN ELLEN

Gaige House 13540 Arnold Dr., 95442; 707-935-0237 (M/E). You'll find memories of Jack London and stories to read in each of the eight comfortable rooms in this 1890 Queen Anne iced in two shades of chocolate. Builder A. E. Gaige's butcher shop was across the road, and Mr. Gaige delivered meats in his horse and wagon to the London family. Today's owners have restored the exterior to its original appearance and have successfully combined modern comforts—such as a swimming pool in the garden and a 5' x 6' Jacuzzi in the Gaige Suite—with a romantic turn-of-the-century ambience. Two house cats occasionally join guests for a full breakfast in the dining room or on the deck, and afternoon refreshments in the parlor.

SONOMA

Sonoma Hotel 110 W. Spain St., 95476; 707-996-2996 (I/M). Located on Sonoma's beautiful tree-lined plaza, this vintage hotel offers accommodations and dining to those who want to escape to an earlier era. If you want to live in the past, you'll choose the Vallejo Room, with its grand hand-carved rosewood bedroom suite once owned by General Mariano Vallejo's family. The Italian Suite overlooking the patio boasts an Italian bedroom set of solid oak inlaid with ebony. Antique lamps, marble-topped dressers, a sleigh and brass beds, and other fine pieces lend an authentic flair to the seventeen rooms. Twelve rooms have washbasins and share bathing quarters and water closets off the hallway.

Victorian Garden Inn 316 E. Napa St., 95476; 707-996-5339 (M). "Escape into the past when entertaining was an art, and gracious hospitality a way of life" is the motto for this small Stick villa surrounded by Victorian gardens. The four country

Vintage Towers, Cloverdale

guestrooms have private entrances and clawfoot tubs in the private baths. A babbling brook, secluded swimming pool, and winding paths to private patios make this a surprisingly intimate retreat within walking distance of the town's main square. Breakfast in bed, by the pool, or in the dining room is the hardest choice you'll have to make during your stay.

Restaurants

Depot Hotel 241 1st Street W., 95476; 707-938-2980. Lunch Wednesday through Friday. Dinner Wednesday through Sunday. Built in 1870 of stone from General Mariano Vallejo's quarries, the Depot was first a three-room house, then a saloon in 1880 to serve the San Francisco and North Pacific railroads. Italian dinners have been served since 1906, when a second story was added for hotel rooms. The Depot is no longer a train stop, and no longer a hotel, but the Northern Italian family-style dinners by

Chef Ghilarducci are still local favorites, and the ambience is pleasingly old-fashioned. In summer, you can even have dinner by the pool. The Depot has consistently received three stars from the Mobil Travel Guide, and Chef Ghilarducci has received the national "Master Chef of America" award.

Sonoma Hotel 110 W. Spain St., 95476; 707-996-2996. Saloon and lunch daily; dinner except on Wednesday; brunch on Sunday. A magnificent oak and mahogany back bar, gaming tables, and florid paintings of tastefully naked ladies lend authenticity to the Victorian Grand Saloon. And standing at the door to the gracious dining room is Frederic Remington's *The Wounded Bunkie*. Did Pony Express riders haul into Sonoma as exhausted as this? The Sonoma Hotel dinner menu changes twice each month and offers seasonal local produce and homemade ingredients in a setting graced by stained-glass windows and Maxfield Parrish prints.

Places to Visit

Depot Historical Museum 285 W. 1st St., 95476; 707-938-5389. Wednesday through Sunday, 1:30 to 4 P.M., and by appointment.

Sonoma Hotel, Sonoma

Fee. The restored North Pacific Railroad Station now houses a spiffy historical museum and pioneer exhibit. A Victorian parlor, dining room, and kitchen have been re-created by volunteers. The nineteenth-century milliner's shop is particularly interesting.

Lachryma Montis Sonoma State Historic Park, W. Spain St. at 3rd St. W., 95476; 707-938-1578. Daily, 10 A.M. to 5 P.M. Fee. Swiss chalet museum on the premises. General Mariano Vallejo's city home, named "tear of the mountain" after the reservoir behind the house, is one of our favorite Sonoma stops. It's an 1852 Carpenter Gothic home, painted a creamy yellow with bright green shutters, wine-dark sashes, and delicious festoons of lacy white bargeboards.

Brought prefabricated from New England, this wonderful home is now a California State Historic Landmark furnished just as it was when Mariano and Francesca Benicia Vallejo lived here with six of their ten children. In 1832, a family toast was "May their progeny be numerous

Lachryma Montis, Sonoma

Lachryma Montis, Sonoma

and worthy of them and an adornment to our beloved California."

Bricks were placed inside the walls of the house in order to keep it warm in winter and cool in summer. Marble fireplaces for each room, crystal chandeliers, lace curtains, and the rosewood concert grand piano were imported from Europe. Some of the paintings were done by one of the Vallejo daughters. Family clothing, photographs, and memorabilia are placed to look as if the family just stepped out.

Suppliers

B & B Exchange 707-963-9756. A referral service.

Victorian Garden Inn, Sonoma

B & B Inns of Sonoma County 707-433-4667. A referral service.

Adrian Martinez Historic Architect. 707-996-9406.

NAPA

Bed-and-Breakfast Inns

The Beazley House 1910 1st St., 94559; 707-257-1649 (M/E). A Napa landmark since 1902, this chocolate-colored Colonial Revival shingle-style mansion was also Napa's first bed-and-breakfast, opening in 1981. White frosting and blue and white awnings accent the exterior. Inside, polished wood floors and paneling have been beautifully restored. The ten spacious bedrooms, all with baths, have garden views.

Five Carriage House rooms also have fireplaces and large spas. Quilts, cheerful wallpapers, beamed ceilings, cedar wood paneling, fresh flowers, and flower prints create the aura of a peaceful era. One guest offered this recipe for a perfect weekend: "Take a lovely inn, add a charming and cozy room. Mix with kind and considerate hosts. Blend well with the beauty of this wine country. Do not save or store, but pass it around."

The Blue Violet Mansion 443 Brown St., 94559; 707-253-2583 (BLUE) (E). This many-gabled, delightfully columned 1886 Queen Anne has been painted in three blues, a white, and a tan. The six comfortable rooms, all with robes and private baths, are decorated with Victorian touches. Guests can wander in the garden or on the widow's walk, can relax in the gazebo, the music room, the game room, or the spa. Bicycles, croquet sets, and kites are on hand. Full breakfasts and afternoon refreshments are served. Picnic baskets and dinners are available.

Churchill Manor 485 Brown St., 94559; 707-253-7793 (M/E). The magnificent 1889 Second Empire residence of Napa banker and vintner Edward S. Churchill is now a National Historic Landmark and an extraor-dinary inn. The pink, white, and wine Ionic columns enthroned on a landscaped acre lead to expansive reception areas and a marble-floored solarium lavished with leaded-glass windows, crystal and brass chandeliers, fine wood paneling, and treasured rugs.

Family portraits on the staircase lead to ten rooms (all with bath). Many of the closets are as big as rooms. The fireplace and bathroom tiles in Edward's Room, once Mrs. Churchill's, glisten with twenty-four-carat gold trim. An antique blackboard and scooter are for play in the Children's Room. The Bordello Room hides a black and red Jacuzzi spa.

The two cats, Tess and Zoe, greet guests in the grand parlor. A buffet breakfast is served in the sun room. Local wines are served in the evening. Tandem bicycles are available. Staying here is almost like visiting a Newport mansion.

Coombs Residence Inn on the Park 720 Seminary Dr., 94559; 707-257-0789 (M). This 1852 shingled Victorian farmhouse is one of the oldest surviving residences in Napa Valley. Restored and furnished with European and American antiques, the four bedrooms, with two and a half shared baths, are extremely comfortable after a hard day of winery hopping. Terry robes and bath sheets are provided. The linen and white duvets are finished with needlework. A full-size pool, Jacuzzi, and bicycles beckon, and your hosts will be happy to arrange hot-air balloon rides. Continental breakfast starts the day, followed by afternoon cheese, fruit, wine, and evening sherry.

Goodman House 1225 Division St., 94559; 707-257-1166 (M). A lovely Painted Lady in Old Town Napa, this 1880 Queen Anne shines in sunny yellow, white, orange, and red. Two of the four guestrooms share a bath, and all share a guest kitchen stocked with complimentary snacks, wine, and beverages. In the parlor the red-flocked wallpaper and the bear rug will grab your attention. A generous continental breakfast brings on the day.

The Hennessey House Bed & Breakfast Inn
1727 Main St., 94559; 707-226-3774 (M). The
star of this cream and white Queen Anne
farmhouse trimmed in two shades of adobe
is the polychrome hand-painted tin ceiling
in the front parlor. This blue-, pink-, gray-,
and gold-flowered marvel is original to the
house. New owners have given the rest of
the place a country-fresh airy ambience
that extends to the ten pleasant guestrooms.
The lovely grape arbor in back and the
surrounding gardens create a feeling of
peacefulness.

La Belle Epoque 1386 Calistoga Ave.,
94559; 707-257-2161 (M). Three shades of
brown and cream adorn this 1893 Queen
Anne landmark in Napa's Calistoga Historical District. Original stained-glass windows
in the transoms and half windows cast
rainbows in the six guestrooms. Each is
appointed with period furnishings and has a
private bath. A decanter of wine or sherry is
a welcoming touch in each room. Wine and
appetizers are served each evening in the
inn's rustic wine-tasting cellar. Breakfast is
served by the dining-room fire on chilly
mornings, or on the garden sun porch, with
its lush display of blooming orchids, African
violets, and fragrant hoyas.

La Residence Country Inn 4066 St. Helena
Hwy., 94558; 707-253-0337 (M/E). The
twenty romantic rooms in this modern inn
are in two houses joined by an arbored pool
and hot-tub area. The barnlike Cabernet
Hall features "suite rooms" with private
baths, fireplaces, Laura Ashley prints, and
patios. American antiques, sitting areas,
fireplaces, and private baths are also found
in the rooms in the 1870 Gothic Revival
residence built by a New Orleans river pilot
who hit it big in the Gold Rush. Guests
mingle during the afternoon wine hour, and
breakfast in the inn's dining room.

Napa Inn 1137 Warren St., 94559; 707-257-
1444 (M). This stately 1899 Queen Anne,
done up in blue, green, white, and burgundy, was a wedding present for Harry
and Madaline Johnston. The present owners
have restored the inlaid hardwood floors,
the wide natural wood moldings and trim,
and retained the Johnstons' original vision.
Antique clocks from the owner's extensive
European collection, including a six-foot
ninety-day Vienna regulator in an ebony
case and an English nineteenth-century
triple fusee eight-ball mantel clock, keep
time throughout the inn. A beautiful 1880s
clock calls visitors to a bountiful breakfast.
Tea is served in the afternoon. Two of the
four rooms have baths and kitchens. Period
lamps and furnishings complement the
intricate fretwork in the hall.

Old World Inn 1301 Jefferson St., 94559;
707-257-0112 (M/E). "Search for Happiness
and You May Never Find It, but Help
Others to Find It, and You Shall Be Truly
Happy."
   "The Sun Rises in a Friendly Way, Shining
on Hard Work, Real Progress, Added Peace,
More Joy in Life, and Your Own Comfortable Home Waiting Round the Corner."
   These happy homilies are stenciled
around the moldings of the living room and
dining room in this cheerful European
Victorian inn, built in 1906 by contractor
E. W. Doughty for himself. The home is an
eclectic combination of architectural styles
detailed with wood shingles, wide shady
porches, and leaded and beveled glass.
   The inn is furnished with painted Victorian and antique furniture. The eight
guestrooms, all with bath, are color-
coordinated in French blue, pink, peach,
and mint green, with decor inspired by the
colors of Swedish artist Carl Larsson. A
substantial breakfast is served in the
Morning Room, where afternoon tea, wine,
and appetizers and an after-dinner dessert
buffet are offered. An oversize Jacuzzi in
the garden will relax you. As the sign says,
"Romance Spoken Here."

Groups and Suppliers

Patrick Lynch P.O. Box 4233, 94599; 707-
255-8597. Custom finish work and fine
carpentry.

La Belle Epoque, Napa

Napa County Landmarks Inc. 1144 Main St., Box 702, 94559; 707-255-1836. A non-profit historic preservation organization, NCL's goal is to use education to protect the heritage of Napa County. House tours in December and on Mother's Day, home-owners and membership meetings, and social events help raise funds. NCL has developed a façade easement program to help property owners protect their historic properties in perpetuity. Five architectural walking tour pamphlets are available here or from the city clerk's office, P.O. Box 660, 94559; 707-257-9503.

Napa Valley Tourist Bureau P.O. Box 3240, Yountville, 94599; 707-944-1557. For information on accommodations, hot-air balloons, wine tours, mudbaths, and dining reservations.

YOUNTVILLE

Magnolia Hotel 6529 Yount St., P.O. Drawer M, 94599-1913; 707-944-2056 (M/E). When Bruce Locken retired as general manager of San Francisco's top-rated Clift Hotel, he bought a rundown 1873 fieldstone hotel that had seen service as a bordello and a 4-H Club meeting place. With his family's help, he transformed the main building and two outbuildings into a homey, gracious country inn.

The eleven rooms and huge suite have antique furniture, floral carpeting, private baths, lots of cut glass and lace, and welcoming bottles of port. Many have fireplaces, balconies, sitting areas, private entrances, and pleasing views. Fine woods and a lavish use of red velvet add a European ambience. Victorian dolls made by Bonnie Locken grace each room.

A garden swimming pool with a Jacuzzi and a wine cellar with rare vintages will add to your pleasure. A bell rung at nine calls everyone to a hearty family-style breakfast in the fireside dining room.

ST. HELENA

The Ambrose Bierce House 1515 Main St., 94574; 707-963-3003 (M/E). Ambrose

Dollhouse in lobby of Hotel St. Helena, St. Helena

Bierce once lived in this 1872 Stick Victorian painted two shades of gray, white, wine, red, and black, and the suites are named after him and three friends: Lillie Langtry, Eadweard Muybridge, and Lillie Hitchcock Coit. Comfortable queen-size brass beds, antique armoires, clawfoot tubs, etched-glass doors, and Bierce's writings combine to defy Bierce's definition of comfort: "A state of mind produced by the contemplation of a neighbor's uneasiness."

Chestelson House 1417 Kearney St., 94574; 707-963-2238 (M). Located in a quiet residential neighborhood a short distance from the main street, this sweet, teal-trimmed white 1904 Queen Anne cottage is a treat. Intricate fretwork, gorgeous armoires, and down comforters bedeck the three sunny rooms. The innkeeper shines with her preparation of innovative family-style breakfasts. Afternoon drinks are offered on the veranda.

Cornerstone B & B 1308 Main St., 94574; 707-963-1891 (M). Across the street from the Hotel St. Helena, this 1891 stone building offers twelve rooms with spare period furnishings. Four of the rooms have shared baths. A continental breakfast is complimentary.

Hotel St. Helena 1309 Main St., 94574; 707-963-4388 (M/E). Since 1881, this imposing sandstone structure with taupe, green, white, and peach wood ornamentation has been a Victorian hotel. Renewed to its turn-of-the-century grandeur, Hotel St. Helena was granted an award for its significant contribution to Napa County preservation.

The lobby wine bar downstairs feels like an overstuffed Victorian toy store. Upstairs, a pink solarium with white wicker furniture provides a peaceful sitting area, with two big fascinating pink and white dollhouses.

The seventeen rooms, four with shared bath, and the Lillie Langtry Suite are decorated in rich tones of burgundy, mauve, chocolate, and gold. Lush carpeting and bright white shuttered windows throughout complement the Victorian

The Rhine House, St. Helena

touches of brass, hand-carved wood, bent willow, and marble. A bountiful fruit bowl comes with the continental breakfast served in the garden patio. Parties, weddings, and catering opportunities are welcome.

The Ink House 1575 St. Helena Hwy., 94574; 707-963-3890. This formidable chocolate and white 1884 Italianate villa built by Theron H. Ink is a state treasure listed on the National Registry of Historic Places. The 12' x 20' observatory on top of the house is a

Sharpsteen Museum and Brannan Cottage, Calistoga

sitting room with 360° views. It gives the inn the whimsical appearance of an inkwell, sans quill.

Places to Visit

The Rhine House Beringer Vineyards, 2000 Main St., 94574; 707-963-4812. Daily, 9:30 A.M. to 5 P.M., later in summer. Beringer Vineyards was established in the Napa Valley in 1876. In 1883, Alfred Schroepfer, a San Francisco architect, built this copy of the old Beringer family home in Mainz, Germany. The house, like most Queen Annes, is a compendium of Victorian architectural styles, with wonderful stained-glass entry doors and windows. Tours of the century-old cellar and tastings in the Rhine House end in the large wine and wine accessories shop.

St. Clement Winery 2867 St. Helena Hwy. N., P.O. Box 261, 94574; 707-963-7221. Tours by appointment. Tastings daily. St. Clement wines are still aged in the original cellar beneath the green and white towered Queen Anne Rosenbaum House now open to the public as a hospitality center. The Victorian, built in 1876, is pictured on the St. Clement Wine label.

Spring Mountain Vineyard 2805 Spring Mountain Rd., 94574; 707-963-5233. This 1885 white, beige, and pink stone towered villa is familiar to millions as Falcon Crest. Tiburcio Parrott, founder of Villa Miravalle—eight hundred acres of olive trees and grapevines—was known for the greatest of all American wine, a cabernet sauvignon, before Prohibition. In 1974, a San Francisco businessman turned winemaker bought and restored the winery, and in 1976 moved his own Spring Valley winery to the property. The original cave is still used. The house is a private home, but visitors can tour the grounds on the hour, 11 A.M. to 4 P.M. daily, for a fee. Winery tours are at 10:30 A.M. and 2:30 P.M. by appointment. The tasting room is open daily.

CALISTOGA

B & B Exchange 1458 Lincoln Ave., Suite 3, The Depot, 94515; 707-942-5900. Reservation service for accommodations in Napa and Sonoma valleys. Represents 150 inns from San Francisco to Fort Bragg, including the Wine Country, Sacramento, and the Gold Country.

Brannan Cottage Inn 109 Wapoo Ave., 94515; 707-942-4200 (M). In 1860, town founder Sam Brannan built seventeen cottages for his Calistoga Hot Springs Resort. This four-room, two-suite inn is the only one still standing on its original site. Even the original palm tree planted in 1875 by Brannan and celebrated by Robert Louis Stevenson in "The Silverado Squatters" still towers over the building. Stevenson jotted his notes for *Treasure Island* while staying at the inn, and several Napa landmarks appear in the book.

Listed on the National Register of Historic Places and recipient of the Napa Valley Historic Preservation Award, the gingerbread gableboard, wraparound porch with arches, and unusual scalloped-ridge cresting have been carefully restored and painted white with forest-green trim. Stencils of sweet peas, wild iris, California poppies, wood violets, morning glories, and wild roses grace each room and provide color themes for the country Victorian furnishings.

All of the rooms have private entrances and baths. Port and sherry are available in the old rose and gray formal parlor, and a full breakfast is served among the apple and walnut trees in the enclosed courtyard.

Culver's: A Country Inn 1805 Foothill Blvd., 94515; 707-942-4535 (M). A flurry of finials top this 1875 landmark Queen Anne. A roaring fireplace in the parlor offers a warm welcome. The six guestrooms are furnished with a European flavor. The sauna, pool, spa, and sitting porch with its view of Mount St. Helena, full country breakfasts, and afternoon sherry and tea make for an agreeable sojourn.

The Elms 1300 Cedar St., 94515; 707-942-9476 (M). Napa County's first circuit judge, Judge A. C. Palmer, built his French Mansard dream home in 1871. That was when he planted the elm seedlings which now stand as the largest elm trees in the Napa Valley. The house is now an eclectically furnished bed-and-breakfast listed on the National Register. The four guestrooms share two baths. Amenities include robes and slippers, decanters of sherry, evening wine and cheese, early morning coffee in the room, and full breakfast in the dining room. The nine cats live outside.

The Inn on Cedar Street 1307 Cedar St., 94515; 707-942-9244 (M). Summer, spring, and autumn provide themes for the three country-style rooms with baths in this cheerful 1880s white, peach, and avocado-green Stick cottage. At breakfast on the deck under the walnut tree, you can pick your own walnuts. The inn is across the street from a picturesque town park.

Places to Visit

Sharpsteen Museum and Brannan Cottage 1311 Washington St., 94515; 707-942-5911. Daily, 12 to 4 P.M. in winter, 10 A.M. to 4 P.M. in summer. Free. One of the last of the gingerbread-laced four-room resort cottages built by Sam Brannan, Calistoga's founder, in 1860, it was moved to its present site, restored, and authentically furnished to show how vacationing Victorians lived.

LAKEPORT

The Forbestown Inn 825 Forbes St., 95453; 707-263-7858 (M). This charming Gothic cottage painted in two greens, cream, and violet was built in 1869 when the town of Lakeport was known as Forbestown. The four rooms are furnished in American oak antiques and are named after local historical figures. Guests enjoy a hearty breakfast, afternoon cheese tastings, the spa, and the swimming pool.

MIDDLETOWN

The Lillie Langtry Collection Guenoc Ranch Winery, P.O. Box 1146, 100 Butts Canyon Rd., Middletown, 95461; 707-987-2385. "The Jersey Lily," Prince Edward's passion, and a renowned actress, Lillie Langtry became a citizen of the United States, and California, in order to shed a superfluous husband. Her California home, once a 4,200-acre horse and cattle ranch, is now a 270-acre vineyard.

In 1888, she invested money made from her acting career and cabled a friend: "Am delighted. Words don't express my complete satisfaction. Join me in Paradise." The simple two-story white frame house, with a fence of white and yellow roses and a white gazebo in the scent garden, is a private home, open to the public one day a year in May.

REDWOOD COUNTRY

Mendocino, Humboldt, and Del Norte Counties

*"No matter how distant
The Highways we roam,
Our thoughts use the Highway
That leads back to Home."*
—Anonymous

The joys of Mendocino and the Redwood Country are many and varied:
- The rugged Mendocino coast is as beautiful as any shoreline in the United States, and even now, so much of the coast seems empty.
- The town of Mendocino is an irresistible example of a nineteenth-century coastal town.
- Ferndale is a polychrome jewel saved from neglect by its Victorians.
- Linden Hall in Ferndale, although a relatively new house museum, is a model of taste and attention to detail.
- The Carson Mansion is the greatest Victorian in California, yet is only part of the fine Victorian stock in Eureka.
- Unless we achieve immortality, the magnificent redwoods will outlive us all.

If any place can tempt you to give up your present life and seek your own form of splendid isolation, this part of California will do it.

GUALALA

Old Milano Hotel 38300 Hwy 1, 95445; 707-884-3256 (M/E). Established in 1905 and deliciously refurbished, the Old Milano Hotel sits on three secluded acres at the ocean's edge and is one of California's Historic Places. Six upstairs rooms—five with spectacular views—share fastidious baths. Queen Victoria would have been right at home in the Master Suite. She might also have enjoyed the Caboose, rustic Engine #9 tucked in the garden, with its own cupola, kitchenette, and private observation deck. The Passion Vine Cottage in the gardens also has a sitting loft.

A generous breakfast is served in your room or in the wine parlor. Intimate hôtel du jour dining nightly, by reservation, helps keep the country-hideaway feeling. Conferences and weddings may be arranged.

ELK

Elk Cove Inn Hwy. 1, P.O. Box 367, 95432; 707-877-3321 (M). This 1883 Mansard home with spectacular ocean views was built as a guesthouse for lumber baron L. E. White. Two cabins and an addition use bay windows and skylights to bring the outside in. There are nine period rooms with sun-dried linens on the beds, six with private baths, several with fireplaces. Hostess chef Hildrun-Uta Triebess enjoys serving bountiful breakfasts and Alsatian dinners, which is propitious, because walking on the private beach will work up a hearty appetite.

LITTLE RIVER

Glendeven 8221 N. Hwy. 1, 95456; 707-937-0083 (M/E). Lumber merchant Isaiah Stevenson built his farmhouse on a head-

Little River Inn, Little River

lands meadow overlooking Little River Bay in 1867. The spacious rooms mix country Victorian with contemporary touches. Most have four-poster beds and private baths and retain the flavor of a New England merchant's home. One favorite, the Eatlin Suite, boasts a rosewood bed, a fireplace, and a distant view of the bay. A Jacuzzi on the grounds offers a welcome respite from the winding Mendocino roads. A continental breakfast is served. Children are welcome in the Barn House Suite. Conferences and catered meetings by arrangement.

Little River Inn 7751 N. Hwy. 1, 95456; 707-937-5942 (M/E). The sweet Gothic 1853 Victorian inn by the sea has blossomed into a hotel complex of fifty-six units (some wheelchair-accessible) and cottages—all with ocean views—along with lighted tennis courts, a nine-hole golf course and pro shop, and a hiking path to the adjacent Van Damme State Park. Only the parlors and rooms in the original home have Victorian accents. An Emerson square grand piano,

which survived its trip around Cape Horn in 1850, presides over the music room.

Nonresidents are welcome for breakfast and dinner in the Victorian dining room overlooking the beach. Critics rave over the Little River Inn's Swedish pancakes and wonderful eggs.

The Victorian Farmhouse 7001 N. Hwy. 1, P.O. Box 357, 95456; 707-937-0697 (M). "Opening a B & B was a dream of my husband's," says Carole Molnar, "but I had to think about it. As an innkeeper, you have to put your heart and soul into the business." The Molnars have restored John and Emma Dora Dennen's 1877 white and blue farmhouse, polishing the pressed tin ceilings and redwood wainscoting. They also added a matching wing to create a comfortable bed and breakfast within walking distance of the ocean.

Children are welcome here, and they love the burbling School House Creek, the cat, and the apple orchard on the grounds. The ten rooms have king- or queen-sized beds, quilts, and private baths. Some have free-standing fireplaces. Breakfast is served in fine china on trays in the rooms, but everyone gathers for afternoon sherry in the parlor.

MENDOCINO

Founded in the 1850s on a bluff overlooking the Pacific Ocean, the town of Mendocino has been lovingly restored. It is now a registered Historic Preservation District and a frequent movie and television location. Galleries and boutiques line the streets and invite a leisurely stroll.

Lodging

Agate Cove Inn B & B 11201 N. Lansing St., P.O. Box 1150, 95460; 707-937-0551/800-527-3311 (M/E). Mathias Brinzing, who established the first Mendocino brewery, built his Stick home in the 1860s, and the original candlestick fence still surrounds the entry garden. His home is the reception area, breakfast room, and treasure-filled living room for guests who stay in a garden complex of dark teal, white, and black cottages with white water views. The ten rooms have four-poster or canopy beds with handmade quilts and country decor. Most have wood stoves or fireplaces. Three have companion showers or tubs. The hearty country breakfast includes fresh baked bread spiked with the sight of migrating whales and crashing waves.

The Headlands Inn Howard and Albion Sts., P.O. Box 132, 95460; 707-937-4431 (M). Built in 1868 as a barbershop on Main Street, this simple creamy gold and chocolate Victorian farmhouse was moved on horse-drawn logs to its present location two blocks from the surf. The four Early American rooms in the main house and cozy cottage in back all have private baths. The fireplaces and parlor stoves have copper surrounds. Jars of hard candies grace each bedside. Annie the dog is happy to share the parlor, where there are fresh apples on the antique sewing machine. Breakfast is served on a tray in your room. The thimble-sized blueberry muffins and curaçao-poached oranges are favorites.

Joshua Grindle Inn 44800 Little Lake Rd., P.O. Box 647, 95460; 707-937-4143 (M). Lovely gardens and a gingerbread porch encircle the home built by the town banker, Joshua Grindle, in 1879. Each of the ten rooms-with-bath in the main house, cottage, and water tower has a sitting area, so you can enjoy the views of the town with glimpses of the bay. Many have fireplaces.

A New England seacoast ambience is reflected in the fine Early American antiques, which include some excellent Shaker pieces. A full country breakfast featuring homemade scones is served on the 1830s pine-harvest dining table. There are cats to pet and a croquet set for playing.

MacCallum House 45020 Albion St., P.O. Box 206, 95460; 707-937-0289 (M). William H. Kelley built this gingerbread-bedecked Carpenter Gothic cottage, now yellow with white frosting and blue cresting and sashes, as a wedding present for his daughter, Daisy MacCallum, in 1882. Daisy served tea and held court in what is now the glassed-in porch until her death in 1953. Her family owned the house until 1970, and some of the Tiffany lamps, Persian rugs, and antique furnishings were hers.

The six rooms upstairs in the house have sinks, but the baths are down the hall, "just like home." Sixteen other rooms and suites are nestled in the greenhouse, carriage house, water tower, gazebo, and barn. Most have private baths, fireplaces, and potbelly or Franklin stoves.

Some of the halls are papered with rotogravures of the period. Old trunks and quilts, some of the MacCallum original furnishings, and family photos keep the place "in the family." Daisy's roses, famous in her time, still bloom in the garden.

One of the town's best restaurants is on the main floor (see below).

The Mendocino Hotel and Garden Cottages 45080 Main St., P.O. Box 587, 95460; 707-937-0511/800-548-0513 (M/E). The

Mendocino Hotel, built in 1878 near the saloons of this logging boomtown, is now a fifty-one-room hotel furnished in Victorian and Early American antiques. Fireplaces and wood stoves keep the bayside rooms cozy, and the lavish use of mahogany and red velvet helps you step back in time. In the main building, the twenty-five Victorian-era rooms and hallways are graced with Victorian pictures and photographs. Don't miss the funeral card for Queen Victoria in the lobby. And although some of the less expensive rooms share baths, all the rooms have sinks, telephones, and room service. The twenty-six rooms in the garden and back buildings are newer and more contemporary. Conference space is available.

A cozy bar and restaurant are on the premises (please see below).

Mendocino Village Inn 44860 Main St., P.O. Box 626, 95460; 707-937-0246 (M). In 1882, Dr. William McCornack decked his graceful blue and white Mansard home with spiraling acroteria. The twelve rooms are an eclectic mix of Queen Anne, whaling skipper, Teddy Roosevelt (his hat is on the door), Navajo, and pink and burgundy Diamond Lil. Ten rooms have private baths, seven have fireplaces, and some have ocean views. Fresh flowers and chocolates greet guests. The full breakfast stars homemade breads, herbed cheesecake, blue cornmeal pancakes, and other surprises. There are turtledoves in the front parlor.

Sears House Inn 44840 Main St., P.O. Box 844, 95460; 707-937-4076 (M). Cozy cottages and a striking newly built water tower next to the 1870 main house provide eight welcoming country guestrooms, some with kitchens, fireplaces, and ocean views.

Whitegate Inn 499 Howard St., P.O. Box 150, 95460; 707-937-4892 (M). A local newspaper called this white and black 1880 Stick Gothic home "one of the most elegant and best appointed residences in town." The house has been refurbished and decorated with antiques, including a graceful pump organ in the second parlor. The pride of the place is the original wallpaper in the front parlor. The original chandelier still uses candles rather than light bulbs. All of the photographs in the house are from the owner's family.

The five gracious rooms have private baths, fireplaces, and ocean or garden views. The French Room, with its pineapple motif bedroom set and multicolored Capodimonte porcelain chandelier, is a favorite. Crystal and Rosenthal china help make the bountiful breakfast, which frequently features Whitegate Eggs Florentine with jalapeño jack cheese, memorable. Jigger Dog is a guide-dog school "flunky." Weddings and receptions are held in the gazebo in the garden. Gift certificates are available.

Restaurants

MacCallum House Restaurant and Gray Whale Bar 45020 Albion St., 94560; 707-937-5673 (M). Daisy MacCallum's private quarters have been turned into the comfortable Gray Whale Bar—even though Daisy was a teetotaler. The ocean can be seen through the windows, with the occasional gray whale cruising by. Delectable California and Mediterranean cuisine is served each evening in the elegant restaurant, where cobblestone fireplaces warm linen-covered tables set with flowers and oil lamps. Many of the pictures on the walls were Daisy MacCallum's.

Mendocino Hotel 45080 Main St., 94560; 707-937-0511 (M). Polished woods, floral rugs, and marbles embellish this Victorian restaurant and bar featuring California cuisine. The dining room is separated from the main parlor of the hotel by a beveled-glass screen imported from England. The cheerful garden room is a pleasant place for lunch and snacks.

Places to Visit/Groups

Ford House Main St., P.O. Box 1387, 95460; 707-937-5397. Monday through Saturday,

MacCallum House, Mendocino

10:30 A.M. to 4:30 P.M.; Sunday 12 to 4 P.M. Groups by appointment. The Mendocino Area Parks Association has established the Mendocino Headlands State Park Visitor Center in the restored 1854 home of Jerome and Martha Ford, who moved in as newly-weds on July 4th. The visitors' center offers volunteer and docent programs and videos, and the gallery has changing historical and natural history exhibits. One of the most popular is the miniature village created by Len Peterson. It is a meticulous reproduction of almost every structure—358 buildings and 34 water towers—that existed in Mendocino exactly as it was on December 14, 1890.

Kelley House Museum 45007 Albion St., P.O. Box 922, 95460; 707-937-5791. Friday through Monday, 1 to 4 P.M., and by appointment. Donation. Housed in the 1861 home of mill owner William Kelley, the museum offers exhibits on the cultural heritage of the Mendocino coast, the town's

logging and shipping industries, and its architecture. Mendocino Historical Research, Inc., operates the museum and maintains an extensive collection of historic photographs, local genealogical data, and research materials.

Kelley House is also home for the Mendocino Historical Society.

Visitors will also want to stop by to see the old Masonic Lodge Hall at Lansing and Ukiah, with its massive redwood sculpture, "Father Time and the Maiden," carved from one piece of redwood.

FORT BRAGG

Lodging

Avalon House 561 Stewart St., 95437; 707-964-5555 (M). The queen of the Weller Addition section of Fort Bragg is a 1905 Victorian built as a wedding present by Horace Weller for his son. Although there are exemplary Victorian embellishments,

Whitegate Inn, Mendocino

the house has been restored to preserve the unique details of the California Craftsman style. The six rooms, painted in clear light colors, mix old and new: canopy beds with fluffy comforters, good reading lamps, and whirlpool tubs under original stained-glass windows.

Country Inn 632 N. Main St., 95437; 707-964-3737 (M). This 1899 residence was built of first-growth redwood by the Union Lumber Company and purchased by L. A. Moody, the mill foreman, in 1893, for $500. The present owners have restored the home and added Alpine gingerbread and stenciled flowers inside and out. Eight country-comfortable rooms, each with private bath and two with fireplaces, are decorated in flowery country wallpaper and white enamel and have brass beds. "Excursion weekends" include Skunk Train tickets and buffet dinners.

Pudding Creek Inn 700 N. Main St., 95437; 707-964-9529 (I/M). Two light-and-dark-peach and white Victorian homes, built in the late 1800s by a man rumored to have been of Russian nobility, have been joined by an enclosed garden court where guests socialize. The ten cheerful country-style rooms have private baths. The Count's Room is inlaid with 1884 redwood paneling, and has a king-sized brass bed, stone fireplace, and cranberry accents. Victorian Valentine is all in pink.

Full breakfasts are served near an old-fashioned stove in the antique kitchen. After breakfast, browse in the small store.

Stewart House B & B 511 Stewart St., 95437; 707-961-0775 (M). A blue, blue and white 1876 simple Victorian farmhouse down the street from the Skunk Train station, surrounded by a private garden, offers six rooms, four with bath. Fine woods and wallpapers, carpets, electrified gas chandeliers, and European replicas give the place a convivial air. A Siamese cat is right at home, and guests enjoy the "outside" dog, a Samoyed who lies in the open door for conversation. A suite of armor guards the

DeHaven Valley Farm, Westport

stairs. And an antique wood stove with pie ovens warms up the dining room, where guests gather for a hearty breakfast.

Places to Visit

The Guest House Museum 343 N. Main St., 95437; 707-961-2825. Wednesday through Sunday, 10 A.M. to 4 P.M., April through October. C. R. Johnson, Union Lumber Company founder and the first mayor of Fort Bragg, built this three-story Victorian in 1892 for himself, then used it to entertain fellow lumber barons and visiting buyers. Artifacts, equipment, and photographs depicting local history are on display.

The museum is in walking distance of the Skunk Train, which travels through the redwoods to Willits. By the way, the Skunk Train, once an old logging train, was given that name because you could smell it coming. Today's riders go into the redwoods through some of California's most spectacular territory—with no untoward odor.

A walking tour map of historic Fort Bragg is available.

WESTPORT

DeHaven Valley Farm Hwy. 1, P.O. Box 128, 95488; 707-964-2931 (I/M). A historic landmark, this 1875 Victorian farmhouse set on twenty acres within sight of the Pacific shelters eight comfortable guestrooms and a cottage. The antique nightstands bear fresh flowers in a variety of rooms. Some have private access. Some share a deck overlooking the sea. Children are welcome in the cottage. They're sure to love the geese, llamas, horses, sheep, and donkeys that browse in the meadow. The state beach is down the road. And the hot tub under the stars offers ocean views.

Everyone shares a bountiful breakfast at the round walnut table in the dining room. The dining room is open to the public for dinner, Wednesday through Saturday.

UKIAH

Bed and Breakfast Inn

Sanford House 306 S. Pine St., 95482; 707-462-1653 (M). Located on a quiet side street, this 1904 Victorian offers five homey air-conditioned rooms with baths.

Places to Visit

Held-Poage Memorial Home and Research Library 603 W. Perkins St., 95482; 707-462-6969. Tuesday, Thursday, and Saturday, 1:30 to 4 P.M., and by appointment. Donation. This 1903 Queen Anne, home of Mendocino County Superior Court Judge William D. L. Held and Ethel Poage Held, was deeded to the Mendocino County Historical Society in 1969 to serve as a community resource dedicated to the collection and preservation of archival materials relating to the county and California. The library houses more than 5,000 volumes, 13,500 negatives of historical photographs, microfilms, documents, maps, scrapbooks, registers, and genealogical references. Volunteers help researchers.

WILLITS

Mendocino County Museum 400 E. Commercial St., 95490; 707-459-2736. Wednesday through Sunday, 10 A.M. to 4:30 P.M. Free. The Mendocino County Museum is a storehouse of memories, dreams, and hard-won lessons of survival in the rugged beauty of California's north coast. Changing exhibits use local artifacts to celebrate the life and times of Mendocino County.

SCOTIA

Scotia Inn & Restaurant Main and Mill Sts., P.O. Box 248, 95565; 707-764-5683 (I/M/E). The town of Scotia was founded in the early 1800s and is one of the last remaining company towns in America. Scotia's original 1880s hotel was the former home of one of the Pacific Lumber Company's officials. In 1923, the old hotel was torn down and replaced by the present building, which was refurbished as a Victorian-era inn in 1985.

The rooms are romantically decorated with European silk wallpaper and some antique furnishings. Many of the private baths have clawfoot bathtubs. The bridal suite with its lacy canopy bed has a hot-tub room as well. A complimentary continental breakfast is served.

The redwood dining room of the Scotia Inn offers fresh California cuisine, a Grand Era atmosphere, and facilities for weddings, banquets, and conferences.

FERNDALE

The village of Ferndale is like Brigadoon, a forgotten town that has risen from the mist of neglect to become a mecca for Victoriana fans. Seth Shaw's home, Fern Dale, was one of the first farms carved out of the valley floor. Immigrants were so successful at dairy farming that their homes were called butterfat palaces.

The steamship run to San Francisco started in 1878, but then salt in the river began to silt it in and the railroad and redwood highway passed the town by. The once-thriving community, lost in "protective neglect," remained unchanged.

Viola Russ McBride, granddaughter of

one of Ferndale's settlers, bought an 1880s commercial building on Main Street for a song and invited artists to rent it cheap. A "paint up" in 1962 helped. By the 1970s, a design ordinance kept the town spruced up and Victorian. Even its bridge over the Eel River remains, narrow and sturdy as ever, the oldest reinforced concrete spandrel bridge in the world.

The Chamber of Commerce provides a walking tour and map of antique stores, crafts shops, restaurants, and historical buildings: P.O. Box 325, 95536; 707-786-4477. Special events take place throughout the year. The entire village is designated a historical landmark.

Lodging

Ferndale Inn 619 Main St., 95536; 707-786-4307 (I/M). Ferndale's first bed-and-breakfast is a yellow, white, and blue 1859 Carpenter Gothic farmhouse offering five sunny rooms, big country breakfasts, afternoon tea, bicycles, and truffles from Sweetness & Light, the old-fashioned candy store on Main Street. The Cottage Suite, in blues and mahogany, features a double-sized Victorian clawfoot tub and private porch. The Marguerite Suite also has a private patio. Colorful gardens add charm to the inn.

The Gingerbread Mansion 400 Berding St., 95536; 707-786-4000 (M/E). Dr. H. Ring's 1899 turreted, carved, and gabled home and hospital has been lovingly turned into the epitome of a romantic Victorian bed-and-breakfast by Wendy Hatfield and Ken Torbert, who found it by accident while on vacation.

Guests from all over the world head for this peach and yellow Painted Lady to find afternoon tea in the four lovely Victorian parlors, and a morning tray of coffee in their room before they sit down to a generous continental breakfast that includes cheese from the local factory, fruit, hard-boiled eggs, and three fresh-baked breads. There are two different jigsaw puzzles of the Gingerbread Mansion waiting to challenge guests.

The nine rooms (all with private bath, cotton robes, turn-down service, bubble bath, and chocolates) have individual charms, such as his-and-her clawfoot tubs by the fire, a fainting couch by a Franklin stove, and garden views. In the Fountain Suite, you fall asleep to the burbling sounds of the fountain in the superb English garden. There's a mirrored ceiling in the Rose Suite. Stained-glass windows in the Lilac Room cast romantic shadows. The hideaway has a single bed nestled in the mezzanine. Peach and yellow bicycles are available. (DPL)

Shaw House Inn 703 Main St., P.O. Box 1125, 95536; 707-786-9958 (M). Town founder Seth Shaw built this light-and-dark-blue and white Gothic Revival cottage for his bride in 1854. With a design based on Hawthorne's *The House of the Seven Gables*, Shaw House is listed on the National Register. Five beautifully wallpapered and eclectically furnished rooms nestle under the many gables. The Honeymoon Room has a private bath. The Shaw Room has a private half-bath and the famed honeymoon bed used by hundreds of couples who stayed over after being married by Justice of the Peace Shaw.

Two balconies overlook the acre of gardens, and a deck overlooks the creek. Afternoon tea is served in the parlor where the gold-leaf overmantel is original to the house, as is the painted paneling in the front parlor. Quilts, fireplaces, flowers, and the owners' art collection add to the homeyness of the place. Copious breakfasts include Victorian specialties.

Places to Visit

Fern Cottage 2121 Centerville Rd., P.O. Box 36, 95536; 707-786-4835. Tours in summer, same hours as Linden Hall, and by appointment. When this gray and white farmhouse, with a red roof and green sashes, was placed on the National Register, the placard noted:

The Gingerbread Mansion, Ferndale

"Retaining a high degree of architectural and historic integrity, Fern Cottage is significant for its simple, gracious architecture which has been carefully preserved."

The original eight-room house was built in 1866 with a wide verandah. Subsequent additions—there are now twenty-eight rooms—have not changed the fabric and content of the house. Joseph and Zipporah Russ and their thirteen children and grandchildren lived in the house from 1866 to 1978. Joseph and Zipporah smile over the piano, Humboldt County's first, in the parlor. There's a hall of family portraits, along with the original architectural renderings. All of the family books, clothing, and every piece of correspondence that ever came into the house is still here. There are toys in the nurse's room. The original washer is still in the laundry room. A nonprofit organization, Fern Cottage and its surrounding ranch, are still owned by Russ descendants.

Ferndale Museum Shaw at 3rd St., P.O. Box 431, 95536; 707-786-4466. Wednesday through Saturday, 11 A.M. to 4 P.M., Sunday,

1 to 4 P.M. Also open on Tuesdays in June through September. Closed Monday and January. Fee. "Working Together to Preserve Our Heritage" is the motto of this volunteer-run association. Four Victorian room settings and changing exhibits portray life in the area in previous eras. Tours, living history outreach programs, research projects, and an oral-history program keep members busy preserving the rich historical heritage of the valley.

Linden Hall 1392 Port Kenyon Rd., P.O. Box 574, 95536; 707-786-4908. Tuesday through Sunday, 11 A.M. to 4 P.M., April through October; Friday and Saturday, 11 A.M. to 4 P.M., Sunday, 12 to 4 P.M., November and December. Groups by appointment. Fee. Eel River Valley dairyman Frans Wilhelm Andreasen built a classic Queen Anne butterfat palace in 1901. Actually, Linden Hall was known as a skim-milk house, because Andreasen picked up all the skim milk that wasn't used at the dairies to feed his pigs.

Mrs. Andreasen's maiden name was Lind. Larry Martin and Jerry Lesandro, director of the Ferndale Museum, have done an outstanding job restoring this 5,000-square-foot home to its Victorian splendor and

Shaw House Inn, Ferndale

getting it on the National Register. They've polished the parquet floors, waxed the curly redwood moldings, repaired the stained-glass windows, and installed Bradbury & Bradbury wallpapers throughout.

Many of the original furnishings, including a wonderful antique-filled sideboard in the dining room, a pump organ in the sitting room, and an 1870 Chickering grand piano in the parlor, remain. The staircase has a gilded banister and oak spindles. The original gas lighting fixtures were found in the attic, along with the vintage clothing now displayed in the sewing room.

At Christmas, Victorian ornaments transform Linden Hall into a wonderland. Martin is a landscape artist who cares for the grounds of Gingerbread Mansion. He's creating a four-acre English country garden around Linden Hall.

Suppliers

Etter's Victorian Glass 476 Main St., 95536; 707-786-4237. Specialists in the matting and framing of old prints and family photos in mats and frames authentic to the era of the picture.

Parlor Crafts 431 Main St., 95536; 707-786-9572. Stephanie Koch. Custom framing, handcrafted gifts, one of the most complete collections of needle art on the North Coast. Brochure.

FORTUNA

Rohnert Park Park St., 707-725-2495. Summer: 12 to 5 P.M. daily. Winter: 12 to 5 P.M. Saturday through Wednesday. Free. Fortuna's 1893 train depot now houses a small museum of period items. Gift shop.

Linden Hall, Ferndale

Suppliers

Hexagram Antiques 2247 Rohnertville Rd., 95540; 707-725-6223. Brass reproduction lighting fixtures, lamps, sconces, and chandeliers, both gas and electric. Restoring, wiring, and polishing. Antique glass shades.

EUREKA

When San Franciscans were building their pleasure palaces after the Gold Rush, they used redwood from the north coast, and Eureka was an important logging port. As the port waned, so did downtown Eureka, although Victorian enthusiasts continued to make pilgrimages to the Carson Mansion. Now the town has realized that there's a future in tourism, and Victorian Eureka is blossoming.

Eureka's Old Town is an inviting brick-top district, lined with gingerbread-laden wood, stone, and brick buildings built in the 1880s and 1890s, housing ice-cream parlors, craft shops, bookstores, restaurants, antiques stores, and bed-and-breakfast inns.

There are fifteen hundred "architecturally significant" structures dating from Eureka's founding in the 1850s to the present. The Eagle House Trolley and the Eureka Trolley, built of redwood by the Blue Ox Millworks, provide horse-drawn carriages for romantic tours of the quarter. Old Town Carriage Co. (707-668-4322) also gives rides around town, starting at the Gazebo in summer, Sunday, Monday and Wednesday, 10 A.M. to 7 P.M.; Thursday through Saturday, 10 A.M. to 10 P.M..

The Chamber of Commerce (2112 Broadway, 95501; 707-442-3738/800-356-6381), offers maps, tours, and lodging information summer weekdays 8:30 A.M. to 7 P.M., weekends until 5 P.M. "Image Tours" of Victorian Eureka are offered twice weekly. There are free books, with pictures, available, such as "Take a Victorian Architectural Tour of Eureka California." Eureka Humboldt County Convention and Visitors Bureau, housed in a 1903 Queen Anne at 1034 2nd St., also has maps and bed-and-breakfast literature.

Lodging

Carter House Country Inn 1033 3rd St., 95501; 707-445-1390 (M/E). Developer Mark Carter followed Newsom Brothers blueprints for an 1884 San Francisco mansion built at Bush and Jones Sts. and destroyed in the 1906 earthquake to build his own redwood shingle dream Victorian. Fine antiques, modern art, Oriental rugs, and pots of flowers embellish a spare, polished decor. Four of the seven bedrooms share a bath.

Afternoon tea, evening cordials, and fresh-baked cookies, a lavish four-course breakfast with herb- and flower-flavored goodies—the apple-almond tart is a winner—and limousine service in Mark's 1958 Bentley pamper guests.

Mark Carter himself made every piece of molding in and on the house, and he does special orders for woodwork.

The brown-stained redwood shingles have been given a stunning coat of many colors by color consultant Bob Buckter, who also designed the two buildings next to the Carter House, which will soon be part of the Carter House Inn block.

An Elegant Victorian Mansion 1406 C St., 95501; 707-444-3144/442-5594 (M). "Come to where history lives" is the motto here, and Doug and Lily Vieyra greet their guests in Victorian dress. They try to make being here an event in living history. When William S. Clark, mayor and county commissioner of Eureka, built this deliciously bedecked Eastlake redwood cottage, a local newspaper called it "an elegant Victorian mansion." It's still exactly that, painted in cream, green-grays, and frosty white. Full gourmet breakfasts are served in the four guestrooms. Lillie Langtry stayed in the Lillie Langtry Room, which has a nice view of the bay. Afternoon tea or evening desserts are shared in the three antiques-filled Bradbury & Bradbury–papered parlors.

Heuer's Victorian Inn 1302 E St., 95501; 707-442-7334 (M). A charming formality reigns in the three rooms of this cream, ochre, and chocolate towered Queen Anne, built in 1894. Breakfast is served in the gracious living room.

Iris Inn 1134 H St. at 12th, 95501; 707-445-0307 (M). William Haw, Humboldt County's first county clerk, built this fully restored Queen Anne in 1900. Today it's painted in two shades of sea green, cream, and bittersweet. There are four airy, homey rooms, one with private bath. Afternoon tea, a warming nightcap, and a full breakfast are offered. Tours of the inn are available, Monday through Friday, at 3:30 P.M. Available for meetings and gatherings.

Old Town Bed & Breakfast Inn 1521 3rd St., 95501; 707-445-3951 (M). The 1871 Stick home of the William Carson family, one and a half blocks from the Carson Mansion, has been restored and opened to guests. The five intimate guestrooms, three with private bath, benefit from the quiet residential setting. The decor combines period pieces with whimsy. Every bed has its own teddy bear, and the antique clawfoot tubs come with bubble bath and rubber duckies. Beds are covered with handmade afghans. A tea tray with apples and truffles greets each guest. Diane Benson's own wedding dress decorates Sarah's Rose Parfait Room.

There are two cats, one for each parlor. All of the artwork in the hallway is done by family members. The Bensons have created fourteen rotating menus, which can include decadent French toast, garlic/cheese grits, cast-iron breakfast pie, or Rum Tum tidy with herbed biscuits. The dining room is crammed with memorabilia and, with eight doors leading into it, is the heart of the home. Afternoon tea and refreshments are served in the parlors.

Shannon House Bed & Breakfast 2154 Spring St., 95501; 707-443-8130 (I). This restored 1890 Queen Anne, painted in three shades of pink, two shades of peach, and chocolate, burgundy, and white, opens to a lavishly papered entry and hall and a cozy parlor with plenty of natural light. Lace and flowers decorate each of the three country-style rooms. Afternoon tea and a full breakfast are served in the formal dining room. A sweet cat is in residence, and children are welcome by prior arrangement.

A Weaver's Inn 1440 B St., 95501; 707-443-8119 (I/M). A Weaver's Inn is the cream, white, and black home and studio of a fiber artist and her husband. It's a stately Queen Anne built by a sea captain in 1883, with Colonial Revival embellishments added in 1907. After admiring the faux-grained entry and hall woodwork created by the captain himself, guests visit the studio, try the spinning wheel before the fire, or weave on the antique loom.

A croquet set beckons in the colorful garden, and a piano in the parlor can help make afternoon refreshments festive. Original fireplaces warm the three lovely rooms and romantic suite. Two rooms share a bath. The Marcia Room, with restored family furniture, also offers a soaking tub.

Restaurants

Hotel Carter 301 L St., 95501; 707-444-8062 (M). A small street-side dining room off the lobby of this neo-Victorian hotel offers the best California cuisine in Eureka. Fresh local seafood, meats and produce, and creative desserts are beautifully presented. Many of the herbs come from the hotel's own gardens. Dinner is served Wednesday through Saturday. The high ceilings, large picture windows, and large abstract paintings create an airy intimacy for romantic dining. A knowledgeable wine list includes lesser-known California labels, with virtually every selection a discovery, at great prices.

The twenty handicapped-accessible, European-style rooms are furnished in English and country-pine antiques and modern art by local artists. Children are

Carter House Country Inn, Eureka

welcome. Complimentary wine and hors d'oeuvres and a continental breakfast are offered in the lobby.

Samoa Cookhouse Samoa Rd., State Route 255 across the Samoa Bridge, 95501; 707-442-1659. Open for breakfast, lunch, and dinner (I). Thrifty full-course, family-style meals are served every day in an old lumber-camp cookhouse, once relief quarters for shipwreck victims. The long tables are set as they were in 1885, with red-and-white-checkered tablecloths and large bottles of catsup, and you can easily imagine yourself sitting here a century ago.

At breakfast, you're plied with huge amounts of orange juice, coffee, French toast, and homemade sausages. Dinner can include thick cuts of ham, slabs of sole, and fresh peach pie with all the fixings. Lunch could be soup, salad, turkey with dressing, mashed potatoes, gravy, peas, and chocolate pudding. There are logging and sailing

exhibits in adjoining rooms, including a steam coffeemaker that once served five hundred men three times a day.

Places to Visit

Carson Mansion 2nd and M St. William Carson hired millworkers to build the ultimate Victorian redwood showplace in 1884, 1885, and 1886 during a depression, when they might have otherwise been out of work. The designers, San Francisco architects Samuel and Joseph Newsom, combined the exuberant architectural elements of the Queen Anne, Stick, Eastlake, and Moorish styles in what has been called a "one-stop example of drop-dead Victoriana." Although the structure is four stories high, there are only three bedrooms, since all of the Carson children had grown up by the time the place was built. The original woodwork and stained-glass windows are spectacular. A Carson descendant sold the property to the Ingomar Club, a private businessman's group, in 1950. You must see it, although you can only view it from the street. (DPL)

Clarke Memorial Museum 240 E St. at 3rd, 95501; 707-443-1947. Tuesday through Saturday, 12 to 4 P.M. Free. Tours by appointment. Regional history, Victorian

An Elegant Victorian Mansion, Eureka

decorative arts, costumes and textiles, and furnishings typical of those used in Humboldt County are well displayed through changing exhibits. There are three very detailed Victorian room interiors drawn from the museum's extensive collection. Included are a parlor, dining room, and sewing-room corner. Walking tours of Old Town, the Victorian commercial district, are given Wednesday and Saturday during the summer at 2 and 3 P.M. The museum is wheelchair-accessible. Museum members enjoy lectures, newsletters, and special events. There is also a gift shop.

The Pink Lady 2nd and M Sts. Lumber baron William Carson built this delectable Queen Anne in 1889 as a wedding gift for his son Milton and his wife, Mary Bell. They lived in the house, also designed by the Newsom brothers, until William Carson's death in 1912, after which they moved into the mansion across the street.

Two sisters living in Germany operated the place as a rooming house, until it was seized as Nazi property in 1942. The house was threatened with demolition in 1963, when Robert Madsen, a former mayor of Eureka, and his wife bought it and restored it, painting it pink and white to highlight the patterned shingles, ornamental carved wood trim, and gingerbread that so grandly decorates its surface. It is now used for offices.

Carson Mansion, Eureka

Lady Anne, Arcata

Groups and Suppliers

Blue Ox Millworks Foot of X St., 95501; 707-444-3437. "You draw it—we'll make it." That's the motto of Eric Hollenbeck, an ex-logger who manufacturers reproduction millwork and does custom woodwork. Gutters, molding, plasterwork siding, and columns are available. Hollenbeck also has a collection of restored vintage equipment from the 1800s and 1900s, and uses the "working museum" of houses in Eureka to make everything from corbels and balusters to full-size trolley cars. Tours. Catalog.

Doll Houses 320 2nd St., Suite 1 B, 95501; 707-443-5481. Lida-Lee miniatures.

Eureka Heritage Society Carson Block Building, 3rd and F Sts., Box 1354, 95502; 707-442-8937. Meetings, preservation programs and conferences, home tours, publications, and heritage fairs.

Eureka/Humboldt County Convention and Visitors Bureau 1034 2nd St., 95501; 707-443-5097. Events and lodgings listings.

FVN Corp. Bob Von Normann, P.O. Box 68, Redcrest, 96569; 707-722-4251. Architectural photographer.

Humboldt County Historical Society 636 F St., P.O. Box 8000, 95502; 707-443-3515. Publishes the *Humboldt Historian* bimonthly, and maintains an office where historical materials may be used for research.

Redwood Community Action Agency 904 G St., P.O. Box 1347, 95502; 707-445-0881. Lloyd Throne, executive director. Historical preservation.

Restoration Hardware 417 2nd St., 95501; 707-443-3152. Skylar Falls, Bayshore Mall, 3300 Broadway, 95501; 707-445-9694.

Nancy Spruance Designs 2241 Burns Dr., 95501; 707-443-1596. Victorian house designs for Counted Cross Stitch. Chartpaks of six houses (including Carson Mansion and Pink Lady) are available by mail order, and include the designs, complete instructions, color photo of the stitched design, black-and-white photo of the house, and historical information.

Stained Glass by Steve 2808 Broadway, 95501; 707-443-8157.

North Pacific Joinery 76 W. 4th St., 95501; 707-443-5788. Premium quality doors and windows.

ARCATA

Lodging

Lady Anne—A Bed & Breakfast Inn in the

English Tradition 902 14th St., 95521; 707-822-2797 (M). Wesley Stone, Arcata's first banker, built this regal creamy yellow, blue, white, and pink Queen Anne on a crest overlooking the town and bay in 1888. Former Arcata mayor Sam Pennisi and his wife, Sharon, welcome well-behaved children, with separate children's suites, toys, crib, high chair, and dining room. Parents will appreciate the quiet music room, the bikes, the full breakfast, and the sherry at sunset on the veranda. There are five rooms and a cottage decorated in bright floral patterns, family pictures, and toys.

The Plough and the Stars Country Inn 1800 27th St., 95521; 707-822-8236 (I). Discover a pastoral retreat in this 1862 gray and white farmhouse with dripping bargeboards. At the door, the sign says "Tourists Treated Same as Home Folks." Five individually themed guestrooms and three sitting rooms filled with books and games afford plenty of space for relaxed mingling or quiet sanctuary. Only the William Morris Room is decidedly Victorian. The others are light, sunny, and contemporary. A regulation-size bent grass croquet lawn is set up at all times in front of the house. The hot tub is popular, too. Family-style breakfasts are served in the country kitchen, and there's a cache of sweets and a basket of edibles for midnight munchers. Receptions and business retreats.

Suppliers

Design/Work 905 H Street, 95521; 707-822-1070. Alex Stillman and Mary Gearheart work on historic projects in public and private sectors. Historic resources, design management, landscape assessment.

Kathleen Stanton 2428 Old Arcata Rd., P.O. Box 185, Bayside, 95524; 707-826-7139. National Register nominations and districts. Historic preservation.

White Rose Designs 940 Samoa Blvd., 95521; 707-822-8822. Cotton night and underclothes of vintage design.

Places to Visit

Arcata is a Main Street town with a Victorian-era plaza lined with stores. Jacoby's Storehouse, on the plaza at 8th and H Sts., Historic Landmark No. 783, houses an Italian restaurant. The Arcata Chamber of Commerce, 1062 G St., 95521, 800-55-ENJOY, offers a walking/driving tour map that takes visitors past the Pythian Castle, the Victorian Bair House, the two Mirror-Image Mansions, and other historic homes.

BLUE LAKE

Blue Lake Museum 330 Railroad Ave., Box 707, Blue Lake, 95525; 707-668-5576/4237. Tuesday through Wednesday, 1 to 4 P.M.; Sunday, 12 to 4 P.M.; and by appointment. Donation. The old Arcata and Mad River Railroad depot is filled with historical photographs, artifacts, and displays in a museum dedicated to preserving the history of the families of Blue Lake and the Mad River Valley. Tools, clothing, household furnishings from first families such as the Chartins and the Douarins, and the High Renaissance carved bed from the Hemphill family are lovingly cherished. There are free maps of town tours. The museum is wheelchair-accessible, and there is a gift shop.

Artisans

Mad River Woodworks 189 Taylor Way, P.O. Box 1067, Blue Lake, 95525; 707-668-5671. Architectural millwork: moldings, pickets, screen doors, and porch parts. Catalog.

CRESCENT CITY

Battery Point Lighthouse 707-964-3922. Wednesday through Sunday, 10 A.M. to 4 P.M. tide permitting, April through September. Fee. The 1856 Battery Point Lighthouse is located offshore from Crescent City on a little island accessible only at low tide. The old logbook, banjo clock, shipwreck photos, display of lighthouses around the world, and nautical mementos add to the enjoyment of a visit. Lighthouse keepers with the Del Norte County Historical Society help bring history to life with a guided tour.

Del Norte County Historical Society Museum 577 H St., 95531; 707-464-3922. Monday through Friday, 10 A.M. to 4 P.M., May through September. Donation. A completely furnished country kitchen, period furniture, quilts, photo carousels, and a research facility are available to visitors in this jam-packed museum, where collections of memorabilia from local residents bring local history to life.

McNulty House 7th and H Sts., 95531; 707-464-5186. Tuesday through Saturday, 10 A.M. to 5 P.M. Donation. This Victorian home is a California point of historical interest. There are antiques to view and to buy, as well as gifts and art. Custom framing is available.

NORTH CENTRAL CALIFORNIA

*"This room is equipped with Edison Electric Light.
Do not attempt to light with match. Simply turn
key on wall by the door. The use of electricity is in
no way harmful to health, nor does it affect the
soundness of sleep."*
—Note in a North Country Bed-and-Breakfast

In the supermarket we call America, the Big Valley is the produce department. Heat, sunshine, and irrigation yield an inexhaustible supply of rice, olives, grapes, and other fruits, and a lot more. The Main Street of the Big Valley is Interstate 5, the gray ribbon that ties Northern and Southern California together.

For the purposes of this guide, North Central California runs along I-5 from the Oregon border to Sacramento. It has more to offer visitors in the way of natural beauty than Victoriana. Near Lake Shasta, there's a mountain to climb and caverns to descend into. Shasta State Historic Park contains a gold-mining town that is being restored.

Two other treats are the William B. Ide Adobe State Historic Park one mile north of Red Bluff, and the Chinese Joss House in Weaverville.

The Victorian star of the area is the Bidwell Mansion in Chico, which, like many California Victorians, was created by gold, pride, and ambition.

YREKA

Siskiyou County Museum 910 S. Main St., 96097; 916-842-3836. Monday through Saturday, 9 A.M. to 5 P.M. in summer; Tuesday through Saturday, 10 A.M. to 4 P.M. in winter. Donation. In this reproduction of the Callahan Ranch Hotel, one of the first stage stops in Siskiyou County in the 1850s, the museum has organized exhibits ranging from the prehistoric era to fur trapping, mining, settlements, lumbering, railroads, and agriculture. Period environments help convey the life and times of early Siskiyou County residents, and special exhibits illustrate the historical features so unique to the county. There is also a two-and-a-half-acre outdoor museum of authentic and reconstructed buildings and a general merchandise store with period merchandise and gifts for sale (open summer only). Research library by appointment.

MT. SHASTA

Lodging

Sisson House 1904 326 Chestnut St., 96067; 916-926-6949/800-369-2497 (M). This restored 1904 Victorian, painted butter-yellow and two shades of blue, is a romantic hideaway. The new owners used a black-and-white photo taken in 1904 to see where the dark and light shades should be applied. Katy Kohn, the great-granddaughter of the original owner, lives next door and visits with interested guests at afternoon tea or breakfast, answering questions about the history of the house and Mt. Shasta.

Four rooms, two with fireplaces, share two baths. Antiques from the area and family glassware, silver, and accent pieces are used with pride. A calico cat may keep you company during the full breakfast in the formal dining room, which was the original kitchen. Vacation packages are available.

Craftspeople

Designs in Tile Dept. J., Box 358, Mt. Shasta, 96067; 916-926-2629. Custom ceramic tiles and murals, historic reproductions, and traditional patterns such as Victorian Foliate, Gothic Revival, Neo-Grec, William DeMorgan Style, Spring Garden, Folk, Art Nouveau, Persian Revival, and Art Deco tiles. Catalog.

The Jeter Victorian Inn, Red Bluff

WEAVERVILLE

Lodging

Granny's House 313 Taylor St., P.O. Box 31, 96093; 916-623-2756 (M). This sweet two-story Queen Anne was built for H. W. Goetze, Sr., owner of the sawmill on nearby Buckhorn Mountain, which provided the wood for the house. In 1905, H. W. Goetze, Jr., moved into the house with his bride, Clara. Although they did not have children, Weaverville children were often found partaking of treats in Clara's kitchen over the years. She died in 1986 at 102. The current owners have renovated the gracious parlors and retained the turn-of-the-century ambience in the three comfortable rooms. Children are still welcome in "Granny's House." The sumptuous breakfasts include smoked meats and cheeses.

The Old Yellow House B & B Inn 801 Main St., P.O. Box 2595, 96093; 916-623-2274 (M). Jack Hall added an early Trinity County Victorian-style addition to his 1876 home shortly after the turn of the century. Keeping with the rural character of homes in the area, the owners of this new bed-and-breakfast chose "country" as the decorating theme. There are five guestrooms and the two upstairs rooms share a bath. Guests have the run of the kitchen. Breakfasts are served in the dining room or on the patio.

During the Gold Rush, thousands of Chinese laborers were brought here, and you can still see a monument to their culture preserved in a restored 1870 temple in Weaverville, the Joss House State Historic Park, also on Main Street.

Places to Visit

Big Ben's Doll Museum Hwy. 299, Main Street, 96093. Irregular hours.

SHASTA

Old Shasta State Historic Park P.O. Box 2340, 96087. Courthouse Museum, 916-243-8194. Daily, 10 A.M. to 5 P.M., March through

The Faulkner House, Red Bluff

October; closed Tuesday and Wednesday in winter. Lischt Store, 916-244-1848. Weekends 10 A.M. to 5 P.M. in summer, and by appointment. Old Shasta State Historic Park is a re-creation in-progress of a small Gold Country and Victorian town. Many of the buildings have been intact and had been completely refurbished as a state park until the early 1980s, when a fire destroyed them. The Courthouse Museum was and is the most important building, and it now holds a vast collection of Victorian-era California art as well as furnishings and mementos of Shasta's early residents. The nearby Lischt Store is a general store of the period, with shelves stocked with articles from the 1880s. Staffed by volunteers, the hours are irregular. Volunteers are also restoring the 1878 bakery next door.

RED BLUFF

Buttons and Bows Bed & Breakfast Inn 427 Washington St., 96080; 916-527-6405 (I). Buttons and Bows decorate the three large country Victorian bedrooms in an 1882 Queen Anne home painted in two creams, white, and dark green. The shared bath—robes are provided—has a large shower and an "antique buffet" sink. Guests enjoy the hot tub in the garden and the wood-burning stove in the living room. Walks along the nearby Sacramento River can help you work up an appetite for the hearty breakfast.

The Jarvis Mansion 1313 Jackson St., 96080; 916-527-6901 (M). This brightly hued blue Italianate was built in 1870 and recently restored. The four rooms mix antiques and continental touches with modern amenities such as remote-control TV and up-to-the-minute private baths. The Eastlake Room in green, rose, and white with an Eastlake bed and a bay window seating area is a favorite.

The Jeter Victorian Inn 1107 Jefferson St., 96080; 916-527-7574 (M/E). A few years ago, Linda Jeter bought a Louis XV armoire, then asked her husband to make an arch in her bedroom ceiling to accommodate it. Cal told her to find a house with taller ceilings. They found the light and dark dusky rose and brown 1881 Queen Anne farmhouse built by G. K. Willard two blocks off Main Street in Red Bluff's Victorian Home Tours area. Much of the house's gingerbread was made by hand and is being added back onto the house.

It took eight months of twelve-hour days to restore the place inside and out—two months just for the brass hardware.

Guests may choose from four extravagantly comfortable rooms that feel old-fashioned but have all the modern conveniences. The tall ceilings are graced by silk and lace window treatments and European touches. The pink-tiled Imperial Room bathroom has a double whirlpool bath, double sinks, a separate shower, large closets, and a hairdryer. Robes are provided for each room as are a nicely stocked amenities basket, nighttime liqueurs, and a handy travel kit. Coffee and banana bread await you in the hall as a pre-breakfast at 7 A.M. Guests choose their breakfast menu in the evening. Lovely grounds offer a perfect setting for weddings and parties.

The Faulkner House 1029 Jefferson St., 96080; 916-529-0520 (M). Jeweler Herman H. Wiendieck built this cream, white, blue, gray, and burgundy Queen Anne in the 1890s. Dr. and Mrs. James Faulkner bought the place in 1933, preserving the wonderful stained-glass pussy-willow window on the staircase landing and in other areas. Today, family heirlooms mingle with fine antiques in a welcoming setting. Of the four rooms, all with bath, the Rose Room boasts a fainting couch, but the cozy Tower Room is the most romantic. Full country breakfasts are served on the beautifully set oak table. Afternoon sherry rests on an ornate sideboard once used to store altar linens and vessels in a midwestern Lutheran church. The front bay window is filled with handcrafted gifts and flower art. Host Mary Klinger is active in the local preservation society.

Places to Visit

Kelly-Griggs House Museum Tehama County Historical Society, 311 Washington St., 96080; 916-527-1129. Summer: 2 to 5 P.M., Thursday through Sunday. Winter: 2 to 4 P.M., Thursday through Sunday. In 1880, sheep rancher Sidney Allen Griggs built this handsome Italianate, with its hipped roof, columned front porch, and symmetrical brackets. It was completely restored and furnished with period antiques and clothing by volunteers and donations from local families. Only the chandeliers, metal fireplaces, and bathroom with a tin tub are original to the house. The painting of the lovely girl in the main parlor was done by John Brown's daughter. Mannequins wear period clothing, and the armoires are fully stocked. The pictures of Ishi, the last of his tribe, at home, and the collection of paintings and work in wood by a man who helped build San Francisco's Palace Hotel help the citizens of Red Bluff remember their past. A band plays occasionally in the nearby gazebo. Residents also enjoy the Kelly-Griggs Christmas party and the August ice-cream summer social. The fence around the house is made from bars of the old jail.

Craftsmen

Matthew Nehrer 916-527-2960. Custom cabinets.

Dick Fletcher 916-527-8193. Custom painter.

Kinner Construction 645 Rio St., P.O. Box 1502, 96080; 916-527-7559. Dave Kinner, exterior restoration and remodeling.

CHICO

Bed & Breakfast Inns of Northern California (BBNC) P.O. Box 7150, 95927; 800-284-INNS. An association of more than one hundred California B & B's, most of them Victorian. Annual seminar and a Frequent Traveler Program in nineteen California B & B's. A travel guide is available as well.

Bidwell Mansion State Historic Park 525, The Esplanade, 95926; 916-895-6144. Daily, 10 A.M. to 5 P.M. (tours on the hour, 10 A.M. to 4 P.M.). Donation. Rancho del Arroyo Chico, covering twenty-six thousand acres, was purchased in 1849 by agriculturalist and politician John Bidwell. His twenty-eight-room "Gull pink and Bidwell red" Italianate villa, designed by Henry W. Cleveland and built in 1865–68 for $56,500, soon became the social and cultural center of the upper Sacramento Valley. Bidwell arrived in California in 1841, worked as a clerk for John Sutter, and then, on July 4, 1848, made the second-largest gold strike of the Gold Rush. He built a model farm and was elected state senator and congressman and even ran for president.

Today, the Bidwell Mansion is one of the finest house museums in the state. Guided tours are offered through the meticulously restored and furnished rooms, admiring Bidwell mementos, and donated furnishings. Portraits of John and Annie Bidwell hang in one of the parlors. Bidwell's stuffed birds, Annie's telescoping organ, her piano, intricate Victorian hair-wreath pictures, fireplace screens, and sidesaddle mix with donated pieces such as the painted bedstand and the quilt collection in the third-floor central sitting area. Bidwell Mansion's intrepid manager, Maggie Gisslow, showed us the turn-of-the-century vacuum cleaner and the twelve servants' bells "below stairs." The love letters in the exhibit area/gift shop provide insights into these pioneers.

The Bidwell Mansion's grounds benefited from the agricultural experimentation and importing carried out by General Bidwell.

Stansbury Home 5th at Salem Sts., 95928; 916-895-3848. Weekends, 1 to 4 P.M., and by appointment. Donation. Weddings: 916-343-0442. The modest, crested 1883 Italianate, filled with period furnishings, is remarkable because only Stansburys have

Kelly-Griggs House Museum, Red Bluff

lived in it and it has never been remodeled or modernized. The original wallpaper and ceiling treatment can still be seen in the front parlor. Some of the rugs are original. The docents can show you untouched samples of wall coverings to show how time has darkened and dulled the walls. Ice-cream socials, Victorian Christmas teas, and weddings help fund the maintenance of this extraordinary glimpse into the past.

The Chico Merchants' Association has put together a "Tour of Community History Through Parks and Architecture," available at the Bidwell Mansion and the Stansbury Home.

The Stansbury Home Preservation Association 307 W. 5th St., 95928. Meetings, newsletters.

OROVILLE

Judge C. F. Lott Historic Home 1067 Montgomery St., 95965; 916-538-2497. Friday through Tuesday, 11 A.M. to 4:30 P.M.;

also Wednesday and Thursday, 1 to 4:30 P.M., in summer; and by appointment. Fee. A forty-niner from New Jersey, Judge Charles Fayette Lott built this Gothic Revival home for his bride, Susan Heyer, in 1856, and it was in the Lott family until 1962. Mr. Sank wooed their daughter for many years, and you can still see the plaque he put up in the trellis leading to the house: "In commemoration of a kiss and a promise given between these columns." In the front parlor, semiprecious stones from the local riverbed spell out "Love," marking his success.

Today, the Lott-Sank home is a museum of furniture and household objects typical of Oroville's pioneer family homes between 1849 and 1910. In the kitchen, you can see Mrs. Lott's handwritten cookbook. A cheerful caretaker will tell you the fascinating stories behind each object.

The gift shop near the kitchen is thoughtfully stocked. The Victorian rose garden and adjoining Sank Park, with fountain and gazebo, are available for weddings and receptions.

Butte County Historical Society Ehmann Historic Home, 1480 Lincoln St., P.O. Box 2195, 95965; 916-533-1010. Meetings are held on the third Sunday of each month at 2 P.M. in the Ehmann Home, which may also be visited by appointment. The society fosters and preserves the history of Butte County and does research into its past.

YUBA CITY

Harkey House B & B 212 C St., 95991; 916-674-1942 (M). William Harkey, sheriff of Sutter County, built his home in 1864 near the Yuba River. Today, painted cream, blue, and burgundy, it's an elegant bed-and-breakfast of four suitably fitted-out guest-rooms with an art gallery, a library, back-to-back marble fireplaces, a pool, and a spa. The Harkey Suite, with its adjoining library room, and the Empress Room, with Oriental antiques, share a bath. For the energetic, there's a basketball court in the garden. You may prefer to read a good book in the hammock. Weddings, dinner parties, and conferences can be arranged. Gift certificates are available.

City of Colusa Heritage Preservation Committee City Hall, 425 Webster St., 95932; 916-458-4740.

Colusa County Historical Records Commission and County Archives 546 Jay St., 95932; 916-458-5146. Prepares a historical calendar with photographs of recreation and leisure activities of yesterday.

Colusa County Historical Society P.O. Box 448, 95932.

Les's Stained-Glass Studio 1734 Wilson Ave., 95932; 916-458-4437. Custom windows, gifts, supplies, and classes by stained-glass artists Eleanor and Les Kaun.

WILLIAMS

Sacramento Valley Museum 1491 E St., Box 290, 95987; 916-473-2978. April through

Bidwell Mansion State Historic Park, Chico

Bidwell Mansion State Historic Park, Chico

November: Wednesday through Saturday, 10 A.M. to 4 P.M., Sunday, 1 to 4 P.M. Winter: Friday and Saturday, 10 A.M. to 4 P.M., Sunday, 1 to 4 P.M., and by appointment. Donation. This twenty-one-room museum, located in a 1911 high school, has captured the past, transforming schoolrooms into a general store, dentist's office, M'Ladies Room, music room, a blacksmith shop and saddlery, an apothecary shop, a barber shop, and restored 1860s California parlor, bedroom, and kitchen filled with memories. An 1850 Chickering square piano and a 1700s twin's cradle are two treasures. The fashion doll collection shows costumes dating from Greek times up to the present, and includes Queen Anne in a jeweled cap, and dolls in patterns from the 1883 and 1893 *Delineator*. The newspaper collection in the documentary room includes the report of George Washington's death. The collection of quilts is remarkable, as are the clothes.

MARYSVILLE

Mary Aaron Memorial Museum 704 D St., 95901; 916-743-1004. Tuesday through Saturday, 1:30 to 4:30 P.M., and by appointment. Free. An 1857 crenellated gray and white Gothic family residence with cresting built by Warren P. Miller for $5,000 has become an early Victorian museum with period furniture and clothing, and an interesting display of dolls, documents, pictures, and photographs. Our favorite: the 1860s wedding cake that was discovered perfectly intact and petrified in a wooden Wells Fargo storage box. The bricked garden has Victorian wrought-iron furniture and plantings.

Will Rogers once quipped: "I'm not a member of any organized party. I'm a democrat." Regardless of your political persuasion, if you're a Victoriana buff, Sacramento has four major attractions to entice you:

- The 1874 state capitol is a magnificent structure.
- The Old Governor's Mansion is an outstanding piece of architecture, with furnishings to suit.
- At the Crocker Art Museum, the art begins with the building.
- With fifty-three Gold Rush buildings, a paddle-wheel hotel and excursion boat, and possibly the best railroad museum anywhere, Old Sacramento will be a treat for the whole family.

WOODLAND

Morrison's Upstairs 428½ 1st St., 3rd fl., 95695; 916-666-0500. It took ninety-five years to complete this restaurant. The Jackson Building was built in 1891 as Woodland's first luxury apartment complex. The attic was never used until now. Although you can take the elevator, diners agree that the food is well worth the climb.

Woodland is a small town with a Victorian center just finding itself again after many years. There are antique shops and walking tours. The Opera House at 320 2nd St. (916-666-9617), an 1891 brick structure, is on the site of the first opera house in the Sacramento Valley.

Be sure to see the Gable Mansion at 659 1st St. Amos and Harvey Gable, pioneer settlers of Yolo County, built it in 1885, and it was one of the last of its size and style built in California.

The Chamber of Commerce, 520 Main St., 95695 (916-662-7327), offers tour maps of the Victorian neighborhoods south of Main between West and East Sts. For a walking tour, call 916-666-6269.

VACAVILLE

Vacaville Museum 212 Buck Avenue, 95688; 707-447-4513. Located in a quiet Victorian neighborhood, this museum preserves and promotes the history of Solano County with its collection of local memorabilia, exhibits focusing on locally significant historical themes, community programs, walking tours, and a bimonthly newletter.

SACRAMENTO

Lodging

Aunt Abigail's 2120 G St., 95816; 916-441-5007 (M). This centrally located blue and white cupola-style Colonial Revival mansion has been transformed into a comfortable "merchant" Victorian guesthouse. The six cozy rooms, four with private bath, are individually decorated and named for family members. A generous breakfast is served on a lace tablecloth in the sunny dining room. Books, flowers, a house cat, and old-fashioned radios make travelers right at home, whether they're traveling for business or pleasure.

Aunt Abigail's is a member of a Frequent Traveler Program sponsored by the Bed & Breakfast Inns of Northern California.

The Driver Mansion Inn 2019 21st St., 95818; 916-455-5243 (M/E). Philip S. Driver, a prominent Sacramento attorney, built this grand Colonial Revival mansion in 1899, and it is still one of Sacramento's most architecturally significant Victorian residences. The property remained in possession of the Driver family until 1977. Fine antiques and marble fireplaces help evoke

Crocker Art Museum, Sacramento

the Victorian elegance of the mansion, while Jacuzzis and other modern amenities add to the guests' comfort. The lush landscaped gardens and Victorian gazebo make this a popular wedding spot.

The Sterling Hotel 1300 H St., 95814; 916-448-1300/800-365-7660 (M/E). This white wedding-cake Queen Anne is Sacramento's most glamorous hotel. Potted palms, fireplaces, four-poster beds, and Oriental touches create a polished Victorian ambience. At the same time, every business need the traveler may have is attended to, and every room has its own Jacuzzi. The hotel conservatory, a unique glass structure made in Europe, is popular for receptions, conferences, and weddings.

Chanterelle, behind art-glass windows, is the hotel's luxurious restaurant, specializng in nouvelle continental cuisine. Reservations are advised; call 916-442-0451.

Places to Visit

Crocker Art Museum 21 O St. at 3rd, 95814; 916-449-5423. Tuesday through Sunday, 10 A.M. to 5 P.M., Thursday until 9 P.M. Tours by appointment: 916-449-3537. Fee. The oldest art museum in the West was built in 1872 to house the paintings and drawings of Judge Edwin Bryant Crocker. The collection is worth seeing, but the building itself, a grand Italianate by architect Seth Babson, rivals the collection. With its frescoed ceilings, rococo mirrors, and curving staircases, the museum itself is a work of art. It was painted in polychrome when it was donated by Mrs. Crocker to the city in 1885.

Old Governor's Mansion 16th St. at H, 95814; 916-445-4209. Daily, 10 A.M. to 4 P.M. Hourly tours. Fee. Architect Nathaniel Goodell built this resplendent Mansard-roofed Italianate, painted white to ward off the heat of the Big Valley, for Albert

Old Governor's Mansion, Sacramento

elected California's eighth governor and shortly after becoming president of the newly organized Central Pacific Railroad. The California Department of Parks and Recreation is in the process of restoring the home and operating it as a house museum. Until the work is complete, tours will focus on the indoor archaeology of the restoration and the architecture of the building.

OLD SACRAMENTO

Visitor Information Center: 1104 Front St., 95814; 916-442-7644. Old Sacramento Citizens and Merchants Association: 916-443-7815. Events hotline: 916-443-8653. Wander down wooden-slat sidewalks and up cobblestone streets to the sound of a horse and wagon going by in this authentic restoration of a period Gold Rush town on the Sacramento River. Walking tours depart each morning from the front of the California State Railroad Museum at 2nd and I Streets (State Park Docent Association: 916-324-0040). A fifteen-minute slide/tape presentation by the Department of Parks and Recreation is given, free, on the hour, 10 A.M. to 4 P.M., on weekends in the Old Eagle Theatre, 916-323-7234.

Gallatin, a local hardware merchant, in 1877, on land owned by John Augustus Sutter. In 1887, journalist Lincoln Steffens's father, Joseph, bought it. From 1903 to 1967, it served as the governor's mansion.

This handsome building still has much of Gallatin's original decor, including the molded ceilings, ornate hardware, marble fireplaces, and inlaid hardwood floors. The music room, formal and second parlors, and master bedroom are wonderfully Victorian, with fine woods, red velvet, and gilt. Furnishings, mementos, and photos show life in the mansion under thirteen governors. The docents often wear period clothing and host special events.

Stanford House 800 N St., 95814; 916-324-0575/445-4209. Tours by appointment. When merchant Shelton Fogus built his two-story polychrome Italianate in 1851, it was the most substantial in the city. Leland Stanford bought it in 1861, just before being

Visitor Information Center, Old Sacramento

Old Sacramento is also a state historic park, and information is offered at 925, The Embarcadero, 95814, 916-446-6761. The Huntington & Hopkins Hardware Store, part museum and part store, offers typical hardware of the mid-to-late 1800s. The Central Pacific Railroad Freight Depot, originally built in the 1860s, shows how the world reached Sacramento then, and the Central Pacific Railroad Passenger Station, originally built in 1876, shows how passengers crossed the country in Victorian times. Boutiques, craftsmen, historical exhibits, and restaurants line the streets.

The Sacramento History Center at the foot of I Street and the Old Sacramento Schoolhouse at L and Front will be of particular interest to Victoriana buffs.

Groups

California Historic Landmark Information Office of Historic Preservation, Department of Parks and Recreation, P.O. Box 942896, 94296-0001; 916-445-8006.

Californians for Preservation Action P.O. Box 2169, 95810.

Central Valley Chapter of the American Institute of Architects 1025 19th St., Suite 8, 95814; 916-444-3658. Maps of historic architecture tours.

Sacramento Heritage 630 I St., 95814; 916-440-1355. Maps of historic architecture tours. Meetings and information.

Suppliers

Decorative Painting by D. M. Cocker 916-363-0866. Faux and decorative paint finishes: wood graining, marbleizing, glazing, antiquing, ragging, gold-leafing.

Linen Lady 885 57th St., 95819; 916-457-6718. Charlene Seipel specializes in lace curtains and handmade linens.

Mac the Antique Plumber 885 57th St., 95819; 916-454-4507. Tuesday through Saturday, 8:30 A.M. to 5 P.M. Order by catalog,

10:30 A.M. to 4:30 P.M. "The most complete antique plumbing shop in the world...and other places too!" Antique plumbing bought and sold. Bryan C. "Mac" McIntire heads a staff of consultants knowledgeable about plumbing, lighting, furniture, hardware, and garden equipment from furniture and sundials to wind chimes and fountains. Porcelain, oak, mirrors, brass—large and small—original antiques, and careful replicas. The object we pined for—a $12,000 wraparound shower. Investigation will yield treasures. Catalog.

Mac the Plumber is in the 57th Street East Antique Plaza, between H & J Streets, a haven for antique collectors.

Medimer 9931 Horn Rd., 95827; 916-363-5846. Fireplaces in six colors of Greek marble.

The Turning Point, 8372 Carbide Ct., Suite 1, 95819; 916-423-4440. Daniel Howle. Stair and door company.

ELK GROVE

The Stair Company 9746-A Dine Dr., 95828; 916-686-4840. Chuck Hampton provides consultation. Modern milling techniques with skilled handwork in wood, metal, and glass for one-of-a-kind stairs.

ORLAND

Swanco Star Rte., Box 7, 95963; 916-865-4109. Handmade fabric picture hangers and tassels. Catalog.

RANCHO CORDOVA

Sign of the Crab 3756 Omec Circle, 95742; 916-638-2722. Brass, chrome, and porcelain plumbing fixtures and accessories. Solid-brass hardware, gifts, and garden items. Catalog.

Wood Gallery 2538 Mercantile Dr., Suite C, 95742; 916-631-0260. Custom-made furniture and architectural interiors. Architectural ornaments for interiors. Brochure.

ROSEVILLE

Fancy Front Brassiere Co. P.O. Box 2847, 95746; 916-791-7733. Victorian millwork authentically reproduced. When the Victorians wanted to make their farmhouses stylish, they simply ordered bargeboards, corbels, gable trim, fan brackets, and anything else they desired by catalog.

Today's Victorian homeowners facing blank spaces after stripping asbestos or other shingles off their homes can do the same thing. Fancy Front re-creates gingerbread, moldings, fretwork, and decorative items using patterns from old houses all over the country.

They have headers, screen doors, corner posts, spindles and dowels, gables and balusters, and pickets custom-crafted in poplar or redwood. Fancy Front can reproduce brackets or moldings to match existing or missing material.

Although Fancy Front is not open to visitors, you may wish to visit the Antique Emporium at 238 Vernon Street in downtown Roseville (916-781-3322), a multi-dealer cooperative of antiques. Another Antique Emporium is located at 11395 Folsom Blvd. in Rancho Cordova (916-852-8517).

"Recipe for a Good Luck Cake:
The ring for marriage within a year;
The penny for wealth, my dear;
The thimble for old maid or bachelor born;
The button for sweethearts all forlorn;
The key for a journey to make all right;
And this to you will see next All Hallow's night."
—Anonymous

"Return with us now to the thrilling days of yesteryear." These opening words from the "Lone Ranger" show capture the spirit of a trip along Highway 49. Gold Country is an area rich in colorful history. But this hilly, rock-strewn country has created a new life for itself by preserving its heritage so that new generations of visitors can enjoy it and learn from it.

It's easy to imagine the Lone Ranger and Tonto riding out of the hills in search of desperados. What's hard to imagine is a greater concentration of well-preserved historic settings or a greater selection of historic B & B's to ease your journey.

The Gold Country's most enduring treasure is its history, and its most important lesson is how preserving the past is right not just for moral and aesthetic reasons but for economic ones as well. A leisurely tour along the path of the '49ers offers an inspiring example of how we can find our future in our past.

QUINCY

The Feather Bed 542 Jackson St., P.O. Box 3200, 95971; 916-283-0102 (M). Painted in peach with off-white trim and brick-red accents, this 1893 Queen Anne boasts fluted columns added in 1907 by the original owner, Edward Huskinson, a Quincy entrepreneur. Four of the seven antiques-filled rooms, all with bath, are named after Huskinson family members. Edward's room overlooks Main Street with its courthouse and the building that housed Mr. Huskinson's office, saloon, and livery stable.

Owners Chuck and Dianna Goubert converted their family home into a bed-and-breakfast in 1983, and many of the antique oak furnishings and watercolors by local artists are family heirlooms. Guests are served a full breakfast, and can enjoy the patio, bicycles, croquet, and the Victorian garden with a fountain and a gazebo with a swing inside. Although there are no feather beds, the inn is named The Feather Bed after the Feather River.

SUSANVILLE

Roseberry House 609 North St., 96130; 916-257-5675 (I/M). Three shades of rose, violet, and white grace this 1902 Queen Anne built by Congressman Thomas Roseberry, who died after a climb on Mt. Lassen. His widow, Viola May, converted their home into a boardinghouse, The Green Tree Inn. She was an artist, and two of her paintings still hang in the house, which is in Susanville's Victorian Row.

The present owners moved in in 1975 and transformed the top story of apartments into four sunny period rooms with bath. Children over ten are welcome. A full breakfast is served in the formal dining room.

The Feather Bed, Quincy

TRUCKEE

Truckee is a mecca for skiers and travelers heading for the outdoor sports found in the Donner Lake and Lake Tahoe area.

Truckee is also the birthplace of the red-light district, because the trains running across the country were run by hand, and brakemen had to be available at all times. While they waited, they found diversion in the cribs, still standing, in the brothel area. They left their red brakemen's lights on the front porches so they could be found easily. Hence, "the red-light district."

The Chamber of Commerce provides an informative Truckee Historic Landmarks map. The tourist information center is in the old train station on the main street.

The White House, a lovely Queen Anne/Eastlake built by W. H. Kruger in 1874, has been a bed-and-breakfast and is now a collection of stores on the main street of town. The house is listed on the National Register of Historic Places.

The Truckee Hotel Commercial Row at Bridge St., P.O. Box 884, 95734; 916-587-4444 (M). This historic Victorian hotel on the main street has been offering rooms to mountain travelers since 1880. There are thirty-seven rooms, eight with private bath. All of the rooms are named after historic Truckee residents, from the McGlashan

suite named after Charles McGlashan, one of Truckee's first citizens, to the Bulette Suite, named after Julia Bulette, a well-known lady of the evening, also remembered for tending to the sick and needy. Period furnishings and sepia portraits add to the authentic flavor. Guests enjoy a full

Red Castle Inn, Nevada City

Red Castle Inn, Nevada City

continental breakfast and afternoon wine and snacks.

The Passage, a bustling "mountain Victorian" restaurant, adjoins the hotel.

NEVADA CITY

In 1852, a visiting journalist wrote: "The city is upon hillsides, on the ridges, among the streams and over them. The muddy waters rush beneath the houses, stores and hotels and through the streets, splashing and gurgling as if uttering self-congratulating hymns for its escape from the torturing cradles and sluices. Not until a personal observation of the natural riches of Nevada City had I anything like an adequate conception of its golden abundance." Nevada City was once the third largest city in California, with many grand homes built for the mining and business millionaires. Today, the gold is found in tourism, generating historical reconstructions with nineteenth-century gas lamps on the streets.

Nevada City puts on a Victorian Christmas festival, with costumed vendors, horse-drawn wagon and buggy rides, fudge, and old-fashioned entertainment. Contact the Chamber of Commerce (916-265-2692/9019) for dates. The Chamber also offers maps and tours of Gaslit Downtown and the historic preservation districts.

Downey House B & B 517 W. Broad St., 95959; 916-265-2815 (M). Beige, white, and a touch of gray grace this 1870 Eastlake home on Nabob Hill. The six rooms with bath are decorated with a Southwest contemporary flair. Guests serve themselves at the generous buffet and eat in the sun room, kitchen, on the curved veranda, or in the garden near the lily pond. Cookies, fruit, and beverages are served in the afternoons.

Flume's End 317 S. Pine St., 95959; 916-265-9665 (M/E). Perched on a rushing creek next to the last surviving piece of flume from the Gold Rush days, this 1877 Victorian, painted in green, white, black, tan, and clay pink, offers a secluded setting close to town. Two of the five rooms have Jacuzzis; two have private balconies; and all have wood stoves. A full breakfast is served in the parlor or on the terrace near the waterfalls. Flume's End's newsletter is named "Creekside Chatter."

Grandmere's B & B Inn 449 Broad St., 95959; 916-265-4660 (M). This plain white Carpenter Stick home boasts an ironwork fence and a Painted Ladies–style door in white, gray, and black, with a touch of turquoise. The A. A. Sargent residence, listed on the National Register of Historic Places, is located on Nabob Hill in one of the earliest residential areas of the town. Senator Aaron Augustus Sargent was a lawyer, owner of the *Nevada Journal*, and champion of women's suffrage. His wife, Ellen Clark Sargent, founded San Francisco's Century Club with Susan B. Anthony in 1878.

Today, cool grays provide a backdrop for quilts and folk art in the six country-style rooms. Full breakfasts are served, and rooms are available for meetings and receptions.

National Hotel 211 Broad St., 95959; 916-265-4551 (I/M). California Historical Landmark No. 899 is a big, rambling, brick building, painted green with white fretwork. Built in 1854 on the site of a log jail, the National is the state's oldest continuously operating hostelry. The forty-three rooms are Victorian hotel rooms designed for miners, gamblers, dance-hall girls, and weary travelers. There's dancing and music in the cocktail lounge, a swimming pool out back and a restaurant downstairs.

The Parsonage 427 Broad St., 95959; 916-265-9478 (M). Once the parsonage for the Methodist church, this blue, gray, and white 1865 cottage in the town's historic central district is a microcosm of California pioneer history as collected by owner Deborah Dane. Guests can relax in a Turkish chair in the front bay window and read *Ghost Town*, a collection of miners' tall tales by

Deborah Dane's father. Family heirlooms are also used on the dining-room Sheraton table when guests gather for the bountiful continental breakfast. The linen used in each of the three rooms and baths is line-dried and hand-pressed, transporting guests back to a gentler era.

Red Castle Inn 109 Prospect St., 95959; 916-265-5135 (M). Nevada City's first bed-and-breakfast, perched on "Prospect Hill" overlooking the town, is also our favorite place to stay in northern Gold Country. This four-story icicle-laden red-brick Gothic Revival was built in 1860 by Judge John Williams, an eccentric miner whose son Loring loved to play his cornet on the white wraparound verandas. The house was paid for with sacks of gold, and two generations of the Williams family lived in and loved the house, which was saved from demolition in 1963 by James W. Schaar. Schaar is honored by a plaque near the entrance naming the Red Castle a state historic landmark.

The present owners, Mary Louise and Conley Weaver, feel privileged to "burnish the same mahogany banister that countless hands since before the Civil War have grasped," and feel a link with that time and this special place. Their continuing restoration and care is designed "to preserve the flavor of the Victorian era without creating a museum." To Mary Louise and her guests, the house produces its own magic. Victorian carved and canopied beds, cozy settees, delicious wallpapers, and whimsical touches delight and comfort.

Each of the eight rooms, six with private bath, has its own appeal. The two-bedroom suite in the garret upstairs, complete with its own comfortable sitting room, is perfect for two couples traveling together.

A bountiful buffet breakfast featuring at least one dish from the gold-mining era is laid out in the hall, and guests can choose to dine in the parlors, in their rooms, or out on the veranda. Afternoon tea features fresh teas from herbs grown in the Victorian garden terraces that protect the house.

The Weavers also host a Victorian Christmas Day feast with champagne, storytelling, music on the parlor pump organ, and eight courses from a cold soup to warming port. The house motto, "Pleasant Dreams and Fond Recollections," is fulfilled in this Gold Country gem.

Restaurants

Michael's Garden Restaurant 216 Main St., 95969; 916-265-6660 (M). California/continental dinners are served Monday through Saturday evenings in the tastefully decorated rooms of this small Italianate painted in white, cream, tan, and brown.

National Hotel Restaurant 211 Broad St., 95969; 916-265-4551 (M). The tavern's pride is its historic back bar. The Veranda Dining Room serves California specialties at breakfast, lunch, and dinner in a historic setting of pink silk walls with marvelous mirrors and wood-framed pictures illuminated by kerosene lamps on each table.

Places to Visit, Groups, and Artisans

Marsh House 254 Boulder St., 95959; 916-265-6716. An Italianate built in 1873 from Sloan's *The Model Architect* and listed on the Historic Register, the building is open by appointment to students wishing to study in what was once the American Victorian Museum.

Nevada City Carriage Company 17790 Cooper Rd., 95959; 916-265-5348. Horse-drawn carriage rides and tours are offered weekends year-round and daily in summer and fall, weather permitting. The Percherons can also be used for specially designed tours.

Nevada County Historical Society P.O. Box 1300, 95959.

Nevada County Historical Society Museum Firehouse No. 1, Main St. at Commercial, 95959; 916-265-9941. Daily, 11 A.M. to 4 P.M. in summer, 11 A.M. to 4 P.M. Tuesday through Sunday in winter. Donation. The striking

Victorian firehouse and belltower, now home for the local history museum, has a friendly ghost on the second floor.

Orey Victorian Tour House 401 N. York St., 95959; 916-265-9250. This authentically furnished pretty pink Victorian can be seen 11 A.M. to 5 P.M. on weekends in summer and by appointment. Fee.

A Work of Heart P.O. Box 1477, 95959; 916-265-4433. Susan Oliver teaches and designs patterns for French "Heirloom" lacemaking, kits and clothing, chatelaine kits, sewing accessories. Correspondence course by mail.

Annie Horan's B & B, Grass Valley

GRASS VALLEY

The Grass Valley and Nevada County Chamber of Commerce, 248 Mill St., 95945, 916-273-4667, provides maps of strolling and driving tours of Grass Valley, a town known for its hard-rock mining until 1950. Cornish Christmas in Grass Valley, reminiscent of the Cornish miners' days in the town, is an annual event. The streets are closed for dancing. Bellringers and choirs make merry. Visitors feast on bangers with potatoes, Cornish saffron cakes, hot roasted chestnuts, and the meat pasties carried into the mines by miners and reheated on shovels held over the candles in their hard hats. Free, collectible postage stamps hand-cancelled with the official Cornish Christmas cancellation mark are also available.

Annie Horan's B & B 415 W. Main St., 95945; 916-272-2418 (M). Builder-miner James L. Horan built this attractive brown, tan, and white Queen Anne in 1874. His daughter Annie turned it into a boardinghouse for Catholic priests, and lived here until 1954. The exterior, parlor, entry hall, and guest quarters remain as they were at the height of the Gold Country's heyday. The four spacious rooms with private baths are decorated in period country-Victorian furnishings. Breakfast is served in the dining room or on the rear deck.

Golden Ore House B & B Inn 448 S. Auburn St., 95945; 916-272-6872 (M). The motto of this gold, white, and brown Queen Anne cottage is "Come as strangers, come again as friends." Owner Wayne Peterson, who does not live on the premises, is a master carpenter. His grandfather and great-grandfather were also carpenters, and he admires the skill of those who built fine Victorians. "I enjoy a good feeling of satisfaction at having restored some classic homes, for the sake of the house and its creators—and for posterity—and to share with the people of today," he remarks.

Fine fretwork and wood floors and skylights add to the attractiveness of the house. The seven rooms, four with shared bath, are comfortable, decorated simply and comfortably. A full breakfast, which often includes scones and Scottish oatcakes, is served, as is afternoon tea.

Holbrook Hotel 212 W. Main St., 95945; 916-273-1353/800-933-7077 (M). "This New Commodious, First Class hotel, just complete with New Furniture and Private Baths. Presidential and Bridal Suite Accommodations Upon Requests."—D. P. Holbrooke, proprietor, 1890.

California Historical Landmark No. 914 was built in 1851, and again after successive fires in 1852, 1855, 1862, and 1890. Presidents

Swan-Levine House, Grass Valley

Edward Coleman built this Gothic Revival classic in 1866. Green window sashes and topiary ivy frame the white spartan exterior in green. The cozy front and back parlors and six rooms in the main house are decorated with carefully chosen antiques. The two suites in the annex across the street are decorated in Laura Ashley country style. Both have a double shower. A huge spa awaits in back beneath a sequoia tree. Full breakfast is provided.

Swan-Levine House 328 S. Church St., 95945; 916-272-1873 (M). Built in 1880 by merchant William Campbell and sold to Drs. John and Carl Jones, who used it as a hospital until 1968, this imposing Queen Anne has been undergoing restoration since 1975, when San Francisco artists Howard Levine and Margaret Swan bought it.

They turned the twenty-room structure into an art gallery, a printmaking studio, a guesthouse for artist and musician friends, a family home—children and pets abound—

Old Town Firehouse, Auburn

Grant, Garfield, Cleveland, and Harrison have stayed here, as have Black Bart, Bret Harte, and Mark Twain. Grass Valley's newly restored grand hotel offers twenty-seven wheelchair-accessible rooms with private bath, air-conditioning, telephones, brass beds, and clawfoot tubs. Two have fireplaces.

Holbrook Hotel Restaurant and Saloon 212 W. Main St., 95945; 916-273-1353 (M). The characteristic old-time saloon has a historic back bar and is said to be the oldest continuously operating saloon in California. The dining room, which is also wheelchair-accessible, has been restored with style and grace in a Victorian manner. Chef Roger Saker graduated from San Francisco's Culinary Academy and serves exceptionally fine California cuisine. Be sure to try the warm cucumber soup and prizewinning chocolate hazelnut cake.

Murphy's Inn 318 Neal St., 95945; 916-273-6873 (M/E). Mother lode gold baron

and a bed-and-breakfast. Guests stay in four large homey rooms, three with bath and one with fireplace. Full breakfasts are made on the antique Wedgwood stove in the kitchen and served on colorful California pottery. The energetic can pick fruit from the trees on the property, swim in the pool spa, or play badminton.

Places to Visit

Empire Mine Cottage 10791 E. Empire St., 95945; 916-273-8522. Tours at 1 P.M. daily in spring and fall, more frequently in summer, weekends in winter, and by appointment.

Willis Polk created one of the most intriguing Victorian homes in California when he designed a summer cottage for the William Bourn family in 1897. Waste granite rock from the Bourns' Empire Gold Mine was used as building blocks. Electricity from the nearby reservoir and indoor plumbing were novel features. The interior was paneled with heart redwood. Velvet leather-backed curtains between the rooms prevented drafts and were soundproofers. Some of the furnishings are original and the paneled walls still gleam.

The Lola Montez House 248 Mill St., 95945; 916-273-4667. Monday through Friday, 8:30 A.M. to 5 P.M.; Saturday, 10 A.M. to 3 P.M. When this was Lola Montez's home, from 1852 to 1855, it was the only house in town with a bathtub. The present house, a state historic landmark, is a replica of the original and is home for the Grass Valley/Nevada County Chamber of Commerce along with a small history museum that includes many things from Lola's time.

The house next door, a private residence at 238 Mill Street, was the home of Lotta Crabtree. Lola Montez taught Lotta to sing and dance. Redheaded Lotta went on to grace the stage for fifty years, and became America's first entertainer to become a millionaire.

Supplier

Deer Creek Pottery 305 Richardson St., 95945; 916-272-3373. Hand-pressed, low-fired, and hand-inlaid ceramic tiles, and custom manufacturing. Brochure.

AUBURN

Auburn, the oldest Gold Rush town in California, nestled in the foothills of the Sierras, is the gateway to the Gold Country on Highway 49. It was founded in 1848 by Claude Chana, who found gold. Historic Old Auburn is California Historical Landmark No. 404. The oldest post office in California is still in its original building. The Auburn Area Visitors and Convention Bureau at 600 Lincoln Way (800-433-7575/ 916-885-5616) provides maps and guides to Historic Auburn and its antiques store–lined streets.

Lodging

Power's Mansion Inn 164 Cleveland Ave., 95603; 916-885-1166 (M/E). Two shades of pink and a tiny bit of green enhance this handsome 1900 Queen Anne/Eastlake mansion built by Harold Power with part of his gold-mining millions. The Powers had six children, and the house was always filled with children and family friends, including young mining engineer Herbert Hoover.

Photographs and memorabilia of the family and Gold Country personalities decorate the halls. Fine art wallpapers, an exceptional Eastlake staircase, and carved wood moldings recall the house's original elegance. There are fifteen period-style rooms with baths, some with fireplaces, Jacuzzi, skylights, air-conditioning, city views, and private entrances. Morning newspapers, nightly turn-down service, phones, plush robes, and thick towels are provided, along with a copious continental breakfast.

The honeymoon suite has a heart-shaped double Jacuzzi and a fireplace. Guests appreciate the clothespress in the hall, the terraced garden patio, and the wraparound porches and decks. Weddings and business meetings can be arranged.

Victorian Hill House 195 Park St., P.O. Box 9097, 95604; 916-885-5879 (M). Two stone lions guard this white Stick home with a red-brick chimney and green gingerbread bargeboards, nestled in the woods overlooking Old Town Auburn. A gazebo, hot tub, pool, gardens, electric organ, and library help provide relaxation. A country breakfast and afternoon libations are offered in the formal dining room or out in the gazebo. Two of the four cheerful guestrooms have a full bath, two have half-baths. There are facilities for small weddings and meetings.

Restaurants

Beverly Inn Restaurant 130 Maple St., 95603; 916-888-6288 (M). Blacksmith John Mills White built the White House, a Stick-style home, in 1870, and the residence was the first building designated an Auburn Historical Building by the Auburn City Council. Today, Joe and Maritza Cordero serve continental lunches on weekdays, and dinner nightly.

Butterworth's 1522 Lincoln Wy., 95603; 916-885-0249. This stately Stick/Eastlake structure, built in 1885 by Sheriff John Boggs, commands a view of Old Town Auburn from its hillside location just south of the handsome Placer County Courthouse. The Butterworths opened the home as a restaurant in 1971, and new owners are in the process of restoring the inside, the outside, and the menu, which features American regional cuisine with homemade sauces, baked goods, and locally grown products. Butterworth's serves lunch on weekdays, dinners every night, and Sunday brunch.

Pullen House Garden Restaurant 729 Lincoln Wy., 95603; 916-823-5588 (M). Romantic country dining in a century-old Victorian. Lunch, dinner, and Sunday brunch.

Places to Visit

Bernhard Museum Complex 291 Auburn Folsom Rd., 95603; 916-885-0204. Tuesday through Friday, 11 A.M. to 3 P.M.; weekends, 12 to 4 P.M. Fee. Part of the Placer County Museum, located adjacent to the county fairgrounds, the Bernhard House was built in 1851 with additions made in 1870. The 1851 structure, Traveler's Rest, was built as a stagecoach stop and is the oldest wooden structure in Auburn. Benjamin Bernhard bought the place in 1868 for $3,500 and turned the property into a productive farm and winery. His descendants lived on the site until the 1960s, but kept the Victorian flavor in the fourteen rooms.

The historic Placer County Courthouse, built as a fireproof structure with a grand monumental dome, was built 1894–98. When the cornerstone was laid, the superintendent of schools noted: "Today we lay the foundation of a building that shall tell the future ages what manner of people we are." The ground floor will be part of the Placer County Museum as soon as reconstruction is complete.

Old Town Firehouse Lincoln Way at Commercial St. Built in 1891, this two-and-a-half-story structure once stood on the opposite end of the block, where it adjoined a now-demolished row of commercial buildings. A Queen Anne influence is evident in the use of patterned shingles in varied styles and colors, although the building is primarily red and white—appropriate for a firehouse. The Auburn Volunteer Fire Department, one of the oldest volunteer groups west of the Mississippi, was organized in 1852 and still fights Auburn fires. The bell still chimes at 8 A.M., 12 noon, and 5 P.M.

Victorian Warehouse 190 Grace St., 95603; 916-823-0374. Everything for the Victorian home is available here, from gazebos, beveled-glass doors, elegant ceilings, and bath fixtures, to light fixtures, satin lampshades, and lace curtains.

NEWCASTLE

Victorian Manor 482 Main St., P.O. Box 959, 95658 (4 miles from Auburn); 916-663-3009 (M). A restored white Eastlake country-Victorian built in 1900, the Victorian Manor offers four rooms, one with private bath, and each reminiscent of a tasteful interlude in our past. The Queen Victoria room, for example, is decked out in shades of mauve, and is graced by an 1860s Regency Revival bed and marble-topped dressing table.

A continental breakfast is served on fine china and crystal by innkeeper Cordelia Sanders, who makes her own quilts, curtains, garments, dolls, and fringed silk lampshades. A talented seamstress, she puts a "one-size-fits-all" Victorian dress and hat in each room, and a closetful in the hall, so guests can play dress-up and take "Victorian" photographs of one another.

Cordelia strives to achieve what she calls "The Victorian illusion." "All of us now are too young to remember those times. And when an era has ended, there's no controversy about it, and we always remember only the good things. The era is a 'golden bloom.' And when you stay in a Victorian bed-and-breakfast, you re-create that bloom. It's a memory of a slower, a softer time."

GEORGETOWN

American River Inn Orleans St., P.O. Box 43, 95634; 916-333-4499/800-245-6566 (M). Nestled in the Sierra Nevada foothills, this large creamy Gothic inn was built in 1853 as a stagecoach stop and boardinghouse for the gold miners. The lode, or natural line of gold, for the Woodside Mine still runs under the inn. At the inn, guests will find traveler's gold in comfortable brass beds with quilts and homey touches. There are twenty-five rooms and suites, most with private bath, some handicap-accessible.

There's something for everyone on the rambling grounds: hammocks, a putting green, bocce ball, a driving range, croquet, ping-pong, badminton, darts, bikes, horseshoes, Jacuzzi, pool, and Victorian gardens. At times, you feel that you're at a family party, at other times, a mountain resort. The gift shop up front is a fully stuffed Christmas toy store.

COLOMA

On January 24, 1848, James Marshall discovered gold in the tailrace of John Sutter's sawmill. This event changed the course of California history and sparked one of the great migrations in history. The Marshall Gold Discovery State Historic Park brings the Gold Rush world to life with museums, replicas, restored homes, and outbuildings. Victorian enthusiasts will want to visit the Noteware Thomas house, an 1860s merchant's home completely refurbished with many of the original furnishings, open weekends and by appointment, and the Emmanuel Methodist and St. John's Catholic churches, Gothic structures run by the State Park and used for weddings.

The Coloma Country Inn 345 High St., Box 502, 95613; 916-622-6919 (M). In 1852, this charming yellow and white Victorian cottage was the home of Hugh Miller, owner of Coloma's Fashion Billiard Saloon. Today's guests can still fish or canoe in the pond behind the house, pick blackberries out back, or loll with lemonade in the gazebo in the garden. Antiques, quilts, and stenciling give the five rooms, three with private bath, an open, airy, cheerful country feeling, and an expanded continental breakfast is served in your room or in the dining room overlooking the pond.

The inn is in the Gold Discovery State Historic Park, which makes seeing the park easy. This is probably the only inn in the country with a resident hot-air balloon pilot. Cindi and Alan Ehrgott are experienced white-water rafters, and Alan also offers white-water ballooning for the adventurous. Bed, breakfast, and ballooning packages are available.

The Vineyard House Cold Springs Rd., P.O. Box 176, 95613; 916-622-2217 (M). Goldseeker Martin Allhoff ended up planting a vineyard and building this plain blue and white Victorian in 1878 a mile from where gold was discovered. His widow remarried

American River Inn, Georgetown

and the family turned the place into a boardinghouse. The seven upstairs rooms, authentically decked out in high wooden bedsteads, silks, velvets, and red flocked walls, all share baths with a wandering ghost. One room with red flocked walls is dedicated to Lola Montez. Breakfast is served downstairs in the restaurant.

The Vineyard House Restaurant is open to the public for hearty four-course dinners and a mouth-watering Sunday brunch. On Friday and Saturday, there's live music on the veranda and in the saloon.

PLACERVILLE

Combellack-Blair House 2059 Cedar Ravine, 95667; 916-622-3764 (M). Mauve, pink, gray, and burgundy highlight the delicious fretwork on this splendid Queen Anne, built in 1895 by William Hill Combellack. New owners are still restoring the building, with Bradbury & Bradbury wallpapers and authentic window treatments. Peach silk and champagne welcome honeymooners in the bridal suite. A resident cat presides over the continental breakfast and afternoon snacks.

The Chichester House B & B 800 Spring St., 95667; 916-626-1882 (M). When D. W. Chichester, partner in the Predmore & Co. sawmill, built this gracious gold and white Queen Anne in 1892, *The Mountain Democrat* announced, "When completed, it will be the finest residence in the City." Supposedly, the house was built over a gold mine with a shaft opening under the dining-room table. It is also thought to be the first house in Placerville with built-in plumbing.

There are three rooms with half-baths. Robes are provided. Guests enjoy a delightful full breakfast in the dining room or conservatory, splendid fireplaces, and relaxing with a good book in the library.

AMADOR CITY

Imperial Hotel Hwy. 49, P.O. Box 195, 95601; 209-267-9172 (M). This brick Gold

Rush Victorian was built as a hotel in 1879 by merchant B. Sanguinetti, and remained a hotel until 1927. In 1988, innkeepers Bruce Sherrill and Dale Martin completely restored the hotel, restaurant, and bar, and added twentieth-century comfort to nineteenth-century charm.

Upstairs, there's a sitting porch–library, and six rooms with private bath. Four are authentically Victorian, with spindle work, gleaming woods, and period pictures. The Art Deco Room with a gorgeous hand-painted bedstead is popular, but our favorite is sunny No. 5, with bed and furnishings hand-painted with whimsical flowers by local artist John Johannsen. Continental breakfast included.

Imperial Hotel Restaurant Hwy. 49, P.O. Box 195, 95601; 209-267-9172 (M). The restaurant on the ground floor is the best in the Sutter Creek/Jackson/Amador area. The large open room with one brick wall has just enough palms, candles, flowers, and wall sconces to give it a Victorian flavor. The food is fresh, inspired California cuisine, served by a knowledgeable, caring staff.

Mine House Inn Hwy. 49, P.O. Box 245, 95601; 209-267-5900 (I/M). Located in the heart of the mother lode, this quaint hostelry is housed in the Old Keystone Consolidated Mining Company's office building, built in the 1870s. Each of the eight rooms is named for what it was originally used for. The Assay Room and the Mill Grinding Room have stories of their own, and they're authentically decked out with furnishings used when the building was a target for bandits and highway men. A pool in the gardens will help you escape the summer heat.

SUTTER CREEK

First a logging camp for John Sutter's fort, and then a camp of gold miners' tents alongside the creek, Sutter's Creek became a town when the first quartz mill and first foundry were established in 1851 and 1852, respectively. Today, the principal industries are lumber, wineries, and tourism, and it's a pretty, bustling town of antiques and gift shops.

The Monteverde Store Museum, a museum of Sutter Creek history, is being put together by the Sutter Creek Area Merchants Association (SCAMA) and the city of Sutter Creek in an 1898 Victorian cottage on Randolph Street donated by Rosa Monteverde.

Walking-tour maps of the town are available from SCAMA or the city offices at 209-267-5647. The Sutter Creek Palace at 76 Main Street is a restaurant, saloon, and hotel dating back to 1891. There are regular annual events, such as the Spring Daffodil Hill Celebration and the Currier & Ives Christmas Open House.

The Foxes of Sutter Creek 77 Main St., P.O. Box 159, 95685; 209-267-5882 (M/E). The Brinn House, built in 1857 and enlarged during the next thirty years, is the most elegant inn in southern Gold Country. Pete and Min Fox make each guest feel right at home. Burnished woods, muted wall coverings, High Renaissance headboards, and armoires evoke an English Victorian atmosphere.

Each of the six spacious yet intimate air-conditioned rooms has its own plush fox mascot and a private bath. Three have TVs hidden in the armoires. The honeymoon suite downstairs has its own wood-burning fireplace, a private entry, and a sixteen-foot bathroom.

Your newspaper arrives at your door at 7 A.M. Award-winning breakfasts, made to order by Pete and Min Fox, are served on gleaming silver trays in your suite or in the gazebo. There are even hand-crocheted booties for the water and juice glasses. Special coffee blends and potpourri are available.

The Gold Quartz Inn 15 Bryson Dr., 95685; 209-267-9155/800-752-8738 (M). Gray, white, and burgundy trim adorn the exterior of this Neo-Victorian inn located just outside of town. The owners bought

English replica antiques and *Godey's Ladies Book* prints to decorate the twenty-four large country-comfortable rooms and suites, with baths and private verandas. Each room has a Rosey the Rabbit on the bed.

Breakfast is served in the two dining rooms. Afternoon teas include ice cream in summer, and snackers will find coffee, soft drinks, and cookies around the clock. Picnics are available. The conference facilities are exemplary. Two of the rooms are totally wheelchair-accessible. They'll even provide the wheelchair for the wheel-in showers.

Suppliers and Groups

Fox Woodcraft Service P.O. Box 846, 95685; 209-267-5051/267-0774. Archie Fox specializes in Victorian design on small and grand scales. Also, custom cabinetry, one of a kind wood carving and kitchen and bath remodeling. Archie has turned an old miner's paycheck house into a turreted, shingled Queen Anne.

Victorian Homeowners Association and **Old House Lovers** P.O. Box 846, 95685. Membership includes a newsletter of sources, informational columns, classifieds, and articles on Victorian lifestyle, and an exquisite Victorian window certificate.

JACKSON

Jackson, a Gold Rush camp dating from 1848 and rebuilt after a fire in 1862, is the heart of Amador County and home of the Kennedy Tailing Wheels, unique in function and size. The four wheels—the remnants of only two exist now—were fifty-eight feet in diameter and lifted the tailings by gravity and flume over hillsides to a dam. Operating models of the wheels and the mine can be seen in the Amador County Museum.

The Amador County Chamber of Commerce, P.O. Box 596, 95642, 209-223-0350, offers event listings and maps of historic walking and driving tours of each town in the county, and a visitor's guide.

Combellack-Blair House, Placerville

For a walking tour of historic downtown Jackson, call local historian O. Henry Mace at 209-223-1966. Tours include admission to the Kennedy Mine Model Demonstration.

Every Saturday night, from mid-May to mid-October, in Drytown on Highway 49, the Claypipers present melodramas of villainy, skullduggery, love, honor, and virtue triumphant. For information, write P.O. Box 155, Drytown, 94599, or call 209-246-4604.

Amador County Museum 225 Church St., 95642; 209-223-6386. Wednesday through Sunday, 10 A.M. to 4 P.M.. Fee. Built in 1859 by politician Armstead C. Brown, this brick Gothic cottage contains Gold Rush history in fifteen exhibit rooms, including a Victorian schoolroom, a Victorian sewing room, and a tribute to Mark Twain.

Lodging

Ann Marie's Country Inn 410 Stasal Ave., P.O. Box DN, 95642; 209-223-1452 (M). This cozy yellow and white Queen Anne cottage was built by Dr. James Wilson in 1892. Once past the art gallery in front, guests can choose from four delightful rooms or the

The Hughes House Inn Bed and Breakfast, Jackson

Windrose Inn, Jackson

The Utica Mansion Inn, Angels Camp

separate cottage in the back garden. A hearty breakfast is served family style. Children are welcome.

The Broadway Hotel 225 Broadway, 95642; 209-223-3503 (M). Established as a hotel in 1904, this blue and white Gold Rush Victorian has fifteen simply decorated rooms and an old-fashioned hotel style. Breakfast is served in the large downstairs dining room. Guests are welcome to share the gardens and the hot tub in the gazebo.

Court Street Inn 215 Court St., 95642; 209-223-0416 (M/E). Painted yellow with white trim and a touch of dark brown, this 1872 Victorian cottage, the Grace Blair DePue house, is listed on the National Register. Guests are pampered by the antiques-filled rooms, a country-style breakfast, hors d'oeuvres, and a spa in the rose garden. Three of the seven rooms have private baths, two have fireplaces.

Gate House Inn 1330 Jackson Gate Rd., 95642; 209-223-3500 (M). This peachy 1903 Queen Anne is set on spacious gardens with

a swimming pool. Parquet oak floors, marble fireplaces, lace curtains, and crystal chandeliers whisper of the past. The five rooms have private baths. The room nestled in the summerhouse behind the main house is for special getaways. Breakfast is served in the formal dining room. There's a ping-pong table on the veranda and a covered barbecue for summer picnics. Business meetings and parties welcome.

The Hughes House Inn Bed and Breakfast 430 Stasal Ave., 95642; 209-223-1117/415-828-4241 (M). County sheriff/tax collector Robert J. Adams built this charming Queen Anne home in 1896, and it is Jackson's newest bed-and-breakfast. Ed Hughes's grandparents and great-grandparents smile down from their portraits in the front parlor, which they share with the house cat and a wonderful Victorian dollhouse.

Judy Hughes has created unique Victorian adornments for their home and inn. In the stairway, great-grandmother's wedding dress decorates a wall. The three upstairs rooms share a clawfoot tub bath, but each is distinctively decorated and each has a mini-refrigerator.

Afternoon refreshments are served in the downstairs parlors. A tantalizing breakfast, served from a Victorian kitchen, may be taken in the dining room, on the balcony, or in the garden. A fourth room with wheel-chair access is planned for the cabin in the garden.

National Hotel 2 Water St., 95642; 209-223-0500 (I/M). A historic hotel in continuous operation since 1862, the National has retained its eleven simply furnished Gold Rush–style rooms. Black Bart stayed here. So did presidents Garfield and Hoover, and John Wayne.

The National Hotel and Louisiana House saloon and restaurant are open for weekend music and reminiscences. Lunch and dinner are served Thursday through Sunday.

The Wedgewood Inn 11941 Narcissus Rd., 95642; 209-296-4300/800-WEDGEWD (M). Although this is a Neo-Victorian, created as a bed-and-breakfast from old floor plans in six months in 1987, born innkeepers Jeannine and Vic Beltz have been collecting family treasures for the inn all of their lives. They have put together a livable and living museum—a memorable B & B.

Each of the six rooms—all with private bath, three with wood-burning stoves—incorporates a piece of family history, whether it's a family photo album, a baby or wedding dress worn by a grandmother, or a trunk full of heirloom books.

Vic has done a lot of the landscaping and stained-glass work himself. Jeannine's needlecraft work and Victorian lace lamp-shades are tastefully displayed throughout the inn. Both prepare the multi-course gourmet breakfasts. Guests are greeted with afternoon cheese and refreshments. Painted in Wedgwood blues and white, the inn is set on five wooded acres ten minutes east of Jackson on the road to Volcano.

Windrose Inn 1407 Jackson Gate Rd., 95642; 209-223-3650 (M). Minutes out of town, across a babbling creek and nestled in beds of flowers under fruit trees, this sweet Victorian farmhouse, scheduled to be a Painted Lady, is a newly popular B & B in the Gold Country. The four rooms with private baths, including the ivy-covered two-story miner's cabin, are adorned with period artifacts. One room is a surprising Art Deco.

Full breakfasts are served in the sunny solarium, on the porch beside the goldfish pond, or in the gazebo. By the way, the house is named Windrose not because of the rose carved in the gables over the front door, but because when Marv Hampton proposed to Sharon—after they met again at a twenty-fifth high school reunion—it was at the Windrose Restaurant in Long Beach. Windrose participates in the BBNC Frequent Traveler Program.

Stained Glass Mountain 115B Main St., 95642; 209-223-4612. Coleen Ireland gives classes and does custom-designed stained glass, etched and beveled windows, and original glass art objects. Antique repairs.

Foxes Window and Wallcovering 1500 S. Hwy. 49, Artful Hand Bldgs. 95642; 209-223-2881. Carolyn and Tony Fox install and create windows and wall coverings.

VOLCANO

Jug & Rose Main St., P.O. Box 232, 95689; 209-296-4696. Closed Monday and Tuesday. Open weekends only, November through March. Making reservations for breakfast in this quaint Victorian ice-cream parlor where sourdough pancakes are the specialty is a good idea. Lunch and original ice-cream sundaes are also available.

The Volcano Community Association sponsors two arts-and-crafts fairs during the year, and an Old Abe Independence Day Celebration parade (209-296-4696).

Supplier

The Bandstand Woodworks Main at Consolation St., 95689; 209-295-1391. Custom woodwork.

ANGELS CAMP

The Utica Mansion Inn P.O. Box One, 1090 Utica Ln., 95222; 209-736-4209 (M). Light- and dark-taupe and white beautify this handsome 1882 inn, listed on the National Register. Tad and Cheryl Folendorf have won the Mother Lode Architectural Award from the Calaveras County Historic Society for their definitive restoration of this 5,000-square-foot mansion.

The interior is a symphony of Bradbury & Bradbury wallpapers. Some of them are reproductions of the original wallpapers found in the house and then used for other restorations by the State of California.

The woodwork is grained, English-tiled fireplaces abound, and the original lighting fixtures remain. The three guest suites, two with fireplaces, have fine antique furnishings. Wine and fruit greet the guests, who are welcome to relax in the Mark Twain Library. Full breakfast is served in the formal dining room. Children are welcome,

with prior arrangement. A cat and four dogs are on the premises.

Dinner is served to the public Thursday through Monday evenings in the sunflower-shiny dining room. A private dining room is available as well. Special theme dinners are also scheduled during the year.

Stop by at the City of Angels Museum on Hwy. 49, 753 So. Main St., 95222; 209-736-2963, 10 A.M. to 3 P.M. daily. Fee. An homage to Mark Twain and a galaxy of horse-drawn carriages and memorabilia.

MURPHYS

Murphys, the Queen of the Sierras, is a center for visits to the local caves and caverns. In town, stop at the Old Timers Museum on Main Street.

Mother Lode tours for up to forty-four people for two to five days are hosted by Diane Campana, P.O. Box 252, Murphys, 95247 (209-728-1190).

Bill Mathis of the Murphys Stage & Cab Co. may usually be found with his horse and turn-of-the-century buggy in front of the Murphys Hotel. To hire his buggy for a special occasion, write to P.O. Box 1503, 95247, or call 209-728-2733.

Lodging

Dunbar House, 1880 271 Jones St., P.O. Box 1375, 95247; 209-728-2897 (M). This dignified white Italianate was built in 1880 by Willis Dunbar for his bride, Ellen Roberts, and is now listed on the National Register. The four rooms with private bath are comfortably furnished with antiques, lace, down comforters and pillows, minirefrigerators, and wood stoves. Breakfast is served by the dining-room fireplace, in the century-old gardens, or in your room. The wicker rocking chairs on the wraparound verandas are inviting.

Murphys Hotel 457 Main St., P.O. Box 329, 95247; 209-728-3444 (I/M). The Murphys Hotel was built by John Perry and James Sperry in 1856, with parlors and suites

The Robin's Nest, San Andreas

available exclusively for ladies. The building has continued as a hotel until today, when it has a two-story modern motel attached to one side. Ulysses S. Grant, Horatio Alger, Mark Twain, Henry Ward Beecher, tea-man Sir Thomas Lipton, and J. P. Morgan have signed the guest register, which now resides in the Calaveras County Museum in San Andreas. Today's guests can stay in period guestrooms, with or without bath, as they might have a hundred years ago.

Supplier

D. E. A. Bathroom Machineries 495 Main St., P.O. Box 1020, 95247; 800-722-4426. Monday through Friday, 8 A.M. to 5 P.M.; Saturday, 10 A.M. to 4 P.M. A mecca for restored and reproduced fixtures and accessories, this is a browser's delight. The pretty Williamsburg light- and medium-blue and white 1900 Italianate houses a treasure trove of Victorian and hard-to-find bathroom plumbing, brass hardware, lighting fixtures, and decorator accessories. Clawfoot tubs range in price from $125 to $2,000. Brass hinges, screws, and inexpensive door keys can be found here. Catalog.

SAN ANDREAS

The Robin's Nest 248 St. Charles (Hwy. 49), P.O. Box 1408, 95249; 209-754-1076 (M).

This teal blue, dusty rose, and white 1895 Queen Anne Victorian blends its dramatic character and old-world charm with modern conveniences. The Calaveras County Historic Society gave the 1984 restoration its Architectural Award of Merit. To celebrate the grand opening of the inn, Rowena Snyder, who was born in the bed in the sunny yellow first bedroom, was the first guest. Each of the eight guestrooms, all with private bath, has a distinctive decor inspired by a mode of transportation at the turn of the century. Complimentary beverages greet arriving guests, who may enjoy badminton, croquet, or volleyball outside, or the grand piano and library indoors. Fresh fruit picked in the gardens accompanies the full breakfast.

The Calaveras County Historical Museum on Main Street (209-754-6579) is open 10 A.M. to 4 P.M. daily. Fee. In the old Hall of Records, there is an elegant turn-of-the-century bedroom as well as photographs and memorabilia from Gold Rush pioneers. The museum focuses on people living in San Andreas during the 1880s.

COLUMBIA

City Hotel Columbia State Historic Park, Main St., Box 1870, 95310; 209-532-1479 (M). Wake up to the sound of horses on the street and pretend you're in another era. Hospitality management students attending Columbia College work with the full-time staff in the operation of the hotels and the restaurant, which are part of Columbia State Historic Park.

The City Hotel is an authentically preserved Gold Rush hotel, with nine high-ceilinged, antiques-appointed rooms. Since all the bathing facilities are down the hall, each room comes with a basket full of towels and soap, terry robes and slippers.

Sherry is served before dinner and a continental breakfast is served each morning in the authentically decorated guest parlor upstairs. There's even a blackjack table for gamesters.

The restaurant downstairs, one of the best

in Gold Country, is noted for its fine food and service and its Victorian ambience.

Fallon Hotel Columbia State Historic Park, P.O. Box 1870, 95310; 209-532-1470 (M). The Fallon Hotel was established in Columbia, then a booming Gold Rush town, in 1857. It has been carefully restored by the State of California to its Victorian grandeur as "a living museum," part of Columbia State Historic Park.

There are fourteen rooms, some wheelchair-accessible, and most of the antiques and furnishings are original to the hotel, from small to the grand bridal suite. Meeting and receptions rooms are available. The Fallon Theatre and an ice-cream salon adjoin the hotel. Continental breakfast is served.

Write for a list of the special festival events that take place at the park throughout the year.

SONORA

Lodging

Barretta Gardens Inn 700 S. Barretta St., 95370; 209-532-6039 (M). This white Victorian, built in 1895 by Albert Kleinecke, superintendent of the Standard Lumber Company, is surrounded by three porches, an old-fashioned glass solarium full of plants, and an acre of terraced gardens. The three second-floor rooms, restored to their historic ambience, share a bath and a delightful reading parlor. A complete American breakfast is served on the porches, or in the formal dining room under a crystal chandelier.

Lavender Hill B & B 683 S. Barretta St., 95370; 209-532-9024 (I). Painted in pale dove-gray, white, and lavender, this 1900 Stick cottage is perched on the hill above Sonora. Pretty gardens, a cheerful parlor and sitting room, and full country breakfasts are in store for guests. There are four rooms, one with a clawfoot tub and pull-chain toilet in the private bath. Another has a private bath with stall shower. Owner

Alice Byrnes won a Golden Nugget Landmark Award for her restoration and "loving care" of the inn. "It's always been a dream to find an old place that needed a lot of tender loving care. This is it."

Lulu Belle's Bed & Breakfast 85 Gold St., 95370; 209-533-3455 (M). Built in 1886 for architect John H. Rother, this rambling Victorian homestead harbors five rooms with private entrances and baths. Touches of red velvet and country calico are comforting, and guests are welcome in the library and music room. Suite Lorraine with its two double four-poster canopied beds, roomy sitting area, and separate dressing room is perfect for families. Youngsters will be entranced by the surrey with a fringe on top and antique Bowman carriage in the garden. They'll also like the porch swing and rockers on the wraparound porch.

The Palm Hotel, Jamestown

Oliver's 56 W. Bradford St., 95370; 209-532-0275 (M). An 1889 Stick cottage, the Keil-Burgson home, painted in two blues and white, is located in the heart of downtown Sonora. Named for the color schemes of the rooms—Rose, Green, Gold, and Blue—all but one of the rooms have a private bath. The Blue Suite, decorated with white wicker, has its own fireplace and sun room. A full American breakfast is served in the oak-paneled dining room, decorated with lace and a jukebox, or on the patio.

The Ryan House Bed & Breakfast Inn 153 S. Sheperd St., 95370; 209-533-3455 (M). "Footsteps from town, a century removed," this cozy 1855 blue and white cottage was scheduled to be torn down for a parking lot. Citizen protest saved it, and an innkeeper purchased it from descendants of the original builder. Nancy Hoffman was restoring Ryan House when we visited, trying to make guests feel that they're visiting their grandmother's house, and attempting to keep the house as original as possible.

All the windows are handmade, with the original old glass. The house was built using handmade square nails. Full breakfasts are served to those who rest under the quilts in the three snuggly rooms with baths.

Serenity: A Bed and Breakfast Inn 15305 Bear Cub Ln., 95370; 209-533-1441 (M). Built as a bed-and-breakfast in 1983, and again after a fire in 1988, this Neo-Victorian farmhouse located east of town offers peace and quiet on six secluded acres. Charlotte and Fred Hoover wanted a B & B in Sonora, but they also wanted to be in the country, so they built exactly what they wanted. The exterior is an interpretation of the Downs Mansion in Sutter Creek.

Fred did all the woodwork himself. Charlotte is a fiber artist, and her cross-stitch and needlepoint enliven the house. Even the sheets have hand-crocheted lace edges. The comforters and spreads are also Charlotte's creations.

There are four spacious rooms with floral themes. The Violet Room, all in blues, has sponge-painted walls, balloon shades, and frothy lace curtains. Breakfast is served in the dining room. Guests can relax in the parlor, library, or on the veranda.

Place to Visit

Tuolumne County Museum and History Center 158 W. Bradford Ave., 95370; 209-532-1317. In summer, Monday, Wednesday, and Friday, 9 A.M. to 4:30 P.M.; Tuesday, Thursday, and Saturday, 10 A.M. to 3:30 P.M.; Sundays, 10 A.M. to 3:30 P.M. Sonora, Queen of the Southern mother lode, was founded in 1848 and became the county seat of Tuolumne County in 1850. The Tuolumne County Museum, formerly the county jail, was dedicated in 1982 and is listed on the National Register. Local history, an antique firearms exhibit, cowboy paintings, and a gold collection fill most of the exhibit space.

The town is a shoppers' delight. A visitor's guide with Sonora's most notable landmarks shown on the map is available from the Tuolumne County Visitors Bureau, P.O. Box 4020, 95370; 209-533-4420/800-446-1333. Tuolumne County Historical Society address is P.O. Box 695, 95370.

Suppliers

Damron Interiors 18701 Tiffeni Dr., Village Square, Twain Harte, 95383; 209-586-1116. Hardwood flooring, window treatments, wallpaper, paints, and fine furnishings.

Don Grover & Associates 20280 Summit Dr., 95379; 209-532-6741. Don Grover is an architect specializing in the restoration and redesigning of historic properties. He is responsible for the restoration of the McHenry Mansion in Modesto, the City Hotel in Sonora, and the Jamestown Hotel in Jamestown. He also created his parents' bed-and-breakfast inn, the Oak Hill Ranch in Tuolumne, using old materials and modern construction.

Eric Eckerstrom, Joiner 4221 Eden Ln., Fiddletown, 95269; 209-245-6735. Custom doors, stairs, architectural woodwork and restoration, design, and execution. Unlike a carpenter who typically uses nails, a joiner uses woodworking joints.

Wendall's Wood Stoves 19964 Inks Dr., 95379; 209-928-4508. Renovation and restoration of wood-burning stoves. Restored kitchen ranges and parlor heaters. Brochure.

TUOLUMNE

Oak Hill Ranch B & B 18550 Connally Ln., P.O. Box 307, 95379; 209-928-4717 (M). Jane and Sanford Grover have turned a small dairy farm, part of the C. E. Connally homestead in the 1850s, into an imposing yellow and white country-Victorian replica using Victorian turn posts, railings, mantelpieces, doorways, and salvaged turn-of-the-century relics collected over a period of twenty-five years. The 1870s walnut and mahogany staircase and the Eastlake fireplace mantels are especially remarkable.

The construction was son Don's senior architectural project at Washington State University. Some of the slate rocks in the foundation are from the Tuolumne River bed. There are five rooms: three with bath, one with fireplace, and one in a 1,200-square-foot private cottage. The Eastlake Room, a favorite, boasts a carved, queen-sized headboard, marble-topped dresser, and matching Eastlake carved chairs with rose velvet upholstery.

There's a gazebo in the flower garden for trysts and weddings, and fifty-six acres to get lost in. Jane cooks full gourmet breakfasts, including crepes Normandy, and both Jane and Sanford wear period clothes every day. They belong to the Horseless Carriage Club of America, so you'll see their vintage 1918 Maxwell touring car on the grounds.

JAMESTOWN

Historic National Hotel Main St., Box 502, 95327; 209-984-3446 (M). Built in 1859 as a hotel for gold miners, the National Hotel is one of the oldest continuously running hotels in America. A recent restoration of the eleven rooms, all with sinks and six sharing bathrooms, has retained the mother-lode flavor of quilts, brass beds, oak furniture, and pull-chain toilets, which is enhanced by modern conveniences such as showers, heat, air-conditioning, and television (available on request).

Historic pictures and mementos line the walls. A generous continental breakfast buffet is served in the dining room or the Garden Courtyard. Guests can relax with jigsaw puzzles, chess, checkers, and a snooze in the grape arbor.

The National Hotel Restaurant on the ground floor offers California dinners and Sunday brunch. The long redwood bar in the saloon is known for the thousands of bags of gold dust that changed hands here.

The Palm Hotel 10382 Willow St., 95327; 209-984-3429 (M). Nestled under a towering palm tree, this stately 1890s towered Queen Anne was once a rooming house for railroad and mining men. Today, there are nine carefully refurbished rooms, five with private bath. The skylights in the tower suites give the place a fairy-tale charm.

Dentist sinks rescued from Columbia enhance several rooms. The stencil wall treatment and Lincrusta is especially fine. One room is handicap-accessible. Televisions are available on request. A full breakfast is served.

Railroad buffs will want to visit Railtown 1887 just a block away. There you'll find steam trains ready to take you for a trip back in time.

MARIPOSA

Granny's Garden Bed & Breakfast 7333 Hwy. 49, N. Mariposa, 95338; 209-377-8342 (M). Dave and Dixie Trabucco have turned his grandmother's 1896 Victorian farmhouse into a simple down-home country retreat that is twelve miles north of Mariposa on the way to Yosemite National Park. Visitors will find two suites, an outdoor spa, and hammocks under fruit trees on the lawn.

Schlagater House 5038 Bullion St., P.O. Box 1202, 95338; 209-966-2471 (M). This cute 1859 Carpenter Gothic cottage welcomes guests as it has the various members of the Schlagater family throughout its existence. Innkeeper Roger McElligott, a sixth-generation Mariposan, was a friend of the Schlagaters, one of whom married Mrs. Leland Stanford's brother. The light fixtures are those used by Stanford when he was a senator in Washington.

Guests in the three rooms, one with private bath, are welcomed with wine, hors d'oeuvres, and fresh flowers. The room downstairs, with a canopied four-poster bed, and the two upstairs rooms with their rag and peg ceilings, are especially quiet. The Mining Camp Breakfast served in the country kitchen includes a Welsh breakfast pastie, like that eaten by the nearby Welsh miners.

Places to Visit

Mariposa Museum and History Center 5119 Jessie St., P.O. Box 606, 95338; 209-966-2924. Visitors follow a self-guided tour through the buildings of this authentic picture of the people and life of the county, from the migration of its first inhabitants to the recent past. Original documents and artifacts are of interest, as are the old print shop, the 1850s street of shops, the one-room schoolhouse, and the home of John C. Fremont and his wife, Jessie. The Gagliardo Store is stocked with Victorian merchandise donated by the heirs of Jennie Gagliardo, whose family operated the store from 1854 to 1960.

FISH CAMP

The Narrow Gauge Inn Yosemite's South Gate Lodging: 209-683-7720. Dining: 209-683-6446 (M). This mile-high escape to the gracious world of yesteryear offers dining and comfortable overnight stays in a unique blend of Victorian- and Western-style architecture nestled in the pine forests of the Sierra.

OAKHURST

Fresno Flats Historical Park School Rd., 427 Hwy. 41, P.O. Box 451, 93644; 209-683-6570. Wednesday through Saturday, 1 to 3 P.M.; Sunday 1 to 4 P.M.; and by appointment. Fee. Designed to show how families lived in the foothills and mountains a century ago, this complex of ten saved buildings displays memorabilia. The Laramore House is furnished in middle-class Victorian style, because Mr. Laramore owned the local general store. Also in the park is a museum located in one of the earliest schoolhouses in Madera County, and an 1880s jail.

More Gold Country Craftsmen and Suppliers

Cottonwood

JB Custom Woodworking 916-347-0902. Drewey "Jody" Bush specializes in fine wood furnishings for the home. Antique plumbing fixtures, windows, and trim work.

Pine Grove

Vintage Leatherworks 13780 Tank Dr., 95665; 209-296-5353. Quality reproductions of period luggage. Saddlery and harness repairs. Trunk restorations. Custom creations.

Drytown

Woodchuck Furniture Works 16701 Hwy. 49 at Hwy. 16., P.O. Box, 95699; 209-245-4293. Geoffrey Kidder. Custom-made screen doors in Victorian and other designs. Catalog.

Most Americans' first contact with the Big Valley was seeing Barbara Stanwyck and Lee Majors in the television horse opera of that name, set in Stockton-on-the-lot. The real Big Valley South stretches from south of Sacramento to Los Angeles. It is hot, flat, rich, and huge.

The unofficial capital of the area is Fresno, which has two excellent house museums: the Meux Home and the Kearney Mansion. The McHenry Mansion in Modesto is also worth a detour.

Fresno also had a splendid surprise for us when we were researching the guide. A block from the Meux Home is the most beautiful Victorian church interior we've seen in California: St. John's Cathedral.

LODI

Wine and Roses Country Inn 2505 West Turner Rd., between Hwy. 5 and Hwy. 99, 95242; 209-344-6988 (M). The rambling 1902 Towne family estate has been turned into a charming inn nestled on five secluded acres of towering trees and flower gardens. The Townes farmed fifty acres of Tokay grapes. Today, wedding parties and corporate gatherings catered by an in-house graduate of the Culinary Academy of San Francisco fill the gardens.

Upon her hiring, Sherri and the owner's son and partner Del immediately fell in love, and a year later were married in the garden. With so much romance, Kris Cromwell has been inspired to write a book called *Love Stories from Wine and Roses*. A breakfast tradition is for the guests to exchange love stories of how they met, proposed, got married, and what their secret is for happiness—and a successful marriage. Everyone takes home a special remembrance of new friends, and sometimes a little extra secret to add to the success of their own marriage.

The nine rooms are filled with old-fashioned rose fabric, lace, puffy hand-made comforters, collectibles, fresh flowers, and turn-of-the-century decor. Afternoon tea and special goodies are served in the sitting room by the fireplace or in the rose-filled garden, where guests can also play croquet, badminton, and horseshoes. A horse and carriage are available for rent. Meeting rooms are fully equipped.

STOCKTON

Old Victorian Inn 207 W. Acacia St., 95203; 209-462-1613 (M). This beautifully restored Queen Anne—a Painted Lady in light and dark cream, tan, dark teal, and barn red—was built in 1890 by Dr. Lester E. Cross. The house contains heirloom antiques, many of which belonged to the original owner, and some of which came from the Haggin Museum. Two parlors, a dining room downstairs, and a third-floor sitting room are for the guests' relaxation. The unique antique lamps and lighting fixtures are the works of one of the owners, who specializes in antique lighting.

There are six rooms, all of which have sinks and lovely chandeliers with polychrome medallions. They share three baths. Two rooms have fireplaces, two have decks. Breakfast is served in the formal dining room. Afternoon refreshments are enjoyed on the lovely deck in the back. Meetings and receptions may be arranged. There's good fishing nearby.

MODESTO

McHenry Mansion 906 15th St., 95354; 209-

577-5342. Tours and rentals by appointment. This dignified 1883 Italianate has been restored and refurbished right down to its William Morris–designed Bradbury & Bradbury wallpapers. The rose brass gas chandelier in the front parlor, the nineteenth-century English wall-to-wall carpeting, and the newly molded columns on the front veranda are especially notable.

The landscape paintings flanking the fireplace in the library and the mirrors hanging above the fireplaces in the front parlor and the dining room are the only original McHenry family pieces. The carpeting was woven by the Stouvale Mills in Kidderminster, England, on nineteenth-century looms that might have made the carpets for Queen Victoria's residences at Balmoral Castle and Osbourne House.

The story of the McHenry Mansion reflects the history of Modesto, because the two evolved together. Today, this restored home is almost all that is left of Modesto's historical past. Special events are held throughout the year. The McHenry Mansion Foundation, P.O. Box 642, 95353, and McHenry Mansion Gift Store are working to keep the building beautiful.

McHenry Museum 1402 I St., 95354; 209-577-5366. Tuesday through Sunday, 12 to 4 P.M. Free. Tours by appointment. A complete doctor's office, a general store, a re-created blacksmith shop using square nails from a century-old house, and changing exhibits of quilts, fans, dolls, costumes, and gold-mining and fire-fighting equipment are part of this historical museum. Photo and paper archives are available for research. There are changing exhibits, events, and traveling exhibits to schools and senior-citizen groups.

MADERA

Madera County Museum Courthouse Square, P.O. Box 478, 93639; 209-674-4535. Weekends, 10 A.M. to 4 P.M. Guided group tours by appointment. Donations. The Madera County Historical Society has restored the county courthouse built in 1900. Twenty-three rooms of displays tell the story of Madera County and its people. A turn-of-the-century parlor, dining room, bedroom, sewing room, and kitchen are included. The knowledgeable docents create entertaining tours.

FRESNO

Fresno City and County Historical Society 7160 West Kearney Blvd., 93706; 209-441-0862. Founded to collect, preserve, and interpret Fresno's heritage, the society administers the Kearney Mansion and the Fort Miller Blockhouse Museum as well as archives and an artifact collection. It presents special exhibits of Fresno history at regional museums. Members enjoy special events and tours, research privileges in the society's archives, the opportunity to record their family's genealogy in the historical society's family registry, a quarterly journal, and discounts on purchases at the Kearney Gift Shop.

Kearney Mansion 7160 West Kearney Blvd., 93706; 209-441-0862. Friday through Sunday, 1 to 4 P.M. Fee. Groups by appointment. Visitors to Kearney Park travel down Kearney Boulevard, designed by Rudolph Ulrich, who planted Australian eucalyptus trees, royal palms, flowering oleander, and pampas grass. The park was open to the public in Martin Theodore Kearney's lifetime, and the peacocks wandering the grounds are descendants of Mr. Kearney's.

Kearney was a raisin grower and agricultural promoter. His French Renaissance mansion was built as temporary quarters in 1900–1903, until his version of Chateau Chenonceaux could be erected. Half of the furnishings now displayed are original, as are the European wallpapers and murals, the Art Nouveau light fixtures, and the hand-carved Black Forest oak furniture.

The servants' quarters, in another chateauesque structure, serve as a museum store.

The Meux Home Museum 1000 R St. at

Tulare, P.O. Box 70, 93707; 209-233-8007. Thursday through Sunday, 12 to 4 P.M. Fee. The Meux Home is one of our favorite house museums, because of the building itself and how it is furnished, and because of the community spirit that made it so successful. This sweet blue and white Queen Anne home, listed on the National Register, is the

---

The Meux Home in Fresno has many creative fund-raising ideas. One is the sale of fans with an illustration of the Meux Home on the front and the following text on the back:

Fans have been used since ancient times. They kept the flies off Pharaoh. The clever Japanese devised the folding fan. Whatever fans are made of, the idea is to COOL the person…Ah! But, there is something exquisitely graceful about a lady waving her fan! And…did you know there are fan signals? Here is a list of signals from 1879. Have fun!

Carrying in left hand	=	Desirous of acquaintance
Placing it on left ear	=	You have changed
Twirling in left hand	=	I wish to get rid of you
Drawing across forehead	=	We are watched
Carrying in right hand	=	You are too willing
Drawing thru the hand	=	I hate you
Twirling in right hand	=	I love another
Drawing across cheek	=	I love you
Carrying in right hand in front of face	=	Follow me
Drawing across the eyes	=	I am sorry
Letting rest on right cheek	=	Yes
Letting rest on left cheek	=	No
Dropping	=	We will be friends
Fanning slow	=	I am married
Fanning fast	=	I am engaged
With handle to lips	=	Kiss me

---

last remaining example of the prominent Victorian homes built during Fresno's first years. The house, an architectural wonder, was built for $12,000 in 1888–89 by Dr. Thomas R. Meux, a former Confederate surgeon and pioneer Fresno physician.

Dr. Meux, who had a swashbuckling Rhett Butler mustache, moved in in 1889 with his wife and three children. The Meux family lived there until 1980, when Anne Prenetta Meux died.

The Meux Home was purchased by the City of Fresno in 1973, and has been completely restored by a volunteer organization, the nonprofit Meux House Corporation. Each part of the building, whether it's a complete room or a single piece of furniture, has been donated by a person or a group. For example, the kitchen was donated by a Fresno couple. The Southern-style breezeway was sponsored by Fresno schoolchildren.

Meux family treasures abound, from Dr. Meux's uniform and surgery tools to family clothing, jewelry, and photographs. In daughter Mary's room, there's a picture of Mary as a bride, and her gown hangs in the closet. Her child was born in this bed.

Funds for the house are raised by the tours, teas, parties, and weddings held here, as well as docent-baked cookie sales and events such as the Teddy Bear Picnic for kids, July 4th Jazz and Hot Dogs, and the Harvest Festival and Jumble Sale. There are regular school tours and storytelling afternoons. The gift shop in the carriage house sells art by local artists, modern Victoriana, memorabilia, and fine antiques, as well as framed lithographs of the Meux Home.

St. John's Cathedral 2814 Mariposa St., 93721; 209-485-6210. An imposing twin-spired red-brick edifice completed in 1902, St. John's is one of the oldest churches still in use in Fresno. The Romanesque ceiling, splendid polychrome paint and wood paneling, Tiffany-school stained glass, and art-glass windows add to the beauty of the American Renaissance interior. During Christmas celebrations, the block between

St. John's and the Meux Home is gaily lit, and jitneys run between the cathedral and the home as carolers help celebrate the season.

Supplier

Linden Publishing 352 W. Bedford, #105, 93711; 800-345-4447. Publishers of new and reprinted books dealing with woodworking and other related crafts. Catalog.

SELMA

Pioneer Village Museum Art Gonzales Pkwy., next to Hwy. 99, 93662; 209-896-8871. Seasonal hours. Fee. Victorian homes and cherished buildings are being moved to and restored at this museum-in-progress. Visitors walk through a museum store and out on the grounds to a 1902 Queen Anne, Selma's 1886 Southern Pacific Depot, a 1901 little red schoolhouse, a steepled church, a doctor's office, a barber shop, a pottery shop, a newspaper office, and the Ungar Opera House. Some of the exhibits are furnished; some are still being developed.

HANFORD

The Irwin Street Inn & Restaurant 522 N. Irwin St., 93230; 209-584-9286 (M). Hanford was founded in 1877 by the Southern Pacific Railroad. The town waned in importance at the beginning of this century, but now it is the center of a newly thriving business community.

The Irwin Street Inn is a coven of four Victorian homes built in the late 1880s and renovated to house thirty antique-embellished guestrooms. Each room also has a telephone, radio, and cable television. A giant Jacuzzi in the garden provides a welcome respite.

The Irwin Street Restaurant serves breakfast, lunch, and dinner. (A stay at the inn does not include breakfast.) Weekday

Kearney Mansion, Fresno

lunches and moderately priced dinners, served Sunday, Monday, Thursday, Friday, and Saturday, emphasize local produce. Conference and party facilities are available.

PORTERVILLE

Zalud House 393 North Hockett, 93257; 209-782-7548. Wednesday through Saturday, 10 A.M. to 4 P.M.; Sunday, 2 to 4 P.M. Parties and groups by appointment. Fee. This remarkably preserved and lovingly cared for Victorian home, built by John Zalud, a prosperous rancher and restauranteur, of brick with a mansard roof, is one of the state's unsung treasures.

His daughter, Pearle Zalud, was born here in 1884 and lived here until 1970. Her world tour, in 1913, was the first of many, and her home still displays the fruits of her souvenir hunting. The house is exactly as she left it—which is exactly as her father liked it when her mother died in 1912.

The art, original furnishings, hats, dolls, collars and laces, antique valentines, photos, linens, and dish collections are so numerous that the curators change the exhibits with the seasons. Indeed, many clothes and linens were found in their original boxes, unopened, in the attic. Even the boxes of spices in the kitchen are original. The beautiful garden, with roses planted in the 1900s, is available for weddings.

VISALIA

Spaulding House 631 N. Encina, Visalia; 209-739-7877 (M). A charming turn-of-the-century house has been converted into a comfortable bed-and-breakfast inn. Each of the three antiques-furnished bedrooms has its own sitting room and bath. A favorite is the Bird Room, a cheery bedroom fronted by a sitting room–veranda edged with colorful tiled small sinks, where the inhabitants of the former aviary took their baths. The whole downstairs, including a well-stocked library, is open to guests, who enjoy a full breakfast in the dining room.

The Meux Home Museum, Fresno

The Meux Home Museum, Fresno

Visalia Convention and Visitors Center 720 W. Mineral King Ave., 93291; 209-734-5876. Monday through Friday. Walking-tour maps with descriptions of Visalia's Victorian district.

BAKERSFIELD

Kern County Museum 3801 Chester Ave.,

93301; 805-861-2132. Event hotline: 805-32-EVENT. Weekdays, 8 A.M. to 5 P.M.; weekends and holidays, 10 A.M. to 5 P.M. Tickets must be purchased by 3 P.M. Group discounts by reservation. More than fifty buildings on sixteen acres represent facets of Kern County history. There are three Victorian structures on the grounds. The Alphonse Weill home, built in 1882, and the simple single-story 1885 Metcalf House, an 1880s tract home, are of interest.

The W. A. Howell House, an 1891 Queen Anne moved to its present site in 1969, is the star of the museum. Visitors will enjoy the kitchen, with gas and electric lighting, and the speaking tubes for communication between upstairs and downstairs. The stained-glass windows and turret are also memorable.

Other buildings of interest include an 1869 log cabin, an 1880s cook wagon, the 1882 Norris School House, Woody General Store, and many others.

BISHOP

Chalfant House Bed & Breakfast 213 Academy St., 93514; 619-872-1790 (I). P. A. Chalfant built this simple Victorian in 1898, and the new owners have restored it and named each room after a Chalfant family member. At one time, the house was a hotel for tungsten miners managed by Big Bertha, a madam. The walls were red-flocked.

Each room has a private bath and is tastefully furnished with lovely antiques, handmade quilts and comforters, ceiling fans, and central air-conditioning. Guests gather in the downstairs parlor for a cup of hot mulled cider in the cool months, frosty orange drinks in the summer. Breakfast includes homemade jams and hot breads. Old-fashioned sundaes are summer afternoon treats. A cleaning sink and freezer are ready for lucky fishermen.

Newspaperman P. A. Chalfant wrote about his home: "It has been Earth's nearest touch of heaven above."

THE PENINSULA AND SAN JOSE

"Night has fled,
Day's begun
When day has sped,
Duty's Done."
—Anonymous

In the heart of Silicon Valley, San Jose offers a remarkable no-tech contrast. First, you can visit the must-see Winchester Mystery House, a spectacular tribute to unlimited wealth inspired by terminal madness.

Not far away, James and Cheryl Fuhring are doing a splendid job with the Briar Rose. Their bed-and-breakfast is a labor of love and a shining example of how to use taste and patience to create beauty on a budget.

San Jose also has the largest and finest Victorian heritage park in California. The San Jose Historical Museum has put together twenty-seven buildings on sixteen acres, and has two hundred volunteer docents to tell you about them.

HALF MOON BAY

Old Thyme Inn 779 Main St., 94019; 415-726-1616 (I/M/E). Three shades of peach have been used to brighten this restored 1899 shingled Queen Anne. The British-born owners run the place like a friendly English bed-and-breakfast. Each of the seven rooms is named for an herb and has a bath. A stuffed toy on the bed greets guests. In the garden suite, you can loll in the double-sized whirlpool tub under the skylight and sip wine from the stocked refrigerator. There are over eighty varieties of herbs in the garden, and the owner uses them in her gourmet breakfasts. Fresh flowers, fireplaces, and sherry around the wood-burning stove in the lounge enhance your visit.

San Benito House Inn & Restaurant 356 Main St., 94019; 415-726-3425 (I/M). Ornate blue-on-white stenciling in the hallways reflects the blue and white façade of the restored 1905 Mosconi Hotel. The twelve rooms, nine with private bath, are being restored with decorative pieces from Europe, contemporary paintings, and historical photographs. Guests may whale-watch from the glass-walled deck off the upper hall, read or chat on the large redwood deck, and enjoy the sauna on the second floor. Rates include a hearty continental breakfast and a 10 percent discount in the restaurant.

San Benito House also draws fans in the wood-lined, down-home saloon in front and the flower-filled Victorian dining room in back. Chef-in-residence Carol Mickelson trained with world-famous chefs, including Roger Verge in France. Along with Sunday brunch, she serves three-course dinners Thursday through Sunday that combine imagination with a liberal use of the herbs from the garden in back. Sunday brunch is served from 10:30 A.M. to 1:30 P.M. Celebratory buffets and wedding receptions can also be arranged in the gardens, deck, and dining room. A firepit and barbecue area are also available.

The Zabella House 324 Main St., 94019; 415-726-9123/800-77BNB4U (M). "The Oldest House in Town," a blue and white Italianate, is Half Moon Bay's newest bed-and-breakfast, brightly decorated in Laura Ashley country-Victorian patterns. The nine cheerful rooms have private baths with antique or double-size whirlpool tubs.

125

Complimentary beverages and buffet breakfasts are served.

REDWOOD CITY

Lathrop House 627 Hamilton St., 94063; 415-365-5564. Tuesday through Friday, 11 A.M. to 3 P.M. Donation. Groups: Redwood City Heritage Assn., P.O. Box 1273, 94063.

In 1863, Benjamin G. Lathrop, the county's first clerk, recorder, and assessor, built this handsome Gothic Revival mansion, "Lora Mundi," on a lot bought from the Arguello and Mezes families. Blue-gray, white, and black define the finial-topped gables, quatrefoil trim on the eaves and porch, and the bargeboard cresting. The building, which is listed on the National Register of Historic Places, has been relocated twice and is maintained by volunteers of the Redwood City Heritage Association, who have restored the interior right down to the top hats on the hall rack.

The ground-floor kitchen is equipped with a wood-burning stove and butter churn. Volunteers run a small antiques shop.

The nearby county courthouse, with its sparkling stained-glass rotunda and finely crafted iron balustrades, is a marvelous example of public Victorian architecture.

Lathrop House, Redwood City

The Victorian on Lytton, Palo Alto

PALO ALTO

The Victorian on Lytton 555 Lytton Ave., 94301; 415-322-8555 (M). Two tones of blue, white, and a touch of pink grace this 1895 Stick residence on a quiet street in downtown Palo Alto. Each of the country-comfortable rooms is named for Queen Victoria or her children, and each has a private bath and a separate sitting parlor for cozy breakfasts. Canopy beds, down comforters, and sherry or port in the front parlor make this a favorite "home away from home" for business travelers. Conference room facilities are in the works.

SANTA CLARA

Madison Street Inn 1390 Madison St., 95050; 408-249-5541 (M). Bittersweet-red window sashes perk up the blue-gray with white and dark-gray color schemes on this cute cottage. Five cheerful rooms, three with

The Briar Rose, San Jose

Or you can sleep under Bradbury & Bradbury stars in the two-story pump-house suite. The five rooms in the house itself are delightful, with lots of fresh flowers, antique lace, and old toys. Two rooms share a bath with a clawfoot tub. Receptions and weddings take place beside the original heart-shaped pond under the handmade arbor.

The original owner of the house was Cornelius G. Harrison, founder of Farmers National Bank, now the First National Bank of San Jose.

The Briar Rose is now a beautiful Painted Lady that reflects the colors of the flower and butterfly garden in front. The inn participates in the BBINC Frequent Traveler Program.

San Jose Historical Museum 1600 Senter Rd., 95112-2508; 408-287-2290. Monday through Friday, 10 A.M. to 4:30 P.M.; week-

San Jose Historical Museum, San Jose

bath, are nestled in this midtown hideaway. Brass beds, lavish wallpapers, tubs for two, cheerful gardens, meeting rooms, a pool, spa, and delicious breakfasts make this an attractive choice. Private dinners and meetings by arrangement.

SAN JOSE

The Briar Rose 897 E. Jackson St., 95112; 408-279-5999 (I/M). James and Cheryl Fuhring have turned their 1875 Victorian farmhouse into a warm, welcoming, authentically and lovingly furnished bed-and-breakfast, a real standout in Silicon Valley. James's eagle eye has sought out antique treasures in flea markets, such as the dining-room table and buffet once owned by John Brown's widow, the Karastan rugs, and the authentic Murphy bed in the suite that was once the stable. The stable suite also has a fireplace, refrigerator, a Jacuzzi bath, and a hammock in its private yard.

ends, 12 to 4:30 P.M. Fee. The San Jose Historical Museum is the largest Victorian Park in California. It brings to life the look and feel of the late nineteenth century. Twenty-seven moved and restored or reconstructed homes and businesses are placed, as nearly as possible, in their original relation to other structures in the plaza in the sixteen-acre complex. Visitors may walk around on their own or join a guided tour with one of the association's two hundred docents (more are always needed). The 1880 Pacific Hotel houses a gift shop and O'Brien's Candy Store, built in 1878 and the first place to serve ice-cream sodas west of Detroit. The print shop, housed in an 1884 residence noted for its extensive false front and corner decorations; Dr. H. H. Warburton's 1870s office; the Coyote Post Office, built in 1862; the 1869 Empire Firehouse; and the 1888 Dashaway Stables are all of interest. You will also enjoy the Timeline Exhibit, San Jose's 115-foot electric tower (first lighted in 1881), and the Trolley Barn, which houses six historic trolleys that will soon run on the downtown Transit Mall loop.

Several Victorian homes are being restored, including poet Edwin Markham's Greek Revival home once on South Eighth Street. Painted Ladies fans will head for the Umbarger House, a delicious gingerbread confection in bittersweet, ochre, and dark green. It's an 1870s Carpenter Gothic cottage which has been completely furnished, right down to the clothes in the closets and the dishes in the sink.

Special events include the Victorian Christmas and Living History Days in May. (Please see the associations listed below.)

Winchester Mystery House 525 S. Winchester Blvd., 95128. Recorded information: 408-247-2101. Special events: 408-247-1313. Groups: 408-247-2000. Guided tours daily except Christmas, 9:30 A.M. to 4:30 P.M. in winter; 9 A.M. to 5:30 P.M. in summer. Fee; reduced rates for groups. In 1884, Sarah Winchester, widow of the Winchester Rifle heir, was told that as long as she kept

building something, she'd never die. So, for thirty-eight years, she kept carpenters working around the clock to create a 160-room mansion filled with mysteries. There are doorways opening onto walls, secret passageways that twist around, a four-story chimney that never gets past the ceiling posts—all done in the finest materials that money could buy.

The number 13 is a constant theme, with 13-stepped stairways, 13-paneled ceilings, a room with 13 windows, 13 lights in the chandeliers, and 13 blue and amber stones in a spider-glass window.

The $25,000 storage room is simply piled high with rare Tiffany art glass for future use. Three elevators, gas lights that operate by pressing a button, modern heating and sewer systems, and forty-seven fireplaces attest to Mrs. Winchester's up-to-the-minute tastes.

The multitowered, turreted, and gabled Queen Anne is gold, ochre, and white, with a cheerful red roof. Six acres of Victorian gardens provide a pleasant way to wait for a truly fascinating visit to California Historical Landmark No. 868.

CUPERTINO

Cupertino Historical Museum Quinlan Community Center, 10185 N. Stelling Rd., 95014; 408-973-1495. Wednesday through Saturday, 10 A.M. to 4 P.M. A small but choice collection of memorabilia that preserves and interprets the history and culture, both past and present, of the Cupertino area. Changing exhibits focus on Cupertino history.

Associations

California Committee for the Promotion of History California History Center, DeAnza College, 21250 Stevens Creek Blvd., 95014; 408-864-8964. A statewide nonprofit organization whose goal is to foster, facilitate, and coordinate efforts that enhance appreciation of our historical heritage, the application of history skills in public and private sectors, and the preservation, interpretation, and management of California's historical resources.

California History Center 21250 Stevens Creek Blvd., 95014; 408-864-8712/864-8964. Cultural resources studies, preservation surveys, exhibit research. Dr. James C. Williams, Executive Director.

Cupertino Historical Society P.O. Box 88, 95015; 408-973-1495. Meetings and fund-raising to support the Cupertino Historical Museum.

Los Gatos Museum and Heritage Guild P.O. Box 1904, 95031. The Los Gatos Museum Association runs two museums, the art museum at 4 Tait Avenue (408-354-2646), and the Forbes Mill Museum at 75 Church Street (408-395-7375), a flour mill built in 1884 and now the site of the local history collection.

Redwood City Heritage Association Box 1273, 94064; 415-365-5564. Member of the California Heritage Council.

San Jose Historical Museum Association 1650 Senter Road, 95112; 408-287-2290. Purpose: to support the San Jose Historical Museum and to promote the preservation of the Santa Clara Valley's heritage. Members receive an annual publication on local history, a bimonthly newsletter, and discounts in the museum shops. There are numerous volunteer activities and special events. For the Archives, call 408-287-2290.

San Jose Victorian Preservation Society 111 W. St. John St., Suite 700, 95113.

Victorian Preservation Association of Santa Clara Valley 1657 Cherry St., 95125; 408-267-7128. Biannual house tours, newsletter, monthly meetings.

San Mateo County Historical Association & Museum College of San Mateo, 1700 Hillsdale Blvd., 94402; 415-574-6441. Victorian Days in the Park, the last weekend in August in Central Park, with fashion shows, carriage rides, mock Civil War fights, food and spirits, arts and crafts, entertainment.

Saratoga Historical Foundation P.O. Box 172, 95070; 408-876-4311.

Suppliers

BESPAQ Corporation Fine & Unusual Miniatures 200 Valley Dr., Suite 4, Brisbane, 94005; 415-468-6650. Out of California: 800-423-7310. J. P. "Pit" Ginsburg.

European Painting and Decorating 868 Burlway Rd., Burlingame 94100; 415-345-2041.

Paper Americana P.O. Box 531, Burlingame, 94901; 415-566-6400. Ken Prag. Memorabilia on paper.

American Home Supply P.O. Box 697, Campbell, 95009; 408-246-1962. Solid-brass reproduction hardware, including cabinet hardware, house hardware—door plates and knobs, reproduction Victorian lighting and glass shades, stair rods and decorations, highly polished brass grills with and without damper controls, solid brass faucets, and bathroom fixtures. Catalog.

Dr. James C. Williams 21250 Stevens Creek Blvd., Cupertino, 95014; 408-864-8964. Executive director, California History Center. Preservation studies, exhibit research, planning and design, cultural resources studies, historic preservation.

Dunn Edwards Paint 2201 Junipero Serra Blvd., Daly City; 415-992-9660. Bill Boes. A computer for color matching paint.

The Doll Factory 1127 Chestnut St., Menlo Park, 94025; 415-326-2496. One of the best collections of miniatures and doll houses on the West Coast. Includes Painted Ladies and English Regency. Some are custom-made right down to wallpaper and molding. Cost: 25 cents to $3,000.

Van-Go-Painting 1125 Palmetto Ave., Pacifica, 94044; 415-359-4000.

Abigail Carriage Co. Palo Alto; 415-851-4711. Elegant horse-drawn carriages.

San Jose Historical Museum, San Jose

Antique Alliance Redwood City; 415-369-0221. John Burke.

Roman Marble Shop 2920 & 2936 Flood Ave., Redwood City, 94063; 415-366-4330. Raymond Arceo. Natural marble and granite, counter tops, fireplace facings, vanities.

Anglo-American Brass Co. P.O. Drawer 9487, San Jose, 95157-9487; 408-246-0203. Solid-brass antiques reproduction hardware. Doorplates, Eastlake design locks, pulls, keys, hinges, embossed hooks for hanging pictures from moldings. Catalog.

Mrs. Glory Anne Laffey 496 N. Fifth Street, San Jose, 95112; 408-295-1373. Historian and administrative assistant, Archaeological Resource Management. Architectural evaluation and surveys, archival research, historical overviews.

Winchester Mystery House, San Jose

Pete's Floors 265 N. 13th St., San Jose, 95112; 408-998-5303. C. Pete Anderson, owner. Hardwood-floor contractor, Restoration, refinishing and installation of hardwood floors.

PMG Plenar USA Marble & Granite 761 Colema Ave., San Jose, 95110; 408-287-7861. Joe Cook. Factory, fabrication, installation.

San Jose Trolley Corp. Santa Clara Transit, San Jose, 95112; 408-299-4141.

Wood Gallery 14770 Charmeron Ave., San Jose, 95124; 800-640-0260/408-552-3049. Custom-made furniture and architectural interiors. Architectural ornaments for interiors.

Karen Brown's Country Inn Guides P.O. Box 70, San Mateo, 94401; 415-342-9117.

Dura Finish 726 S. Amphlett Blvd., San Mateo, 94402; 415-343-3672. Specialists in antiques repair, restoration, refinishing, and paint-stripping on all types of interior and exterior wood and metalwork, chair caning, stained-glass windows, pillars, railings, and gingerbread. Metal de-rusting and etching. Literature.

Polla Sales 1134 Humboldt, San Mateo, 94401; 415-621-1870. Woodwork.

Beverly Kitchen 12820 Saratoga-Sunnyvale Rd. Saratoga, 95070; 408-867-4800. Realtor specializing in historic preservation and vintage properties, and offering consultation on interior design and landscaping.

In sunshine or fog, the Santa Cruz–Monterey area has much to offer visitors. It has two of the finest historical settings in the state, both of which capture the enduring importance of our Mexican heritage.

San Juan Bautista is a beautifully preserved slice of California history.

Monterey's Path of History is a model of how to keep history alive and make it a pleasure to learn.

Santa Cruz has one of the most irresistible attractions to the young at heart. Established in 1868, the Santa Cruz Beach Boardwalk is the only operating amusement park on the West Coast. Be sure to see what passionate local-color consultant Doni Tunheim has done with the 1907 casino.

Pacific Grove, Monterey, and Carmel are a constellation of three distinct towns, whose existence is predicated on pleasing visitors. With bed-and-breakfasts like the Seven Gables Inn, they succeed admirably.

BEN LOMOND

Chateau des Fleurs 7995 Hwy. 9, 95005; 408-336-8943 (M). Nestled under the redwoods in the historic San Lorenzo Valley, this 1879 gabled Victorian, painted in French blue with white trim, was built by Assemblyman David Bowman. Three rooms, Orchid, Rose, and Violet, have antique brass beds, down comforters, baths, lacy curtains, ceiling fans, and flowery wallpapers.

A big breakfast is served in the formal dining room. Guests are welcome to play the pump organ and games in the parlor. There's a magic wishing well in the garden, and a three-tiered fountain topped by the Three Graces.

SANTA CRUZ

Cliff Crest Bed & Breakfast Inn 407 Cliff St., 95060; 408-427-2609 (M). Situated in the historic Beach Hill area of Santa Cruz a few blocks from the ocean, Cliff Crest combines old-world charm with pampered elegance. Built in 1890 by William Jeter, lieutenant governor of California, this Queen Anne is a Painted Lady decked in three blues, cream, and wine, and sparkles with stained-glass windows. Jeter helped establish the Cowell Redwoods State Park, and his half-acre garden here was designed by his friend John McLaren, who also designed Golden Gate Park in San Francisco.

The owners have furnished the parlors and five spacious rooms—all with bath and robes, some with fireplaces—with family remembrances and antiques. From the Eastlake bed in the Rose Room, you can see Monterey Bay and the Santa Cruz board-walk. All of the guests can see the ocean and listen to the birds at the bountiful breakfast served on the second-floor porch. Receptions and celebrations are held on the main floor and in the garden.

Chateau Victorian 118 1st St., 95060; 408-458-9458 (M). Painted in pumpkin orange, brown, and white, this turn-of-the-century Stick dwelling was renovated in 1983. The seven rooms with bath, fireplace, and queen-sized beds are all countrified. One has an ocean view; two are in the garden cottage. Afternoon libations and a continental breakfast are served in the European parlors, where the house cat presides.

Artisans

Doni Tunheim 123 Green St., 95060; 408-426-6415. Exterior/interior building colors. Doni delights in bold, clear, "tasty" colors. Her work has appeared in *Daughters of Painted Ladies* and *How to Create Your Own Painted Lady.*

APTOS

Apple Lane Inn 6265 Soquel Dr., 95003; 408-475-6868 (M). *Un Chat Gentil* welcomes guests to this 1876 Victorian farmhouse, painted in two grays, white, and blue, overlooking distant Monterey Bay. The travertine fireplace in the period parlor, tin ceilings, quilt collection, bright rugs, and Laura Ashley prints give the place a country flair. Two of the five rooms share a bath in the attic. There are parties in the wine cellar, and wedding parties use the gazebo, which is also a favorite breakfast spot.

Bayview Hotel Bed & Breakfast Inn 8041 Soquel Dr., 95003; 408-688-8654 (M). This elegant white and blue Mansard mansion in the center of Aptos was built as a hotel in 1878 by Joseph Arano, who married the youngest daughter of General Rafael Castro, grant owner of the 6,680-acre Rancho de Aptos. Lillian Russell and King Kalakaua of Hawaii were among the distinguished visitors. Arano imported many of the carved wooden beds from Spain, and several are still in use today. The eight rooms—one a two-room suite—have been nicely renovated, with art wallpaper borders, modern lamps, and private bath-rooms. The formal garden is a holdover from the time the hotel was the social heart of Aptos Village.

Mangels House 570 Aptos Creek Rd., 95001; 418-688-7982 (M). This gracious 1886 mansion, built by Claus Mangels, who established the California sugar-beet indus-try, offers five cheerful rooms with bath and a spare turn-of-the-century decor. The inn's four acres of lawns and orchards are bordered by the Forest of Nisene Marks—ten thousand acres of redwoods, creeks, and trails.

The Veranda—Dining at the Bayview Hotel 8041 Soquel Dr., 95003; 408-685-1881 (M). The spacious Victorian dining room at the Bayview Hotel specializes in innovative American cuisine. Corn fritters and Smith-field ham on bitter greens, fresh mushroom salad, and smoked sausage with Hopping John have appeared on the lunch menu. At dinner, the chef offers dishes such as lobster sausage, apple vichyssoise, pastas, and tempting desserts.

CAPITOLA

Lodging

The Inn at Depot Hill 250 Monterey Ave., 95010; 408-462-3376. The 1901 Southern Pacific Railroad Depot has been converted into an old-world-style inn with high ceilings, moldings, corbels, and vintage touches. The eight welcoming rooms have spacious baths. Although there's a pond in the garden and the inn is two blocks from the beach, it's right in the center of town, for easy browsing.

Dining

Country Court Tea Room 911-B Capitola Center, Carriage House Center, 95010; 408-462-2498 (M). Take tea in an English cottage or under the magnolia tree or by the trellis under the oak tree in an English garden. The cottage itself was the carriage house for the Castro family. Now, round tea tables gleam with fine silver, vivid flowers, and flowered china. High tea here includes soup, salad, bacon biscuits, scones, cucumber sand-wiches, cream, berries, shortcake, home-made ice cream in summer, and individual pots of tea in tea cozies. Since one of the owners is from the South, cheese grits or fried apples may appear on the menu. Teaposts, books, cups, and cozies are for sale. A string quartet in Renaissance costume plays on weekends.

WATSONVILLE

Pajaro Valley Historical Association and Volks Museum 225 East Beach St., 95076; 408-722-0305. Tuesday through Thursday, 11 A.M. to 3 P.M., and by appointment. A cute Victorian cottage is home for this commu-nity museum crammed with treasures from local families, including a large tinted 1887 photograph of two young girls who grew up to be leading members of the historical society. Reticules, bisque dolls, glove boxes, filled candy jars, and photographs are part of the changing displays.

SAN JUAN BAUTISTA

Mariposa House Restaurant 37 Mariposa St., 95045; 408-623-4666 (M). An adorable blue and yellow Stick cottage offers comforting country cooking in this historic town. Lunch Tuesday through Saturday, dinner Wednesday through Sunday, Sunday brunch.

Places to Visit

Zanetta House San Juan Bautista State Historic Park, 95045; 408-623-4881. Daily, 10 A.M. to 4:30 P.M. Fee. One of the nicest places to visit in San Juan Bautista, a mission and

Gosby House Inn, Pacific Grove

Gatehouse Inn, Pacific Grove

antiques-store haven, is the two-story Italianate built by Angelo Zanetta, owner of the adjacent Plaza Hotel in the square that is the center of San Juan Bautista State Park. It was originally used as housing for the unmarried Indian women who worked at the mission and in the hotel. Zanetta built the house thinking that San Juan would be the county seat of San Benito, but the railroad bypassed San Juan, and Mr. Zanetta was left with this building and hall. He then added the dining room and kitchen and made it his home. The top floor was used as a dance hall and a place for meetings and minstrel shows. Today, the rooms have been restored to their Victorian splendor. The children's room and singing bird in the front parlor make you feel that the family will soon return.

PACIFIC GROVE

The Centrella 612 Central Ave., 93950; 408-372-3372 (M/E). There are twenty-six peaceful rooms, suites, and cottages in this historic Queen Anne painted light and dark gray, white, and dark rose. Many of the rooms have clawfoot tubs and fireplaces with candles near the bedside.

Full breakfast buffets and fresh-baked

cookies with tea or sherry in the afternoon help bring guests together. A large needlework piece in the lobby is an eternal work in progress, with guests adding stitches with each visit. A cat rules the roost. The garden courtyard is frequently used for weddings. The Centrella has been a hotel since 1889 and is now listed on the National Register.

Gatehouse Inn 225 Central Ave., 93950; 408-649-1881 (M/E). This elegant Painted Lady, an 1884 towered Stick villa in light rust, dark brick, lime, cream, and ochre, has been renovated with a feast of Bradbury & Bradbury wallpapers. The eight individually themed guestrooms are furnished with Victorian and twentieth-century antiques with touches of Art Deco. Most rooms have an ocean view, and all have private baths. One is handicap-accessible with a private patio. The tasseled Turkish Room has its own sun porch. There are binoculars for whale-watching from the parlor, and bountiful appetizers to nibble on at twilight.

The Green Gables Inn, Pacific Grove

Stained-glass windows and monarch-butterfly memorabilia add to the airy charm of the place.

Gosby House Inn 643 Lighthouse Ave., 93950; 408-375-1287 (M/E). A Pacific Grove

Seven Gables Inn, Pacific Grove

Heritage House, which won an award for its restoration, this yellow and white 1887 Queen Anne is listed on the National Historic Register.

J. F. Gosby, a gregarious cobbler from Nova Scotia, opened his home to lodgers in 1894, when the Del Monte Lodge burned down, and it has been a hotel ever since. Most of the twenty-two rooms have fireplaces and private baths, and each is named for a local hero or heroine.

The Green Gables Inn 104 Fifth St., 93950; 408-375-2095 (M/E). William Lacy built this many-gabled Queen Anne with Tudor accents in 1888 and painted it red. Today, in white, green, and ochre to blend with its more staid neighbors, the mansion is the award-winning centerpiece for the Four Sisters Inns, a collection of six romantic country inns named for the four Post family daughters.

Most of the eleven glorious guestrooms—five are in the carriage house—have ocean views, fireplaces, and private baths. Fresh flowers and fruit welcome the guests who gather in the English Victorian parlors, notable for its unique stained-glass paneled fireplace and carousel horse. Breakfast is served in the dining room, which also has a superb ocean view. Green Gables is listed on the National Historic Register.

Pacific Grove Inn 581 Pine Ave., 93950; 408-375-BUCK (I/M/E). LaVerne and Ella Buck's 1904 cream and yellow Queen Anne still boasts the marvelous interior woodwork and fretwork designed by Robert Gass in 1905. Fountains, flowers, and historic photographs decorate the ten countrified rooms, each with bath, and most with gas fireplaces and heated towel racks. The top-floor rooms have ocean views. The inn is a national historic landmark.

Seven Gables Inn 550 Ocean View Blvd., 93950; 408-372-4341 (M/E). The large Flatley family extends its warm welcome in this European-style inn, a yellow and white 1886 Queen Anne mansion, where the sound of the surf sings you to sleep. Sun porches and gables added at the end of the nineteenth century and cottages in colorful gardens and carriage-house rooms added in the late twentieth century take advantage of the home's closeness to the ocean.

Each of the fourteen rooms has an ocean view, a private bath, and a queen-sized bed. A grand tea is served at four o'clock every afternoon, and a generous full breakfast is laid out with crystal and lace in the sparkling dining room. Stained glass, Tiffany windows, European antiques, and family treasures give the place a true Victorian feeling of nurturing comfort and plenty.

Restaurants

Consuelo's 361 Lighthouse Ave., Pacific Grove/New Monterey, 93950; 408-372-8111 (I). Dine on fine Mexican food in the nicely wallpapered Victorian dining room of this 1893 towered and furbeloved Eastlake mansion.

Gernot's Victoria House 649 Lighthouse Ave., 93950; 408-646-2477. Dinners only. Closed Monday (M). Owner/chef Gernot Leitzinger served as the private chef to Prince Ausersperg of Austria. Originally Dr. Hart's residence, this handsome Queen Anne is in its original brown and white. Gernot serves continental Austrian food such as wild mushrooms and cream in puff pastry and fresh wild boar from the Carmel Valley.

Old Bath House 620 Ocean View Blvd., Lovers' Point Park, 93950; 408-375-5195 (M). Pacific Grove began as a small religious retreat that convened during the summer to sing praises to God in the open air, a haven between heaven and earth. The original name for the point was Lovers of Jesus Point. The town was surrounded by a wooden fence, which had only one entrance and one gatekeeper, "to keep out the Devil."

The gray-shingled, towered, restored Old Bath House stands on the site of the original Bath House, a California landmark since the late 1800s, and offers California cuisine garnished with panoramic ocean views. Dinner served daily.

Victorian Corner Restaurant 541 Lighthouse Ave., 93950; 408-372-4641 (I). Healthy breakfasts, lunches, and dinners are served in this deliciously multicolored 1893 Eastlake, one of the oldest commercial sites in the city. The first floor displays original pilasters, segmented windows, and stained glass. The chandeliers are from the original interior of 613 Lighthouse Avenue. Many historical pictures show the site over the years.

SALINAS

The Steinbeck House 132 Central Ave., 93901; 408-424-2735. Luncheon 11:45 A.M. and 1:15 P.M., Monday through Friday, by reservation only. Parties and group house tours by appointment. (M). The Best Cellar gift shop open 11 A.M. to 3 P.M. Monday through Friday; 408-757-3106. John Steinbeck's childhood home, built in 1897, is now a lunch restaurant. Here's where Steinbeck wrote *The Red Pony* and *Tortilla Flat*. In *East of Eden* he recalled it affectionately as "an immaculate and friendly house, grand enough but not pretentious, and it sat inside its white fence surrounded by its clipped lawn and roses and cotoneasters lapped against its walls…The pleasant little bedroom was crowded with photographs, bottles of toilet water, lace pin cushions, brushes, and combs and the china and silver bureau-knacks of many birthdays and Christmases."

Today, that bedroom is the reception area. Guests dine in other rooms of the house on Salinas Valley produce. Bradbury & Bradbury and other period wallpapers enliven the rooms, which are decorated with Steinbeck memorabilia.

The Best Cellar features Steinbeck's books and Victorian gifts. The Valley Guild is a volunteer organization which uses its profits to keep the house open to the public and for other Valley charities.

The Steinbeck House is in the center of an area of newly painted Victorians. (DPL)

First Mayor's House 238 East Romie Ln., 93901; 408-757-8085. First Sunday of the month, 1 to 4 P.M. Free. Isaac Harvey, the first mayor of Salinas, built this Queen Anne cottage of redwood hauled from Moss Landing on the coast. The cottage has been moved to its present location and restored with some of the original family furnishings.

MONTEREY

The Stevenson House 530 Houston St., 93949; 408-649-7118. Tours on the hour, 10 A.M. to 4 P.M. daily, except Wednesday. In 1879, before becoming a famous author, Robert Louis Stevenson spent a few months in a second-floor room of what was then a boardinghouse. He had traveled from Scotland to visit his future wife, Fanny Osbourne. Stevenson wrote the stories "The Old Pacific Capital," "An Amateur Emigrant," and "Across the Plains" in Monterey. The house has been restored to look as it did then, with several rooms devoted to Stevenson memorabilia. The doll collection upstairs is also of interest.

Suppliers

Cedar Valley Shingle Systems 943 San Felipe Rd., Hollister, 95023; 408-636-8110/ 800-521-9523. Decorative hand-cut shingles of red cedar in twelve shapes. Brochure.

Glorious Moments Stained Glass P.O. Box 222440, Carmel, 93923; 408-624-8081. Glory Ushakoff.

Ken Hinshaw 747 Short, Pacific Grove, 93950; 408-375-0816. Fine cabinetry.

Oak Leaves Studio P.O. Box 2356, Carmel Valley, 93924; 408-659-0652. Custom wood-sculpting of doors, entryways, room dividers, mantels, and high-relief and freestanding sculpture by William J. Schnute.

Victorian Corner Restaurant, Pacific Grove

Ambrose Pollock 9 Delfino Pl., Carmel Valley, 93924; 408-679-5435. Cabinetry.

Dr. Lois J. Roberts 24694 Upper Trail, Carmel, 93923; 408-625-5635. Archival research, cultural resource studies, and preservation surveys.

Roses of Yesterday and Today 802 Brown's Valley Rd., Watsonville, 95076. Nursery.

Kent L. Seavey 310 Lighthouse Ave., Pacific Grove, 93950; 408-375-8739. Historic preservation, museum interpretation.

Somerset Building Supplies 4005 Cory St., Soquel, 95073; 408-476-4693. Peter Carr. Custom milling of columns, doors, and windows.

The Steinbeck House, Salinas

"The ornaments of a home
are the friends who frequent it."
—Anonymous

The Central Coast area encompasses three remarkable visionary architectural achievements, two of which are not Victorian.

The state's largest collection of antiques may be gathered in William Randolph Hearst's castle of dreams, San Simeon. Designed by Julia Morgan, San Simeon is a not-to-be-missed slice of Americana.

You will be amused by the Madonna Inn on Highway 101 in San Luis Obispo. A popular restaurant and motel, the Madonna Inn is the working-man's San Simeon, the product of as much passion and ambition as its grander cousin on the coast.

You will be amazed by California's ultimate example of the Victorian spirit of play: the Victorian Annex to the Union Hotel in Los Alamos. Dick Langdon is an extraordinary individualist, and the six rooms that he has created in the Annex are the most imaginative use of a Victorian that we've ever seen.

Santa Barbara is as close as America comes to the French Riviera. It's a small, posh, beautiful, cosmopolitan, and seductive enclave sandwiched between the mountains and the sea. Its fine collection of sedately colored, freestanding Victorians reflects the town's self-assurance. They are solid and comfortable rather than flamboyant.

For the purposes of this guide, the Central Coast area stretches from Paso Robles to Los Olivos inland and from San Simeon to Ventura on the coast.

CAMBRIA

Olallieberry Inn 2476 Main St., 93428; 805-927-3222 (M). Olallieberries are on the menu every day in the baked goods, jams, and jellies here. Olallie is the Chumash Indian word for blackberry, and the Cambria strain is a hybrid of blackberries and raspberries. This cream with olallieberry trim 1873 house near Hearst Castle sheltered by a coast redwood Sequoia offers six welcoming rooms with private bath. Breakfast is served in the white-wicker gathering room or on the back porch, and afternoon refreshments are served in the front parlor. The tea kettle is always on.

Victoriana 1 Arlington St., 93428; 805-927-3833. 10 A.M. to 5 P.M. Tuesday through Saturday. Cambria, with its galleries, antiques stores, and ocean views is a small-scale Carmel. Victoriana is a store, a potpourri of miniatures, dolls, collectibles, and country-Victorian gifts in a flamboy-

Victoriana, Cambria

antly bric-a-bracked and furbelowed blue and white mini–Queen Anne built entirely by hand in 1985. The owner has created other elaborate mini-Victorians and has others planned.

PASO ROBLES

Roseleith B & B 1415 Vine St., 93446; 805-238-5848 (M). A happy dog rules the roost in this white Stick close to the center of town. The three rooms, two with shared bath, are cheerfully decorated in "B & B Victorian."

Guests will also enjoy visiting the nearby Booth House Gallery, the home of the Paso Robles Art Association (open Wednesday through Saturday, 11 A.M. to 4 P.M., Sunday until 3 P.M.). Set in colorful gardens, the Queen Anne cottage, bristling with spindlework, is listed on the National Register and painted in three shades of orange with green trim. At Thirteenth and Vine, it's across the street from the 1840s church that is now Joshua's Restaurant.

TEMPLETON

Country House Inn 91 Main St., 93465; 805-434-1598 (M). Pretty in pale gray, white, and pink with lots of cresting, the 1886 Eastlake home built by town founder C. H. Phillips now offers six airy rooms, three with bath. Three of the rooms are in the "servants' wing" and have floating canopy beds. There are plenty of games to play in front of the fireplaces. Children are welcome, and the wonderful rose-bordered gardens are perfect for weddings and parties.

The Templeton Chamber of Commerce, Fifth and Crocker Sts. (805-434-1789), offers a map of a historic walking tour of Templeton that includes an 1888 Presbyterian church and an 1891 Lutheran church.

SAN LUIS OBISPO

Apple Farm Inn 2015 Monterey St., 93401; 805-544-2040/800-255-2040 (M/E). "A blend of charm, comfort, and convenience" is the motto of this large Neo-Victorian inn. Cozy turreted reading areas with wingback chairs or window seats, canopy, four-poster, or brass beds, crown moldings, chair rails, and gas fireplaces mix with modern amenities such as oversized tubs and the bubble bath to go with them, terrycloth robes, flowering plants, books, hidden TVs, and complimentary coffee with your personalized wake-up call.

Most rooms have convertible sofas. Many of the sixty-seven rooms overlook San Luis Creek or the Mill House, where you can watch wheat being stone-ground or apple cider being pressed. Guests receive a shiny wooden apple as a memento. The pool and spa are easy to get to, and all of the rooms are wheelchair-accessible. There are conference facilities available.

The Apple Farm Restaurant and Bakery features homestyle food that is extremely popular with locals as well as tourists. The applesauce Belgian waffles and hot spiced cider are breakfast favorites. Apple dumplings are a house specialty. The gift shop offers tasteful and tasty items including many Apple Farm products.

Noland's Carriage is on-hand for twenty- and forty-minute tours of San Luis Obispo's historic homes and the Old Mission.

Carmel Beach 450 Marsh St., 93401; 805-541-FISH (M). Creative California cuisine with an emphasis on fresh fish is served in this blue, gray, and white Stick cottage built in the early 1900s between Carmel and Beach Sts.

Garden Street Inn 1212 Garden St., 93401; 805-545-9802 (M). To celebrate their marriage, Kathy and Dan Smith transformed their peach, maroon, white, and gray-taupe Italianate Queen Anne into a distinctive, hospitable bed-and-breakfast, restored to look like it did when the Goldtrees owned it in 1887. The nine rooms and four suites all have armoires, spacious baths, and carefully selected antiques. Wine and cheese are offered in the library each evening. Guests are welcome to browse through the books, which were requested wedding presents from friends all over the world. A sumptuous breakfast is served under the stained-glass windows in the McCaffrey Morning Room.

Heritage Inn B & B 978 Olive St., 93401; 805-544-7440 (M). The Herrera family of San Luis Obispo built this 3,000-square-foot home at the turn of the century. After several incarnations and a move, the house has been restored and painted in three shades of dark gray-green. The nine bedrooms, three with bath, are furnished eclectically, some with fireplaces and canopy beds, clawfoot tubs, and views of the San Luis Mountains or Creek. Evening wine and cheese are offered in the welcoming parlor; continental breakfast is served in the dining room.

Places to Visit

Jack House and Gardens 536 Marsh St., 93401; 805-549-7300. Wednesday and Friday, June through September, 1 to 4 P.M.; first Sunday of the month, October through May; and by appointment. Donation. This fine two-story crested Italianate, freshly painted in five historically authentic colors, was deeded to the City of San Luis Obispo in 1975 by the heirs of Nellie Hollister Jack and Robert Edgar Jack to use in a manner that enhances and celebrates its place in the development of the town. Friends of the Jack House, volunteers working with the Parks and Recreation Department, enjoy sharing the house and gardens.

Nellie Jack worked with a catalog company and drew up the architectural plans for the Jack House, which was built in 1876. Most of the furnishings, such as the Eastlake dining-room set, the petticoat table, and the Steinway grand piano, are those used by the Jack family. The two-thousand-volume library is a fabulous resource for town scholars.

The garden is filled with trees and plants and is available for parties and weddings.

San Luis Obispo County Historical Society Museum 696 Monterey St., Mission Plaza, 93401; 805-543-0638. The historical society works to preserve the past for the present and helped save the Jack House. They run the Museum and have meetings and a newsletter.

ARROYO GRANDE

The Rose Victorian: A Country Inn and Restaurant 789 Valley Rd., 93420; 805-481-5566 (E). Looming above the farmlands just outside Arroyo Grande, this 1885 four-story, towered villa gleams in four shades of rose, with touches of white and dark green. Cuttings from the more than two hundred rose bushes in the gardens cheer the eight rooms, three with private bath.

Rosewood, mahogany, and oak gleam on floors, doors, moldings, and antique furniture. Whether or not there's a friendly ghost in the tower depends on who's visiting or telling the tale. Behind the main structure are two cottages converted to guest suites, a carriage house, and a tack room.

Koi ponds surround the thirty-foot rose arbor, backyard gazebo, and sundial. Guests are greeted in the front parlor, which boasts an onyx fireplace, an old-fashioned pump organ, and a marvelous view of the surrounding fields. Upstairs, you can see the ocean. A full breakfast is served in the family dining room, and dinner in the restaurant in the garden behind the house.

The Rose Victorian Restaurant serves California cuisine in view of the fireplace and kitchen inside, the sparkling lights on the rose arbor and gazebo outside. Banquets, garden parties, and romantic weddings are house specialties. (DPL)

There are several Painted Ladies in town, including the Old Arroyo Church, housing businesses and stores (80 E. Branch). Burnardo'z Candy Kitchen, at 100 E. Branch (805-481-2041), is an old-fashioned ice-cream parlor and Victorian card and candy shop. Open Sunday through Thursday, 10 A.M. to 9 P.M.; Friday and Saturday, 10 A.M. to 10 P.M.

Craftman

Dimensions in Glass 680 Tierra St., 93420-4145; 805-473-3020. Larry Wintermantel. Custom stained glass.

NIPOMO

Kaleidoscope Inn B & B 130 E. Dana St., P.O. Box 1297, 93444; 805-929-5444 (M). Blue, gray, and white, with burgundy stars and circles, cheer up the façade of this 1887 Victorian farmhouse. Inside, the stars can be found in the bevy of old and new kaleidoscopes found in each room. The three lacy cheerful bedrooms share two large baths, one with a Jacuzzi. Breakfast is served in the dining room or outside in the garden or gazebo. Ralph the cat rules the veranda. Hidden in the parlor, near the fireplace, is the TV and library.

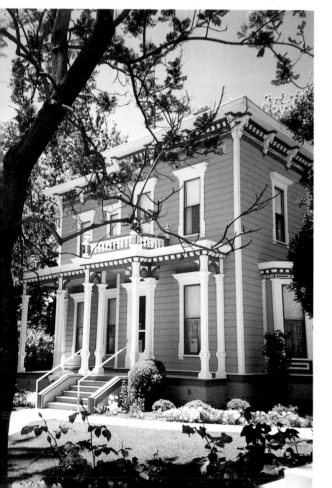

Jack House and Gardens, San Luis Obispo

The Rose Victorian, Arroyo Grande

LOS ALAMOS

Union Hotel and Victorian Annex 362 Bell St., P.O. Box 616, 93440; 805-344-2744 (I/M/E). The Victorian fan with a sense of humor has a revelation in store just off Highway 101, fifty miles north of Santa Barbara at Dick Langdon's 1880 Union Hotel. The hotel itself is a great hulk of a building, with a red velvet-draped lobby, dining room, authentic saloon, and thirteen small "wet" and "dry" bedrooms upstairs. There are reading lamps, books galore, and beautiful bonnets in each room, and the parlor upstairs has a fringed billiard table.

Family-style dinners are served in the

Kaleidoscope Inn B & B, Nipomo

Union Hotel and Victorian Annex, Los Alamos

Union Hotel and Victorian Annex, Los Alamos

large period dining room on Friday, Saturday, and Sunday nights.

The splendid back bar was rescued from the Crystal Ballroom in Nevada City, Nevada. There's a hand-carved shuffleboard table nearby. The immense hand-carved Carrara marble and mahogany ping-pong/dining table at the rear of the saloon is a work of art. Some of Dick Langdon's favorite sayings are carved on each side of the table, in Greek, Chinese, and Egyptian hieroglyphics.

Out back there's a big, sleek, swimming pool, a twenty-person Jacuzzi in the Victorian gazebo, and a barbecue, steam table, and wet bar for weddings and parties. After-breakfast rides in the hotel's yellow 1918 White touring car parked outside are yet another treat.

But next door, in the bedecked yellow and white Queen Anne, dreams come true. Dick Langdon is a gregarious welcoming host who believes in sharing his dreams with the world. It took him and two hundred

Union Hotel and Victorian Annex, Los Alamos

friends nine years to create the Victorian Annex.

First, the house had to be moved in five pieces from forty miles away. The front door is three thousand pounds of local yellow brick covered with hand-carved mahogany that swivels on a central divet. In leather bas-relief, the interior façade of the door is covered with portraits of ten people who helped on the project. The three-story farmhouse has been transformed into six suites, each a world in itself.

In the Gypsy Suite, you can sleep in a real Gypsy wagon in a garden and bathe in the sunken pool by a waterfall.

In the '50s Drive-In, you sleep in a '56 Cadillac convertible and listen to '50s rock 'n roll. In a Sheikh's tent overlooking a desert oasis, you pull King Tut's beard to open the bathroom door.

Modern Ben Hurs can sleep in a Roman chariot and bathe in a marble bath while Rome burns in the background. A Pirate captain can sail the seven seas while his captive bride plays with the jewels in the treasure chest.

Or you can step into a Montparnasse garret, complete with easel and paints, where a bed in the loft overlooks the lights of Paris.

Each suite has a soaking tub for two, a fireplace, a reading nook, books, costume robes, tapes, videos, games, and hidden hand-tiled bathrooms—everything chosen to suit the room's theme. A hidden serving compartment prevents you from being disturbed when breakfast is served. You operate switches with a remote-control system. The hardest thing will be to choose which fantasy to indulge yourself in.

Next on Langdon's agenda is a tree-house room, a room in the King of Denmark's sixty-six-foot yawl beached out back, and a hedgerow maze leading to a squash court. But other fantasies may unfold, so be prepared for surprises.

LOS OLIVOS

Los Olivos Grand Hotel and Remington's Restaurant 2860 Grand Ave., P.O. Box 526, 93441; 805-688-7788/800-446-2455(E). Set in the vineyards of the Santa Ynez Valley thirty-five miles north of Santa Barbara, Los Olivos is a tiny village of galleries and crafts stores. The new Los Olivos Grand Hotel, a light- and dark-pink and beige Neo-Victorian, is a luxurious getaway spot.

The twenty-one spacious rooms, each named for an American western or a classic impressionist artist, offer modern amenities along with antique and reproduction Victorian touches. Bicycles, box lunches, and backpacks are available, or you can stay close and relax in the spa and pool. Most rooms are wheelchair-accessible. Meeting, banquet, and reception facilities are available.

Frederic Remington's Bronco Buster rides on at the entrance to Remington's Restaurant, which serves breakfast and hearty portions of "California Continental" cuisine for lunch and dinner, with an emphasis on fresh local produce.

Mattei's Tavern Railway Ave., Frontage Rd. off Hwy. 154, 93441; 805-688-4820 (M). Felix Mattei built this tavern in 1886 to serve the stage and railroad passengers. The narrow-gauge line went out of business in 1934, but the town continued to grow, and hearty old-fashioned dinners are still served daily. Family pictures and mementos brighten the Victorian dining room. The sun porch off the rose gardens and grapevine arbor are cheerful for weekend lunches.

GOLETA

Stow House 304 Los Carneros Rd., 93117; 805-964-4407. Saturday and Sunday, 2 to 4 P.M. Fee. This pattern-book Victorian, built in 1872, is the oldest frame house in Goleta. It became Stow Ranch headquarters when Sherman Stow married Ida Hollister in 1873. The Stow family lived in the house until 1967, when they gave it to the Goleta Historical Society. The Society restored the house with Victoriana and now shares its history with visitors.

The oldest piece of Stow furniture is the table in the parlor, which was the only piece left in the Stow San Francisco mansion after the 1906 Earthquake and Fire, but the place looks like it did when Sherman and Ida's children were growing up.

The Goleta Valley Historical Society based here operates the Stow House, and the Sexton Museum Compound of Goleta History. Members are volunteers and receive newsletters and participate in year-round functions, raising funds with parties and weddings on the Stow House grounds.

SANTA BARBARA

Lodging

The Bath Street Inn 1720 Bath St., 93101; 805-682-9860 (M). This historic 1873 Queen Anne with a curved "eyelid" balcony and hipped roof was built by Richard Hails, a merchant tailor from Massachusetts, for his wife, Abigail. The present owners have expanded and rebuilt the inn, taking great care to preserve the 1800s atmosphere of the original home, so the rooms are comfortable, with interesting alcoves and sloped ceilings. A few nice pieces are highlighted amid cozy English furnishings.

The Cheshire Cat 36 W. Valerio St., 93101; 805-569-1610 (M/E). A beige and white 1892 Queen Anne and adjoining Colonial Revival home, both built by the Eberly family, offer ten spacious rooms with baths, chocolates, liqueurs, and flowers, some with extras such as a fireplace, patio, or spa. President McKinley slept here, but not in the Eberle Suite, with its glossy dark-blue tile Jacuzzi tub for two, and brick fireplace. The rooms are designed in a light, airy, Laura Ashley–English Victorian style, many with tasteful touches of *Alice in Wonderland* memorabilia. The landscaped rose gardens have a spa nestled in a lattice gazebo. A gourmet breakfast buffet is served in the elegant dining room. There's a cute little dog on the premises. A Romantik Hotel.

The Glenborough Inn 1327 Bath St., 93101; 805-966-0589 (I/M/E). Two grays and wine highlight the 1906 main house and 1880s cottage of this hideaway in the heart of Santa Barbara. The nine lace-filled country-Victorian rooms, most with bath, are cozy, cheerful retreats. There's a hot tub in the garden, and guests enjoy the evening wine and appetizer get-togethers as well as a mouth-watering breakfast served in the garden or in your room.

The Ivanhoe Inn 1406 Castillo St., 93101; 805-963-8832 (M). A retired sea captain built this stately 1880s structure. There are two cheerful, flowery upstairs suites, one with a sitting room in the tower, and a separate private two-bedroom cottage. With the ready-to-use kitchens in each suite, you can supplement the breakfast basket delivered to your door each morning.

The Parsonage 1600 Olive St., 93101; 805-962-9336 (M). A gracious soft-brown and white with blue sashes, this Queen Anne, built in 1882 for Trinity Episcopal Church, is now an art-filled bed-and-breakfast presided over by Hilde Michelmore. The living areas and six rooms, each with bath, combine Victorian chinoiserie and modern furnishings. There's an outdoor deck with a gazebo for lounging; and a full European breakfast, frequently featuring apple pancakes, is served outside on sunny days. The honeymoon suite, with its solarium and large bath, has ocean and city views.

Simpson House Inn 121 East Arrellaga St., 93101; 805-963-7067 (M/E). Taupe, white, and blue highlight this stately 1874 Eastlake inn screened by sandstone walls and tall eugenia hedges. Magnolias and mature oaks grace the tastefully landscaped gardens. Inside, a spacious book-lined sitting room welcomes visitors, who gather in front of the fireplace or on the wicker-furnished garden verandas. They'll appreciate the English lace, Oriental rugs, fresh flowers, and down comforters. Leisurely breakfasts and afternoon tea and wine gatherings are served in a variety of settings. English croquet setups are on the lawns, and bicycles are available.

The Tiffany Inn 1323 De La Vina St., 93101; 805-963-2283 (M/E). Tiffany the dog greets visitors to this shingled 1898 tobacco,

The Parsonage, Santa Barbara

The Upham Victorian Hotel and Garden Cottages, Santa Barbara

Amasa Lincoln built his dream house, a cupola-topped redwood Italianate with sweeping verandas, in 1871. One of the oldest continuously operating hostelries in Southern California, the taupe, white, and black Upham nestles in an acre of gardens in downtown Santa Barbara. The forty-nine simply decorated rooms and suites in the main house and adjoining buildings all have private baths, TVs, radios, and fresh flowers. A continental breakfast buffet is served in the lobby and garden veranda, and wine and cheese round out the day in front of the fireplace. Valet service and fax machines are available, and banquets and meetings can be arranged.

Louie's Restaurant (805-962-0058), on the veranda adjoining the main lobby, serves California cuisine in an intimate setting.

Places to Visit

Fernald House 414 W. Montecito St., 93101; 805-966-1601. Sunday, 2 to 4 P.M. Donation. A mix of many styles and remodelings from 1862 to 1892 to 1905, the gray, black, and white home of Judge Charles Fernald is being carefully restored on a new site to its 1880s splendor by the volunteers of the Santa Barbara Historical Society under the guidelines of architectural restoration specialists David Bisol and William Troi-

Fernald House, Santa Barbara

cream, and green mansion. Lovingly restored, the parlors greet you with polished silver, fresh flowers, and fine antiques. Most of the seven comfortable, antiques-filled rooms have baths, and some have fireplaces and Jacuzzis. The High Renaissance bed in the Somerset Room is remarkable, and Victoria's Room is delightfully romantic. An expanded continental breakfast is served in the formal dining room or on the veranda.

The Upham Victorian Hotel and Garden Cottages 1040 De La Vina St., 93101; 805-962-0058/800-727-0876 (E). Boston banker

La Mer, Ventura

the author of the popular family history *Fourteen at the Table.*

Groups

Professional Association of Innkeepers International P.O. Box 90710, 93190; 805-965-0707/569-1853. A trade association of innkeepers, this offers complete information on opening and operating a bed-and-breakfast or country inn.

Santa Barbara Historical Society P.O. Box 578, 93102. Museum and Library: 136 East De la Guerra St., 93101; 805-966-1601.

VENTURA

La Mer 411 Poli St., 93001; 805-643-3600 (M/E). This blue and white 1890 Cape Cod Victorian, a city landmark, is a cozy European bed-and-breakfast. Each of the five rooms, decorated in French, Norwegian, Austrian, English, and German styles, has down feather beds and private baths. Most have a private entrance, and the front rooms have a view of the ocean. Complimentary wine and a bountiful Bavarian

The Victorian Rose Historical Wedding Chapel, Ventura

ano. Fernald made his money in the California gold fields, then practiced law in San Francisco. Princess Louise, daughter of Queen Victoria, visited in 1883.

Many of the furnishings and paintings are the family's. Note the twenties photo of Hanna Fernald by Jessie Tarbox Beals, and the curved mahogany staircase. The stained-glass window in gold and blue with red and purple flowers over the front door was a wedding anniversary present. The four eggs represent the four children, and the bird is the mother, Florence, who lived in the house into her nineties.

The Joseph and Lucy Sexton House Quality Suites Complex, 5490 Hollister Ave., 93111; 805-683-6722/800-338-6722. The Sexton Family mansion, an elegant Italianate built in 1880, is being restored and refurbished as a centerpiece for the new Quality Suites Complex and is California Historical Landmark No. 14. Painted in five authentic colors, including green, peach, and light yellow, the house is now both a combination museum of Sexton family artifacts and meeting rooms.

The surrounding garden, designed by pioneering nurseryman Joe Sexton, boasts a large historical clump of birds of paradise and rare wine palm, cork, redwood, and oak trees. Joe's eleventh child, Horace, founded the Sexton Historical Museum with the Goleta Historical Society and was

breakfast is included. Bikes, buggy rides, picnic baskets, and therapeutic massage are available.

Gisela Baida feels that personal attention is important. She says "At a B & B, you're coming into somebody's home and staying with them just like a member of the family, and each guest is different from the others." Packages are available.

The Victorian Rose Historical Wedding Chapel 896 East Main St., 93001; 805-648-3307. By appointment. This delightful cream, pink, and lilac Gothic church was built as St. John's Methodist Episcopal Church on the outskirts of town in 1888. Although no longer affiliated with any denomination, the gracious Gothic chapel is a city landmark available for weddings. Now in the center of town, this is the last of the original seven churches in the City of San Buenaventura. You provide the spouse, and the staff will help with minister, photography, flowers, music, printing, and other necessities.

Suppliers

Antique Baths & Kitchens 2220 Carlton Way, Santa Barbara, 93019; 805-962-8578. Craftsman Chris Rheinschild, who restored his own 1905 home, makes and sells fine baths, kitchens, fixtures, and faucets, and he can copy and design to order. Special fixtures available. Catalog.

Architectural Antiques & Salvage Co. 726 Anacapa St., Santa Barbara, 93109; 805-965-2446. Roger Corta specializes in doors and windows.

David Bisol Santa Barbara Museum of Art, 1130 State St., Santa Barbara, 93101; 805-963-4364. Restoration preservationist.

Alexandra C. Cole Preservation Planning Associates, 519 Fig Ave., Santa Barbara, 93101; 805-962-1715. National Register nominations, restoration plans, historic preservation.

Dr. Rebecca Conard PHR Associates, 725 Garden St., Santa Barbara, 93101; 805-965-2357. Architectural and historic resource surveys for planning purposes and/or for National Register nominees. Tax Act manager, and historical architecture and cultural resources management.

Country Plumbing 5042 7th St., Carpinteria, 93013; 805-684-8685. Authentic antique and reproduction plumbing. Pedestal sinks, clawfoot tubs. Refinishing and restoration services.

Mary Louise Days Asst. Planner, City of Santa Barbara, 2833 Puesta del Sol Rd., Santa Barbara, 93105; 805-564-5470. National Register nominations, cultural resources studies.

Alvin Fernhart 50 Prado, San Luis Obispo, 93401; 805-544-9013. Wood carving.

General Wood Turning 120 6th St., Templeton, 93465; 805-434-2182. Central Coast wood turning. Newels, banisters.

Glass Shack 332 Peir Ave., 93109; 805-473-2954. Donna German does decorative carving and monogramming in glass and on lamps.

Hiteshew Studio & Design 7105 Portola Rd., Atascadero, 93400; 805-466-1766. Mark Hiteshew creates etched glass for doors and windows.

Homespun Fabrics & Draperies P.O. Box 3223-PLG, Ventura, 93006; 805-642-8111. 100 percent cotton, ten-foot-wide fabrics for vintage clothing and linings. Catalog.

Moriarity's Lamps 9 W. Ortega St., Santa Barbara, 93101; 805-966-1124. Restores and sells antique lamps.

Lorin Watson 816 Main St., Cambria, 93428; 805-927-4127. Wood carving.

THE LOS ANGELES AREA

"My Guest"
Sweet be thy Sleep, My Guest,
Peace Come to Thee, and rest
Throughout all the Quiet Night;
And with the Morning Light
Awake Thee, and rise Refreshed.
—Anonymous

Los Angeles has made itself a great city not by looking back but by looking ahead. Nonetheless, the greatest sprawl of them all has many organizations dedicated to preservation and pockets of unforgettable beauty:

- Behind the original, eye-catching color scheme for the Hale House lies a colorful story you will learn shortly. Behind Heritage Square lies a great deal of volunteer time and effort.
- Another original paint scheme with no less than fifteen colors on it is the Morey Mansion, a spectacular old Victorian in Redlands. (With that many colors, you know it had to have been built by a San Franciscan.)
- Also in Redlands and equally remarkable is the Kimberly Crest House and Gardens, a fairy-tale French chateau that is Los Angeles's answer to San Francisco's Chateau Tivoli.
- The scale, architecture, furnishings, and spacious grounds of the General Phineas Banning Residence Museum would make it stand out anywhere. But to come upon it in isolated splendor in a Los Angeles suburb we had never even heard of made it all the more striking.
- Monrovia is an outstanding example of a town out of harm's way that is lucky enough to have both an enviable collection of Victorians and a concerned, active group like the Monrovia Old House Preservation Group to protect them.

SIMI VALLEY

R. P. Strathearn Historical Park 137 Strathearn Pl., P.O. Box 351, 93062; 805-526-6453. Tours on weekends, 1 to 4 P.M.; Wednesday at 1 P.M., and by appointment. The Simi Valley Historical Society and Museum, an organization formed to preserve local history, has gathered nine historical buildings together on the site of a Native American Chumash village named Shimiji.

Colony House is one of twelve cottages shipped by rail in 1888 for a new town, "Simiopolis," but the town never got under way, and the houses became the nucleus of the new Simi. Colony House, one of only two remaining, was moved to the park and furnished with the belongings of Simi Valley's early families.

Also on the property is the Strathearn House, built by farmer Robert P. Strathearn, who added a Victorian frame to the original Simi Valley adobe in 1893. Family furnishings and a fine quilt collection have been used to restore the home. The gardens are also laid out as they were originally designed by Mrs. Strathearn in the 1890s.

CALABASAS

Leonis Adobe 23537 Calabasas Rd., 92000; 818-712-0734. Wednesday through Sunday, 1 to 4 P.M. Donation. Standing under the oaks in Calabasas in the San Fernando Valley is the lovely home of one of the most colorful figures of early Los Angeles. Built in 1844 and restored to its original beauty by the Leonis Adobe Association, it is a superb example of gracious living when the San Fernando Valley was ranching country and Los Angeles still a dusty settlement.

The Plummer House, "the oldest house in

Workman and Temple Family Homestead Museum, City of Industry

Hollywood," a tiny two-tone green Gothic cottage built in 1875 by Eugenio Plummer, a friend of Miguel Leonis, was moved to the present location to save it. This state historical landmark now serves as a museum of Victorian clothing, photos, and memorabilia from the area's families. Photographs of Espiritu Chijulla Leonis dressed in her black satin 1880s best are shown next to the actual dress, gloves, shoes, and shawl. The adobe and Plummer House are furnished as they were in the 1880s. Farm animals still roam the pasture and gardens.

CITY OF INDUSTRY

Workman and Temple Family Homestead Museum 15415 E. Don Julian Rd., 91745; 818-968-8492. Tuesday through Friday, 1 to 4 P.M., Saturday and Sunday, 10 A.M. to 4 P.M.

Closed fourth weekend of the month. Free tours hourly. This six-acre historic site preserves several restored historic buildings, the oldest of which is the Workman House. Built by William and Nicolasa Workman as a simple adobe in the 1840s, it was remodeled by architect Ezra F. Kysor in the 1870s into a picturesque country home, featuring Italianate, Gothic Revival, and Normanesque elements as well as a marvelous faux-finish exterior. The interior restoration is under way. Nearby is El Camp Santo, a cemetery established by the Workmans in the 1850s that survives with its original Gothic Revival cast-iron fence.

Rowland House 16021 Gale Ave., 9174; 818-336-2382. By appointment. President Ruth Rogers and the La Puente Valley Historical Society are working to restore the 1855 Rowland House, the oldest two-story brick structure in Los Angeles County. This Greek Revival house was remodeled about 1900 and is currently in the process of restoration. Particularly noteworthy are the two-story Corinthian columns at the entrance, the interior floors painted to resemble grass matting, and the dining-room walls painted with a wisteria vine–covered arbor. Its High Victorian furniture and art are exhibited in a nearby building.

CATALINA ISLAND

With the colorful town of Avalon, the historic ballroom complex, and stretches of beach and empty hills, the island has been a playground for Angelenos for decades. A few of the guesthouses are being done up in Victorian style. For information, call 800-4-AVALON.

LOS ANGELES

B & B of L.A. Reservation Service 32074 Waterside Ln., Westlake Village, 91361; 818-889-8870. Homestays in over one hundred homes in the Greater Los Angeles area. Along the coast from San Diego to San Francisco, bed-and-breakfasts and inn stays. Directory available.

Eastlake Inn 1442 Kellam Ave., 90026; 213-250-1620 (M/E). Built in 1887 in Los Angeles's oldest suburb atop a hill overlooking downtown, this stately Eastlake home offers a bit of quiet close to the business hub of L.A.

Murray Burns had been doing extensive business traveling as a management consultant, and the hotel chains, with their "institutional service and smiles were driving me mad." He tried a bed-and-breakfast and was hooked, so when he purchased the mansion with Planaria Price, who has also been very influential in preserving nearby Carroll Avenue, they transformed it into a bed-and-breakfast inn. The house was built as a double house, with two separate staircases splitting the house down the middle, for two sisters, one of

whom is said to have poisoned her Northern California harbormaster husband.

The rooms have been restored in an uncluttered straightforward Victorian style. Antique decorations and clothing are used to decorate the hallways. The North Star Room has a view of the Hollywood hills from the queen-sized canopy bed set in an alcove. The Sunrise Room's beveled glass catches the sunrise on an antique walnut double bed. Four rooms have private baths; three share two baths, which even have stocked medicine cabinets. Fluffy robes hang in the closets, where alarm clocks are also tucked away.

An eclectic collection of books, a comfortable reading chair, fresh flowers, and a bottle of wine await guests. Ceiling fans and original and fine reproductions of flashed glass adorn each room. The Hummingbird and skylight suites downstairs have private baths.

The garden is used for weddings and parties. Special weekend celebrations, from the Dickens Christmas to Gondola Getaways, keep the place busy throughout the year. Murray and Planaria both own houses on Carroll Avenue and both share in preservation-entrepreneurial ventures, purchasing and saving endangered Victori-

Heritage Square, Pasadena

ans, moving them to safe sites, and restoring them.

Although they do not live at the Eastlake Inn, one or both are always on hand to welcome you with sherry in the parlor and to serve a savory breakfast of fresh-squeezed juice, eggs, fruit, cheese, and baked goodies.

Places to Visit

Grier Musser Museum 403 S. Bonnie Brae Ave. (two blocks east of Alvarado north of 3rd St.); 213-413-1814. Wednesday through Saturday, 11 A.M. to 4 P.M. Fee. Groups by appointment. Mail: 219 So. Irving Blvd., 90004. A restored and furnished polychrome 1898 Queen Anne home, this museum recalls an earlier, slower time. Anna Krieger and her daughters Susan and Nancy established the museum in honor of Anna's mother, Anna Grier Musser, whose great-uncle came West from Pennsylvania to establish one of the first seed companies in Los Angeles.

Three generations of family heirlooms and curios, including Haviland china, seed catalogs, and antique postcards of Los Angeles, fill the house. Changing holiday decorations are also from the family collections. There are monthly exhibits to show Victorian life. Colorful stencils and painted ornamentation by Pinson & Ware of Monrovia enhance the authentic restoration. Lectures and seminars offered; parties, meetings, and receptions arranged. The museum also offers antique clothing rental, a catalog of antiques and collectibles for sale, and appraisal and restoration consulting. Gift shop.

Sepulveda House Visitors' Center for El Pueblo de Los Angeles Historic Park 420 N. Main St., 90012; 213-628-0605. Park: 845 N. Alameda, 90012. Daily, 10 A.M. to 3 P.M. Free. This 1887 Eastlake commercial and residential building is now being restored as a Victorian boardinghouse, like that owned by Señora Eloisa Martinez de Sepulveda. The bedroom and kitchen downstairs are finished, and painted ornamentation by

Pinson & Ware already gleams in the parlors and hallway. To visit, enter on Olvera St. or on Main St., where the two front rooms are still storefronts that function as a gallery with changing exhibits and a visitors' center.

Free guided tours and self-guided tours of El Pueblo de Los Angeles Historic Park are available. Docents also offer historical bus tours of the city, which include Carroll Avenue.

PASADENA

Heritage Square 3800 Homer St., 90031 (Ave. 43 exit on Pasadena [110] Freeway); 818-449-0193. Wednesday through Sunday and holidays, 12 to 4 P.M. Closed Thanksgiving and December 1 through January 1. Guided tours on weekends. Fee. Heritage Square Museum is a sanctuary for historic buildings threatened by the wrecker's ball. When all exterior and interior restorations are finished, the museum will boast a complete neighborhood with a bandstand, drugstore, 1887 Carpenter Gothic Methodist church, carriage barn, 1885 Gothic railroad depot, a French Mansard-style home, an octagon house, and an Italianate home built in 1876. The 1887 Beaudry House, a small Queen Anne, was the home of famed wood-carver John J. Ford.

The showpiece is the Hale House, built in 1888, probably by the Newsom Brothers. The redwood mansion combines Queen Anne and Eastlake styles with fish-scale shingles and massive brick chimneys. James and Bessie Hale moved in in 1901, and Mrs. Hale lived there until 1967.

When it was threatened with demolition, the house was moved to Heritage Square. Its restoration now stands as a landmark study in the State Historic Preservation records, and the house is listed on the National Register. Furnishing the interior will always be a continuing process. The ground floor is nicely done in furnishings of the period.

In 1978, a paint company painted the house for free in thirty-nine nonclashing colors as part of an advertising campaign.

After the campaign, the paint company, working with a specialist in chemical microanalysis, painted the house in its original 1888 stripes of bright greens, clay pink, and raspberry. This colorful scheme graced the front cover of *Daughters of Painted Ladies* and of the *1992 Painted Ladies Calendar.*

There is a museum shop on the grounds. The Cultural Heritage Foundation of Southern California is a volunteer organization.

SANTA MONICA

Angels Attic 516 Colorado Ave., 90401; 213-394-8331. Thursday through Sunday, 12:30 to 4:30 P.M. Fee. A museum of antique dollhouses, miniatures, dolls and toys, Angel's Attic is a nonprofit enterprise. It contributes to the Brentwood Center for Educational Therapy—a center for developmentally handicapped children and young adults. Heavenly blue, white trim, and red accents dress up this 1893 Queen Anne, the oldest house in Santa Monica. It was a rundown building when bought and restored by the present owners.

Visitors will see a miniature Chinese Store, the "Shoe House" from England, fabulous antique and new dollhouses from around the world, precious and well-loved dolls, and a galaxy of old toys. At Christmas, Santa's Workshop is on view.

Tea, with cake and cookies, is served on the enclosed wicker-furnished front porch and in the Victorian garden, which is also available for parties. Handicap-accessible. Gift shop.

ARCADIA

"Lucky" Baldwin's Queen Anne Cottage Los Angeles State and County Arboretum, 301 N. Baldwin Ave., 91007; 818-821-3222. Daily, 9 A.M. to 4:30 P.M. Fee. Speculator Elias Jackson "Lucky" Baldwin built this cottage in 1885 for his fourth wife to entertain in. Unfortunately, she left before it was completed, so the house became a memorial to Baldwin's third wife, lovely Jennie Dexter. Baldwin made a fortune in gold and silver mines and was the largest— and most colorful—landowner in the San Gabriel Valley. When he died in 1909, the house was neglected until 1951, when the Historical Committee of the California Arboretum Foundation restored it inside and out. It gained fame as Mr. Rourk's house in the TV series "Fantasy Island."

Today, the frilled and turreted gingerbread cottage is a fantasy in white, outlined in cherry red. Portraits of Jennie Dexter and "Lucky" Baldwin hang in the parlor, and you can see a bottle of E. J. Baldwin's Santa Anita sherry in the music room. Authentic polychrome wall treatments, period furniture, and dressed mannequins can be seen through the windows as you walk around the outside of the house.

The white and red Gothic Coach Barn was built for Baldwin's fourteen vehicles and horses. In 1891, historian H. H. Bancroft described this area as "Calm and peaceful as the fabled realm of Rasselas, where soft vernal airs induce forgetfulness of the din and turmoil, the crowded streets and selfish intensity of city life." Surrounded by lush greenery, you will agree that Bancroft was right. Gift shop.

BURBANK

Gordon R. Howard Museum Burbank Historical Society, 1015 W. Olive Ave., 91505; 818-841-6333. Sunday, 1 to 4 P.M., and by appointment. Fee. This 1887 Queen Anne, painted in two blues and a white, houses an exhibit about the moviemaking industry. Volunteers are hard at work restoring and refurbishing two other old buildings in this Victorian enclave.

WILMINGTON

The General Phineas Banning Residence Museum 401 E. M St., P.O. Box 397, 90748; 213-548-7777. Guided tours on the half hour, Tuesday through Friday, 12:30 to 2:30 P.M. A 3:30 P.M. tour is offered on weekends and by

Angels Attic, Santa Monica

sents a different decade to show the eclectic nature of a home lived in by several generations. The dining room is a fine formal example of late nineteenth-century decorative arts. The master bedroom, with a Cuban mahogany four-poster, and an opulant armoire given to Banning by General Mariano Vallejo, is a High Victorian gem. Phineas's son Hancock lived here until his death in 1925.

Friends of Banning Park, a private, nonprofit foundation, raises funds for the continuing restoration and educational programs at the museum. The most popular programs are the seasonal kitchen demonstrations in the Victorian kitchen, featuring Banning family recipes and cooking techniques of the period.

appointment. Groups by appointment. Donation. General Phineas Banning, town founder and father of Los Angeles Harbor, built this imposing columned Greek Revival showcase in 1864 near the end of the Civil War.

Each of the twenty-three rooms repre-

Luncheons on the first Friday of most months also help raise money. The house is set on twenty acres of park owned and operated by the City of Los Angeles. The museum shop is open during public tour hours and special programs.

"Lucky" Baldwin's Queen Anne Cottage, Arcadia

MONROVIA

George H. Anderson House 215 East Lime Ave., 91016; 213-208-5069. Third Sunday of each month, 12 to 4 P.M. Built by John C. Anderson, the Ohio-born contractor who built Monrovia's first hotel, this modest 1886 Carpenter Gothic cottage is one of the earliest buildings in Monrovia. The furnishings are of the period. The sweet yellow, light green, dark green, white, and burgundy make it a charming Painted Lady. The house was occupied by the Anderson family until 1974 and is now a city museum.

The Monrovia Old House Preservation Group P.O. Box 734, Monrovia, 91017; 818-358-7822. Meetings, information exchange, newsletter, tours.

REDLANDS

Edwards Mansion California St. Exit, Interstate 10, 92373; 909-793-2031. Citrus grower James S. Edwards built this salmon pink fourteen-room Queen Anne in 1890, using ready-made plans, and his family lived there until 1958. In 1973, it was bought for $1, cut in two, and moved five miles down the road. Today, the house caters parties, meetings, and business dinners. A chapel and gazebo make this a popular spot for weddings and other private parties.

Georgianna Manor 816 E. High Ave., 92374; 909-793-0423 (M/E). In 1888, Isaac Newton Hoag and his wife Georgianna built this charming towered Queen Anne in the middle of an orange grove. Today, dressed in yellow, brown, and white, it's close to downtown and Sylvan Park. Ione Hansen started small with three carefully appointed bedrooms, but is expanding and restoring. She loves sharing her home and its history.

The burled-walnut grand piano in the front parlor won a gold medal at the 1880 Vienna Festival of Music, and the mahogany four-poster bedroom set in Hopalong Cassidy's Room—where President McKinley once slept—came from the William Boyd ranch just down the road. Guests may use the hidden TV, VCR, stereo, phone, and

The General Phineas Banning Residence Museum, Wilmington

stocked refrigerator. A golden retriever and two cats keep you company during the family-style breakfast.

Historical Glass Museum 1157 N. Orange, P.O. Box 921, 92373; 909-797-1528/793-7190. American-made glassware, Cambridge,

Edwards Mansion, Redlands

Heisey, Fenton Art Glass, Steuben, and other fine glass is displayed in a 1903 Victorian. The Historical Glass Museum Foundation gives classes and tours. The visitor will find a gift shop, library, and research facilities at the museum.

Kimberly Crest House & Gardens 1325 Prospect Dr., P.O. Box 206, 92373; 909-792-2111. Tours Thursday and Sunday, 1 to 4 P.M., and by appointment. Donation. One of the finest examples of the American Renaissance in California, Kimberly Crest overlooks Italian gardens and terraces, lily ponds, and a pergola. Built in 1897 to resemble a French chateau, the castle was home to the Kimberlys of Kimberly-Clark Paper, from 1905 until 1979. One relative who visited frequently was Carole Lombard.

The French Parlor, with gilded furniture, damask wall panels, and gilded chandelier with etched shades, was supposedly created and installed by the Tiffany Studios of New York. There are Tiffany lamps in abundance. Rose damask covers the walls of the Musician's Gallery. The authentic faux-finish glazing on the walls in the library, with chinoiserie furnishings, is also exceptional.

Lavender Blue 22 E. State St., 92373; 909-793-0977. A delightfully cozy antiques and Victoriana store filled with wicker ware, lace, and flowers, serving lunch and scrumptious teas.

The Morey Mansion 190 Terracina Blvd., 92373; 909-793-7970. Tours supporting the YWCA on Sunday, 12 to 3 P.M., and by appointment. Fee (M). San Francisco shipbuilder David Morey built this magnificent edifice in 1889 so he could retire on his orange ranch. He spent $20,000 and carved and inlaid the golden oak woodwork, including orange blossoms, ship's wheels, and his wife's favorite calla lilies in the woodwork and art glass. The house has been through tough times and glorious ones in the last century. At one point, it appeared as a wilting gray ghost in John Maass's book *The Gingerbread Age*, and fans wrote so

many letters that Maass called it "America's Favorite Victorian." In the early 1980s, new owners transformed it into a luxurious bed-and-breakfast restoring the carpets, antique furnishings, red velvet draperies, and polished woods. When we visited, the house was in need of a new savior to restore it to its much deserved glory. The fifteen colors on the exterior are those chosen by David Morey himself.

Redlands Area Historical Society Regular meetings, house tours, oral archives, and documentation of Heritage Homes. The Redlands Chamber of Commerce, 1 E. Redlands Blvd., 92373 (909-793-2546) offers an audio and historic drive-by tour of the city. Heritage Room, A. K. Smiley Library, P.O. Box 1024, 92373; 125 W. Vine, 909-798-7632. Oral history archives, documentation and a walking tour of Downtown Redlands.

Tours of Redlands 402 Via Vista Dr., 92373; 909-793-9497. Karen Flippin: Redlands historical tour guide.

Turn of the Century 501 N. 5th St., 92373; 909-793-9215. Wood turning for Victorian restoration. Furniture design and manufacturing of turned posts, corbels, molding.

RANCHO CUCAMONGA

Christmas House 9240 Archibald Ave., 91730; 714-980-6450 (M). Palm trees stand sentinel next to this blue and white Queen Anne bed-and-breakfast built in 1904 by H. D. Cousins on eighty acres of citrus groves and grape vineyards. The red and green stained-glass windows throughout the house—and gala yuletide parties—gave it its name. The house was restored in 1985 and given historical landmark status by the town, which is thirty-seven miles east of Los Angeles.

Seven fireplaces and a wicker-filled veranda welcome visitors to the two suites and three bedrooms in teal, cabernet, or Wedgwood blue, two with shared bath. Terry robes make guests feel at home. The Garden Suite, in English garden florals, has its own garden and private spa in a gazebo. Weddings and business conferences accommodated.

RIVERSIDE

Heritage House 8193 Magnolia Ave., 92501; 714-689-1333. Tuesday through Thursday, 12 to 2:30 P.M.; Sunday, 12 to 3:30 P.M.; and by appointment. Fee. When Mrs. James (Catherine) Bettner, widow of a prominent Riverside citrus grower, built this Moorish Queen Anne in 1891, it was one of the first homes to have gas lighting, then powered by a backyard generator. Visitors can still see the original fixtures, which were converted to electricity in 1906. Designed by L.A. architect John A. Walls, the house cost $10,755 to build.

Although the gasolier and white and gold furnishings in the parlor are Mrs. Bettner's, the house is intended to reflect life in a typical wealthy home in 1891 Riverside, and other families have provided furniture and artifacts.

Highlights include the bread-making room, brick-walled pantry, cozy writing alcove, 1898 Edison cylinder player, tea service, and library. The garden and carriage house have also been restored.

DESERT HOT SPRINGS

Travellers Repose 66920 1st St., P.O. Box 655, 92240; 619-329-9584 (I). Marian and Sam Relkoff built this two-story Neo-Victorian, designed by their son Brian, in 1985 themselves, and painted it blue, gray, and white. Sam hand-turned and carved the gingerbread frills, and made the cupboards, moldings, oak paneling, and some of the furniture by hand. There are three comfortable rooms. "Button & Bows" has a private bath. A country look prevails, with hearts, dolls, and teddy bears everywhere. Tea is served each afternoon, and a continental breakfast is served in the dining room. Guests relax on the patio or in the pool and spa, with a panoramic view of the desert

and 9,000-foot San Jacinto and San Gorgonio mountains. Twelve miles north of Palm Springs, it's the only place like it in the Coachella Valley.

Newspapers

The Historic Traveler 19400 Vintage St., Northridge, 91324-1149. Editor: Allan Mann. A newsletter about travel to America's architectural and historic landmarks.

YesterYears P.O. Box 341228, Los Angeles, 90034; 213-559-0880. Main office: 3735 Canfield Ave., Suite 1, Los Angeles, 90034.

Publisher: Tom Ito. Antiques advertising and interest.

Groups

Angelino Heights Community Organization 213-481-1986.

California Historical Society 1120 Old Mill Rd., San Marino, 91320; 818-449-5450.

Carroll Avenue Restoration Foundation 1300 Carroll Ave., Los Angeles, 90026; 213-250-2869. Priscilla Morales. Tour usually given in May. Established in 1975 to aid in the preservation of Carroll Avenue. *A Moving Experience*, the film on saving endangered Victorians and moving them to the 1300 block of Carroll Avenue, won the 1978 National Trust for Historic Preservation's film award. Vintage street lighting has been installed, ornamental trees have been planted, and the area has been designated Los Angeles's first historic preservation district.

Cultural Heritage Foundation of Southern California 100 Ave. Los Robles, Pasadena, 91101; 818-796-2898. The foundation is restoring Heritage Square.

Downtown Walking Tours 213-623-TOUR. General information: 213-623-CITY.

L. A. Conservancy 727 W. 7th St., Suite 955, Los Angeles, 90017; 213-623-2489. A nonprofit organization that rescues significant

Kimberly Crest House & Gardens, Redlands

buildings. Lectures, tours, meetings. Provides community groups and individuals with technical assistance on the intricacies of preservation law, historic resource surveys, and landmark designation programs. Offers a list of restoration architects.

National Institute for Architecture and Preservation Studies 213-734-3938.

Pasadena Cultural Heritage Commission Pasadena City Hall, Room 111, 100 No. Garfield Ave., 91109; 818-405-4228.

Pasadena Heritage 54 W. Colorado Blvd., 91105; 818-793-0617.

Pasadena Historical Society & Museum 470 West Walnut, 91105; 818-577-1660.

Society of Architectural Historians Southern California Chapter, c/o The Hollyhock House, 4808 Hollywood Blvd., Los Angeles, 90027; 213-662-7572.

West Adams Heritage Home Association 2263 S. Harvard Blvd., Los Angeles, 90018; 213-735-WAHA. House tours.

Artisans and Services

American Architectural Preservation Group 631 Cross Avenue, Los Angeles 90165; 213-749-2600. Jim Dunham, president. Preservation real estate consultant who conducts classes and advises on how and where to invest in historic properties.

Arcadia Area Painters 818-359-0545. Bill Marino.

Architectural Heritage, Ltd. 7201 Melrose Ave., Hollywood, 90046; 213-935-3111. Monday through Saturday, 10 A.M. to 7 P.M.; Sunday, 12 to 5 P.M. John Timarkin. Turn-of-the-century architectural elements: columns, doors, doorknobs, mantels, glass, windows, lights, cabinets, and hardware. Salvage and estate sales.

Architectural Museum Services P.O. Box 86938, Los Angeles, 90086; 213-626-6046. Peter J. Snell, president. Restoration of homes and public buildings, interior restoration and interpretation, landscape restoration, historical research, and long-term planning.

The Morey Mansion, Redlands

Christmas House, Rancho Cucamonga

American Deluxe Lighting 13543 Alondra Blvd., Santa Fe Springs, 90760; 213-802-8910. Hand-blown art-glass shades with bronze bases, lamps, and wall fixtures. Catalog.

Artistic Brass 4100 Ardmore Ave., South Gate, 90280; 213-564-1100. Decorative, solid-brass lavatory faucets with matching tub and shower fittings. Catalog.

Robert Bauman History Associates, 9214 Ives St., Bellflower, 90706; 213-974-2639. Historical records surveys, research in support of litigation, administrative history.

Yvette S. Berthel P.O. Box 1393, Monrovia, 91017; 818-359-8544. Preservation surveys, architectural inventories, oral histories, and local history research.

Bruce Boehmner, Architectural Photography, 1547 Council St., Los Angeles, 90026; 213-250-7252.

Brass Reproductions 9711 Canoga Ave., Chatsworth 91311; 818-709-7844. Solid-brass Victorian and traditional lighting: sconces, chandeliers, floor-, and table-lamp designs. Catalog.

Christopher D. Brewer Vintage Resources, P.O. Box 96, Exeter, 93221; 209-592-6576. Historic preservation plans, local-history publications, resource relocation, collections evaluations.

California Glass Bending Corp. 320 E. B St., Wilmington, 90744; 800-223-6594. Specialists in bending glass for Victorian-style curved windows, cabinets, etc.

Carroll Avenue, Los Angeles

David Cameron P.O. Box 611, Santa Monica, 90406–0611; 213-454-0914. Historic research and real-estate writing.

Canterbury Designs P.O. Box 5730, Sherman Oaks, 91413; 213-936-7111. Outdoor furnishings in period style: clocks, benches, tree grates. Catalog.

Class Painting 818-358-3621. Jim Johnson, exterior painting.

Coppa Woodworking, Inc. 1231 Paraiso Ave., San Pedro, 90731; 213-548-4142. Wood screen doors in stock or made to order. Brochure.

Craftsman Shop 528 Fair Oaks Blvd., Pasadena, 91104; 818-304-9387. Antiques sold and restored.

Crown City Hardware 1047 N. Allen Ave., Pasadena, 91104; 818-794-1188. Hard-to-find original and authentic reproductions of hardware, brass, iron, crystal, and porcelain. Will reproduce to order. Cabinets, furniture, doors, and windows. Catalog.

Designer Resource 5160 Melrose Ave., 90038; 213-465-9235. Period architectural detail in stock and made to order. Columns, mantels, ceilings, ornaments, plaster details, carved and embossed wood moldings, plaster cornices. Catalogs.

Willy Disselhof, Lampmaker P.O. Box 65918, Los Angeles, 90065; 213-227-9002/ 225-7515. Tiffany lamps, reproductions, stained glass.

Elegant Plaster Designs 3436 Brandon St., Pasadena, 91107; 818-578-0293. Richard Rose designs, sells, and installs plaster casts, fireplace surrounds, cornices, and center pieces. He also imports from England. He specializes in Victorian, Elizabethan, Adamesque, and French reproductions, and imports simulated marble fire surrounds.

Raymond Enkobell Designs 16506 Avalon Blvd., Carson, 90746; 213-532-1400. Architectural accoutrements carved and sculptured in solid woods. Inlays, rosettes, panels. Catalog.

Eurocobble 4265 Lemp Ave., Studio City, 91604; 213-877-5012. European cobblestone from Alpine quarries available in preassembled modules. Brochure.

Fairwind Pattern Co. 819 No. June St., Hollywood, 90038. Historical garment patterns. Antique buttons, laces, ribbons, gloves, and hats. Catalog.

Lynn Goodpasture 1757 Franklin Canyon Dr., Beverly Hills, 90210; 213-271-8070. Custom decorative painting, gold leaf, marbleizing, stenciling on floors, walls, furniture, and screens. Custom design for etched glass and carved wood.

Greg's Antique Lighting 12005 Wilshire Blvd., West Los Angeles, 90025; 213-478-5475. Monday through Wednesday, Friday and Saturday, 11 A.M. to 5:30 P.M. Greg Davidson buys and sells table lamps, wall sconces, and chandeliers, vintage 1850–1930.

Helphand Restoration 1537 Berkeley St., #1, Santa Monica, 90404; 213-651-1885. David Helphand. Antiques restoration, furniture maker. Polishes, waxes, fine finishes. House-call service.

Historic Resources Group 1728 North Whitley Ave., Hollywood, 90028; 213-469-2349. Christy Johnson McAvoy, architectural historian and preservationist; William F. Delvac, tax specialist. They specialize in historic resources evaluation, preservation planning and development, National Register designation, and the use of tax incentives. Published materials on the rehabilitation and reuse of historic structures.

House of Moulding 15202 Oxnard St., Van Nuys, 91411; 818-781-5300. A large selection of hardwood and softwood molding, corbels, wood turnings, decorative plaques, fireplace and mantel moldings. Catalog.

The House Relocator 631 Cross Avenue,

Los Angeles, 90765; 213-749-2600. Jim Dunham, author of *Moving Buildings for Profit*, president. Consulting firm that conducts classes and advises clients on how to evaluate and execute the relocation of historical buildings.

International Terra Cotta 690 N. Robertson Blvd., Los Angeles, 90069; 213-657-3752. European terra-cotta and sandstone statuary, fountains, urns, vases and planters, bronze figures, and fountains. Catalog.

Kerry Joyce Fine Architectural Detail 5160 Melrose Ave., Los Angeles, 90038; 213-465-9235. Fireplace mantels made of Novostone, imitation-French limestone, and Novocon, a paintable composite.

Bessy M. Kong 2560 W. Olympic Blvd., Suite 250, Los Angeles, 90006; 213-385-6564. Land-use and environmental planner. Assistance in old-house relocation.

La France 2008 S. Sepulveda Blvd., Los Angeles, 90025; 213-478-6009. Importers of French ceramic tile, natural limestone, marble, and granite. Custom orders. Showrooms in L.A., Beverly Hills, San Francisco, and Costa Mesa. Brochures.

Dr. Portia Lee 8013 Blackburn Ave., #7, Los Angeles, 90048; 213-653-7466. Historic building reports and evaluations, historic building nominations, evaluations of funding and capital needs for historical organizations.

Tom Levine 213-250-5092. Fireplace repair.

Manchester Sash & Door Co. 1228 W. Manchester Ave., Los Angeles, 90044; 213-759-0344. Bud Wolski. Manufacturers and dealers of sashes, doors, and screens.

Michael's Classic Wicker 8532 Melrose Ave., Los Angeles, 90069; 213-659-1121. Reproduction Victorian wicker furniture, including rockers, armoires, headboards, tables, and étagères. Catalog.

The Next Stage P.O. Box 35269, Los Angeles, 90035; 213-939-2688. Marlene Gordon, tour director, organizes Victorian and historical tours in Southern and Central California and occasionally in other parts of the country. Examples: a historic house tour of Redlands and a horse carriage/train tour of San Diego.

Old House Restoration 1400 Calumet St., Angelino Hts., 90026; 213-250-2253. Ron Ross. General contractor specializing in restoration.

Old Riverside Foundation P.O. Box 601, Riverside, 92502; 714-683-2725. Salvages old houses. Holds house-parts sales periodically. Works to protect and preserve "built history."

Paul Osekowsky 213-530-3205/714-898-7967. Custom-made fretwork.

The Painted House/Sage & Associates 2272 W. 29th Pl., Los Angeles, 90018; 213-733-5459. Consultation and design work for Victorian homes. Instruction for floor, wall, and mural design.

Painting Exteriors/Interiors 488 E. Washington, #205, Pasadena, 91104; 818-798-5693. Azaria Stone.

Robert H. Peterson Co. 530 N. Baldwin Park Blvd., City of Industry, 91744; 818-369-5085. Brass fireplace furnishings. Catalog.

Pinson & Ware: Painted Ornament & Architectural Art 145 N. Mayflower Ave. Monrovia, 91016; 818-359-6113. Ed Pinson and Deborah Ware conserve, restore, and recreate antique, ornamental painted work on architectural surfaces and furniture. They specialize in Victorian, Craftsman, and early twentieth-century styles of decorative painting, especially stenciling and polychrome. Pinson & Ware also create new ornaments in historic styles for friezes, floors, door panels, and other interior spaces. Their newest project is a series of decorative borders, hand-painted onto canvas that can be installed like wallpaper.

Platt Construction 818-700-1880. Landmark commercial and residental restoration and rehabilitation. Mold makers.

Pinson & Ware, Monrovia

Plexacraft Metals Co. 5406 San Fernando Rd., Glendale, 91203; 818-246-8201. Hand-cast solid-brass knobs and pulls in traditional styles. Custom duplication. Porcelain hardware for doors and furniture. Catalogs.

Renaissance Designs 251 Kettering Dr., Ontario, 91761; 714-395-8953. Glass-fiber-reinforced gypsum and concrete furnishings such as mantels, tables, sconces, columns, and moldings. Custom orders. Catalog.

Renovators Club 6475 Victoria Ave., Riverside, 92506; 714-684-0596. Bill Kleese. Network for exchanging information on restoration and salvage.

Rinaudo's Reproductions, Victorian Lighting P.O. Box 4472, Glendale, 91202; 818-957-2077. Joe Rinaudo. Reproduction and custom Victorian lighting, including solid brass.

B. Ring Painting 4510 Forman Ave., North Hollywood, 91602; 818-506-1641.

Alan R. Rose Plastering Imperial Fire Showroom, 132 W. Colorado Blvd., Suite 14, Pasadena, 91105; 818-248-8043. Interior and exterior plastering, installation, and restoration.

SEAY Industrial, Inc. 8664 Rheem Ave., South Gate, 90280; 213-564-7777. Joe Heatherington has moved hundreds of Victorians since 1927.

Betty Short El Monte; 818-444-5728. Makes custom lampshades and bases. Restores antique lampshades and bases.

South Coast Shingle Co. 2220 E. South St., Long Beach, 90805; 213-634-7100. Fancy-cut shingles and roofing materials. Brochure.

Swan Solid Brass Beds 2417 East 24th St., Los Angeles, 90058; 213-584-8905/800-421-0141. Reproduction brass beds, head-boards, nightstands, mirrors, tables, and cribs. Catalog.

Through the Woods William Ruddock & Assoc., 333 Raymond Ave., Glendale, 91201; 213-667-2592. Specializes in restoration of hardwood floors.

J. Troup & David 4310 Melrose Ave., Los Angeles, 90029; 213-666-5786. Victorian and Empire furnishings.

Victoria Gardens 18639 Newburgh, Covina, 91722; 800-827-8042. Garden-dried flowers including roses, lavender, hydrangea, caspia, and baby's breath; baskets, ribbons, lace, trims, floral supplies. Design kits for wreaths, sprays, and topiary trees. Catalog.

Vintage Plumbing and Bathroom Antiques 9645 Sylvia Ave., Northridge, 91324; 818-772-1721. By appointment. Donald Hooper. Authentic Victorian and Art Deco bathroom fixtures. Buys, sells, restores, and repairs antique bathroom fixtures.

J. P. Weaver 2301 W. Victory Blvd., Burbank, 91506; 818-841-5700. Ornaments for the decoration of mantels, furniture, walls, doors, and ceilings. Videocassettes and seminars on how to steam and self-bond the flexible ornaments. Catalog.

Helen Williams, Delft Tiles 12643 Hortense St., Studio City, 91604; 818-761-2756. Importer of antique seventeenth- and eighteenth-century tiles from Holland, England, Spain, and Portugal. Brochure.

Lawrence E. Winans Architectural Preservation Consultant/Restoration Services. P.O. Box 4164, Downey, 90241; 213-560-3098. Fourth generation of preservationists.

Win Balance, Inc. 818-401-2788. Gary Richter, general contractor. Restoration and painting.

Yesteryear/Old Tyme Picture Frames P.O. Box 4791, Downey, 90241; 213-803-1236. English walnut, antique gold, country-white, country-pastel, and fruit wood handcrafted frames with glass and easel backs. Catalog.

ORANGE AND SAN DIEGO COUNTIES

"Building on the past, in the present, for the future."
—Motto of the Santa Ana
Historical Preservation Society

Besides being blessed with some of America's best weather, San Diego has four of the state's top Victorian attractions:

- "The Del," the Hotel Del Coronado, is the coast's reigning Victorian hostelry, a magnificent seaside resort that has hosted presidents for a century.
- Both inside and out, the Villa Montezuma is a feast for the eyes.
- The Gaslamp Quarter is a fine example of how to turn an eyesore into a tourist attraction.
- Heritage Park is making preservation pay for itself by using the Victorians it has saved from demolition for offices.

SANTA ANA

Howe Waffle House Santa Ana Historical Preservation Society, 120 Civic Center Dr. W., 92701; 714-547-9645. Tours by appointment. Free. The Santa Ana Historical Preservation Society has worked to save, move, and restore this twelve-room California Redwood 1889 Queen Anne now on the National Register.

The house was built for Willella Howe, Santa Ana's first woman doctor, and her husband, Dr. Alvin Howe, Santa Ana's second mayor. Her second husband, Edson Waffle, owned a livery business. She delivered over one thousand babies, called "Waffle babies," and was known for her skill and charity.

The period furnishings and medical equipment have been donated by volunteers as well as the family, and all of the contributors are listed in a plaque on the front porch. The leader of the Santa Ana Historical Preservation Society explained, "It's important that children understand history. It's important that they understand what came before, so they can go on from here. This house helps them understand how people lived years ago. That's important."

Down the block is the Episcopal Church of the Messiah (614 Bush, 92701), where the doctor sang in the choir. The oldest public building in continuous use in Orange County, it was built in 1886 in medieval Gothic, Classical, and late Queen Anne styles, with a fabulous polychrome wood-carved interior.

NEWPORT BEACH

Doryman's Inn B & B 2102 W. Ocean Front, 92663; 714-675-7300 (E). Founded in 1891 and designated one of California's historical landmarks, this luxurious inn faces the Pacific Ocean near the McFadden Wharf and the Doryman fishing fleet. Half of the ten rooms have ocean views. All have down comforters, fireplaces, and sunken marble or Jacuzzi tubs in the well-stocked bathrooms. Although the European portrait art clashes with the controlled period decor, visitors will enjoy sounds of the sea, the rooftop sunbathing, and breakfast in the fern-filled dining room.

EL TORO

Heritage Hill Historical Park 25151 Serrano Rd., 92603 (north from Hwy. 5); 714-855-

2028. Guided tours Wednesday, Thursday, and Friday at 2 P.M., weekends at 11 A.M. and 2 P.M.; and by appointment. Free. Four historical early Orange County structures including a church, a one-room school, and two Victorian houses show in this fine restoration how our ancestors lived.

SAN DIEGO

Sixteen blocks of downtown San Diego from the waterfront to Broadway has been transformed into the Gaslamp Quarter, a national historic district on the site of the "new town" founded by Alonzo B. Horton in the 1870s. (The Old Town was that founded by the Californios, where Mission San Diego was founded by Father Junipero Serra in the 1700s.) Red-brick sidewalks, Victorian benches, and gaslight-style street lamps grace buildings restored for use as stores, galleries, theaters, and restaurants.

Headquarters for the Gaslamp Quarter Foundation is in the William Heath Davis House at 410 Island Ave., an 1850s prefabricated New England saltbox house, shipped around Cape Horn, and painted yellow, white, and green.

Lodging

Britt House 1887 406 Maple St., 92103; 619-234-2926 (M/E). This grand white, orange, and black Queen Anne, on a hill near the downtown area, is a comfortable bed-and-breakfast inn. The stained-glass window in the stairwell and the magnificent carved-wood staircase are the stars here. Eight individually decorated fan-cooled bedrooms in the house share four bathrooms; some rooms have private entrances or private balconies. Fluffy robes and baskets of plump towels are provided, as are fresh flowers and fruit and cookies. The separate cottage, with its canopied bed, breakfast nook, bath, and garden is best for those traveling with children. The house cat stands guard duty. (DPL)

Britt House is known for its food, from the special breakfast and afternoon teas to the custom picnic baskets or romantic dinners that are ordered in advance and served in your room.

Coronado Victorian House 1000 Eighth St., Coronado, 92118; 610-435-2200 (E). This engaging 1894 blue-gray, white, and burgundy Victorian is a bed-and-breakfast with a difference: the innkeeper offers dance and exercise lessons as part of the package and serves health foods and ethnic foods such as baklava and grape leaves for breakfast. The six rooms are named after dancers and have private baths. There is handicap access. Bonni Marie Dance Studio offers tap, ballroom, ballet, jazz, Hawaiian and belly dancing on the first floor. Upstairs, you'll find stained-glass windows, quilts, sleigh beds, balconies, and a sun porch.

Heritage Park B & B 2470 Heritage Park Row, 92110-2803; 619-295-7088 (M/E). In 1890, *The Golden Era* magazine called Harfield and Myrtle Christian's Queen Anne, built in 1889, "an outstandingly beautiful home of Southern California." Today, its tower, veranda, bay windows, alcoves, and many chimneys shelter an antiques-crammed bed-and-breakfast painted white with brick and black trim. Each of the nine rooms, five with bath, has its own theme. The Turret Room has a queen-sized Victorian Renaissance bed and a tower sitting room overlooking the city, perfect for made-to-order romantic dinners. Vintage film classics are shown, with refreshments each evening, and breakfast is served in bed or on the veranda. (DPL)

Horton Grand Hotel 311 Island Ave., 92101; 619-544-1886/800-999-1886 (M/E). Threatened with demolition, San Diego's two oldest hotels, the 1886 Horton Grand and Wyatt Earp's home, the Kahle Saddlery, have been taken apart brick by brick and then rebuilt and connected by a glass atrium. Decked in lacy ironwork and painted in two pinks, cream, rose, turquoise, and gray-blue, the new Horton

Heritage Park, San Diego

Grand was reopened on its hundredth anniversary. Each of the 134 rooms and suites has a gas fireplace, fine furniture, overstuffed pillows, bath, hidden TVs, and a diary or memory book written in by past visitors. Some of the rooms are light and furnished in wicker. Some of the suites are dark and handsome, with kitchen facilities and private balconies. But they all have something special. Room 309 even has the ghost of a gambler named Roger, who was shot while hiding inside an armoire in a nearby hotel room.

A garden courtyard, meeting rooms, and private dining rooms are available. High tea is served every afternoon in the saloon.

Ida Bailey's Restaurant and Palace Bar (619-544-1886) downstairs is named after the "Queen of the Stingaree," a madam and hostess par excellence whose establishment once stood on the exact spot of the Horton Grand. The gentlemen's bar, with its wood-paneled walls and oversized Rubenesque paintings, is a genteel hideaway. The restaurant has a turn-of-the-century ambience and occasionally serves Victorian-era dishes along with California cuisine.

Hotel del Coronado 1500 Orange Ave.,

Villa Montezuma, San Diego

Britt House, San Diego

a national historic landmark. Convention Center.

The Crown Room's (619-435-6611) sugar-pine paneling and thirty-three-foot ceilings surrounded by views of the sea and gardens make dining in this huge room a pleasure. The bountiful Sunday buffets are a tradition.

Places to Visit

Heritage Park Juan and Harney Sts., adjacent to Old Town, 92110; 619-565-3600. Heritage Park is a 7.8-acre historical preserve dedicated to the preservation of San Diego's Victorian heritage. The six Victorian buildings have been rescued and moved to a hillside overlooking Old Town. County-owned, they are leased to private or commercial organizations that are responsible for interior renovation in keeping with the Park's Victorian theme. Heritage Park is not only an architectural museum, but also a

Britt House, San Diego

Coronado, 92118. Rooms: 619-522-8000 or 800-HOTELDEL. Sales: 619-522-8011 (E). Since its opening on February 19, 1888, the legendary "Del" has been visited by twelve American presidents, thousands of celebrities, and royalty, including Edward, the Prince of Wales. He later married a Coronado housewife, Wallis Warfield Spencer Simpson. Thomas Edison is said to have personally supervised the installation of the electric lights. And Marilyn Monroe stayed here for the filming of *Some Like It Hot.*

The four hundred guestrooms in the main building are furnished in a constantly refreshed Victorian style. The three hundred in the new complex are modern but are closer to the beach. Aim for the Victorian part of the hotel on the ocean side, with a balcony. Guests revel in the tennis courts, spas, swimming pools, sandy beaches, bikes, and shops. The Hotel del Coronado is

functioning center of commercial and social activity.

- Temple Beth Israel, the second oldest synagogue in the West, an 1889 Classic Revival structure and painted in ethereal French gray and sky blue inside, is now a community center.
- The nineteenth-century Vernacular Senlis Cottage, 1896, is now headquarters for SOHO, Save Our Historic Homes, offering information on historic preservation and a resource library.
- The Sherman-Gilbert House, built by architects Comstock and Trotsche for John Sherman in 1888, a towered eclectic Victorian painted tan with brick, white, and green details, now houses a doll shop.
- The light and dark rose-beige with white Stick Bushyhead House, built in 1887 as a boardinghouse for newspaperman Edward W. Bushyhead, is home for several stores, including "The Wedding Casa," which plans and produces weddings and offers pre-wedding workshops.
- Offices and a travel agency maintain the Burton House, a Classic Revival 1893 Victorian.
- The 1889 Queen Anne Christian Mansion is the Heritage Park Bed & Breakfast Inn (see below).

Villa Montezuma The Jesse Shepard House, 1925 K St.; 619-239-2211. Tours Wednesday through Sunday, 1 to 4:30 P.M., and by appointment. Fee. In 1887, the citizens of San Diego built Villa Montezuma for then famous author-musician Jesse Shepard in an effort to bring culture to the town. In 1889, the *San Diego Sun* described it as "the most ornately finished and artistically furnished house in the city...itself a museum." By that time, a national crash had sent Shepard to Europe, and the town had to take over this richly designed towered Moorish–Queen Anne, eventually turning it into a cultural center that failed. Today, Villa Montezuma has been rescued by the San Diego Histori-

cal Society and is one of the most beautiful house museums in the state. A fire in 1986 set back restoration, but now the house is remarkably alive, and rooms are being restored to their original design with the help of photographs taken during Shepard's stay.

Large blowups of the original black-and-white photos on easels show the "before" so you can appreciate the "after." The interior with original and period furnishings, glorious woodwork, and made-to-order stained-glass windows is a marvel. The eighteen-foot bay window in the drawing room, with portraits of Shakespeare, Goethe, and Corneille in art glass created for Shepard in San Francisco, is an eyeful.

Each of the five fireplaces is different, with elaborate overmantels and handmade tiles in the surrounds. In the music room, the largest room in the house, stained-glass windows depict Sappho, Beethoven, Mozart, Rubens, Raphael, and allegorical representations of the Orient and the Occident. The handsome face of the Oriental knight is Shepard's.

Shepard's life is as romantic as his novels. His fiancée, a Russian princess, died just before the wedding. He himself died in 1927 at the piano. He had just played the last piece at a benefit evening given on his behalf.

The kitchen in the basement has been restored as an ample Victorian kitchen, right down to the filled spice rack. The society holds educational programs for young and old here, and offers the space for meetings. The gift shop is imaginatively stocked. Like most wooden structures, the house does have to be painted every ten years or so. We look forward to the day when Villa Montezuma will be painted in the gold and burgundy symphony chosen by Jesse Shepard.

Tours

Cinderella Carriage Co. 619-239-8080. Horse-drawn tours around San Diego.

Gaslamp Foundation 410 Island Ave.,

92101; 619-233-5227. Walking tours of the restored downtown historical district. Two-hour walking tours Saturday at 11 A.M.

Molly the Trolley Express 619-233-9177. Colorful red and green "trackless" trolleys take you to San Diego's most popular destinations in style. Enjoy a two-hour narrated tour or hop off on any stop, walk around, and reboard at leisure. Day pass.

Old Town Trolley Tours of San Diego 619-298-8687. Relive San Diego's history for an hour or two.

NATIONAL CITY

Dickinson Boal Mansion 1433 E. 24th, 91950; 619-477-5363 (M). This noble 1887 Queen Anne bed-and-breakfast is a city landmark. According to owner Jim Ladd, who is also a National City planning commissioner, "Our city does have a beautiful cross section of Victorian homes, and fortunately many people are restoring them to their original luster." The comfortable rooms, with bath, are decorated with period touches.

JULIAN

Julian Hotel 2032 Main, P.O. Box 806, 92036; 619-765-0201 (M/E). Freed slave Albert Robinson built a gabled Stick farmhouse in 1897 with a loan from his former master, a Civil War major. At first, people came for his wife's hot apple pie made with Julian apples. Today's guests in the eighteen rooms, five with bath, enjoy apple-filled pancakes at breakfast or hot cider at tea time.

At one point, the place was known for its two bathtubs, shipped around Cape Horn, and rented to miners before they enjoyed the Southern cooking. Then society came to the "Queen of the Back Country." The U.S. Grant Suite, Scripps Room, and the Governor's Suite still reflect the dreams and traditions of genteel hospitality in an earlier era.

Many of the American antiques are

original to this Gold Rush hotel in the Laguna Mountains, now painted cream with burgundy-red trim and black sashes. The Julian is listed on the National Register, and is a California State Historic Point of Interest.

A walking tour of Julian town site starts at the Julian Hotel and includes rustic Victorian buildings, town mining history, and a museum.

Craftsmen, Groups, and Newspapers

Antique Collectibles 1000 Pioneer Way, P.O. Box 1565, El Cajon, 92022; 619-593-2925. Sandy Pasquam, managing editor. Events and store guide.

Antique Music Box Restoration 1825 Placentia Ave., Costa Mesa, 92627; 714-548-1542. Christian and Kathleen Eric are music-box historians, restorers of all types of antique musical boxes, and contributing editors to the "Music Box Society International."

Architectural Originals P.O. Box 8033, Newport Beach, 92658; 714-551-4325. Limited-edition miniatures, calendars, and gifts for lovers of historic architecture and Victorian design. From mailboxes and birdhouses to heirloom quality wicker, collectibles, fine prints, and calendars. There are posters, pins, porcelains, books, cards, and drawings by Michael Ward and other artists. Catalog.

ASL Associates 18004 Sky Park Circle, #250, Irvine, 92714; 714-251-8852. Architectural plans for making your own gazebo.

The Association of American Historic Inns P.O. Box 336, Dana Point, 92629; 714-496-6953. Tim and Deborah Sakach publish *The Official Guide to American Historic Inns.*

Barbara Bastrup Studios 813 E. 21st St. Santa Ana, 92706; 714-542-5031. Hand-painted prints, in prismacolor and watercolor, matted in any color. Original renderings of Victorian homes, by commission. Limited and unlimited editions of

Horton Grand Hotel, San Diego

color-your-own houses, bookmarks, Christmas cards, and gift tags. Catalog.

Brad and Tony Restoration Painting 619-437-1254. Bradley Brisk and Tony Alvarez. Exterior and interior restoration painting, woodworking, staining, varnishing.

Burdoch Victorian Lamp Co. 1145 Industrial Ave., Suite E, Escondido, 92025; 619-745-3275. Reproduction lampshades, hand-sewn in brocade or embroidered designs. Also reproduction floor, table, and vanity bases.

Paul G. Chase & Associates 1823 Kenora Drive, Escondido, 92027; 619-743-8609. Paul G. Chase. Historic site assessments.

Classic Ceilings 902 E. Commonwealth, Fullerton, 92631; 800-992-8700. David and Donna Morgan. "The quality of yester-year." Embossed English wall coverings

such as Lincrusta and Anaglypta, traditional classic friezes, Nomastyl and Arstyl flexible architectural moldings, ceiling medallions. Cornice work. W. F. Norman sheet metal Hi-Art steel and tin ceilings from original molds in antique copper, pewter, brass, painted, and original tin finish. Catalogs.

Decades 619-563-5686. Garry Mollenkopf. Antique furniture and interior wood restoration.

Walt Diebold 619-448-5830. Furniture maker. Manufactures and installs custom cabinetry. Door and window design and manufacturing.

Jerry Erewett 619-691-9771. Electrician.

Robert D. Ferris, Architect, Inc. 3776 Front St., San Diego, 92103; 619-297-4659. Architectural design services for interior and exterior restoration and rehabilitation of all types of buildings. Adaptive reuse studies and planning.

Frank's Cane & Rush Supply 7252 Heil Ave., Huntington Beach, 92647; 714-847-0707. Caning and upholstery supplies, tools, and instruction books. Brass hardware and wood parts. Chair caning, seat weaving, and wicker repair.

Jim Gibson 180 Mace St., C-9, Chula Vista, 91911-5878; 619-422-2447. Jim Gibson. Restoration design/project management. Includes color selection and decorative finishes.

Gibson & Gibson Antique Lighting 180 Mace St., C-9, Chula Vista, 91911-5878; 619-422-2447. Antique ceiling and wall sconces (1880–1930), glass shades, fixture repair, polishing, reproduction of period fixtures, copper, brass, nickel, silver, gold plating and lacquering.

Robert Goe 619-445-4111. Carpentry, wood carving, façade design and installation. Furniture maker.

Great Gardens 7520 Eucalyptus Hill, La Mesa, 91941; 619-697-7151. Eunice Ventura. Design and installation of flower gardens

Hotel del Coronado, San Diego

and landscaping with a focus on drought-tolerant plants. English perennial flower garden.

Dan Gregory 619-447-7596. Stenciling, mural restoration, decorative painting.

James Houghton 619-462-7334. Plumbing for historical projects.

International Wood Products 10883 Thornmint Rd., San Diego, 92127; 800-468-3667. Decorative hardwood doors, sidelights, transoms, and trims, using oak and mahogany with distinctive finishes. Entry components available either finished or unfinished.

Rurik Kallis 619-460-8048. Restoration and fine carpentry. Architectural antiques.

Liz's Antique Hardware 704 J St., San Diego, 92116; 619-284-1075. Liz Gordon. An extensive collection of antique hardware.

Nevers-Oak Fireplace Mantels & Gallery 933 Rancheros Dr., Suite B, San Marcos, 92069; 619-745-8841. Designing and handcrafting fireplace mantels of all kinds. Catalog.

Paper Magic 619-281-6979. Gail Knoll installs and repairs wallpaper, and can supply period papers such as Bradbury & Bradbury wallpapers.

Promar Sales–Tiffany Lamps & Glass P.O. Box 6554, Huntington Beach, 92615; 714-963-2474. Handmade reproduction Tiffany-style lampshades using genuine stained and cut glass. Custom stained-glass panels. Etched, sandblasted and beveled-glass work. Literature.

Raiments P.O. Box 6176, Fullerton, 92634-6176. Historical clothing patterns from nineteen different companies, corset supplies and kits, hoopskirts, bustles, hatmaking patterns and supplies. Catalog.

Greg Richard 619-691-9116. Master wood refinishers, painting, graining, staining, interior wood stripping and refinishing.

Rumpelstiltskin Designs 1714 Rees Rd., San Marcos, 92069; 619-743-5541. Hand-beaded fringe designed and sold. Antique metallic guimpe and rayon thick fringe.

San Diego Historical Society–Ticor Collection 1649 El Prado, P.O. Box 81825, 92138.

S.G. Plastering 14475 Old Hwy. 80, El Cajon 92021; 619-390-7023. Steve Grassa.

Harry Simpson Studios 7657 North Ave., Lemon Grove, 92045; 619-461-2464. Design and manufacture of ceramic tiles. Can match and re-create any style of ceramic tile from any period.

SOHO: Save Our Heritage Organization P.O. Box 3571, 92103; 619-297-9327. SOHO is committed to preserving whatever is historically and culturally significant in the community. Meetings. Newsletter.

Stefano 619-390-7023. Plaster and stucco restoration.

Tower Mortgage Historical Restoration Division 5241 Lincoln Ave., Suite C-4, Cypress, 90630; 213-435-0326. Gary Prince.

Heather Trimlett Studios 8678 La Mesa Blvd., La Mesa, 92041; 619-460-7855. Custom stained glass. Etched/sandblasted glass. Period designs.

BIBLIOGRAPHY

PERIODICALS

Antique Collectibles, 1000 Pioneer Way, P.O. Box 1565, El Cajon, Cal. 92002, 619-593-2925.

Art, Antiques & Collectibles, P.O. Box 5856, Santa Rosa, Cal. 95402, 800-648-0526.

Journal of San Diego History. "The Villa Montezuma," Special Centennial Issue, Thomas I. Scharf, editor, San Diego, Cal., 1987.

West Coast Peddler, P.O. Box 5134, Whittier, Cal. 90607, 213-698-1718. Listings of antiques sales, fairs, and stores.

BOOKS

AAA Bed & Breakfast Inns of North & Central California. California State Automobile Association, San Francisco, Cal., 1990.

American Heritage Guide to America's Greatest Historic Places. The editors of *American Heritage* magazine, American Heritage Press, New York, N.Y., 1985.

Annual Northern California Guide to Art & Antiques & Collectibles. Art, Antiques and Collectibles Guide, 40 4th St., Petaluma, Cal., 94952, 1990.

Bare, Colleen, and Bare, Stanley, *The McHenry Mansion: Modesto's Heritage.* McHenry Foundation Press, Modesto, Cal., 1985.

Bay Area Historic House Museums. BAHHM, Hayward, Cal. 1990.

Beal, Laurence. *The Carson Mansion*, Times Printing Co., Eureka, Cal. 1973.

Britain, Kilbee. *General Phineas Banning Residence Museum*, Friends of Banning Park Publishers, Wilmington, Cal., 1984.

Brown, Clare, Brown, June, and Brown, Karen. *Karen Brown's California Country Inns & Itineraries*, Travel Press, San Mateo, Cal., 1989.

The Complete Gold Country Guide Book. Indian Chief Publishing, Tahoe City, Cal., 1989.

Directory 77. Foundation for San Francisco's Architectural Heritage, San Francisco, Cal., 1977.

Edeline, Denis P. *Ferndale: The Village, 1875–1893*, Eureka Printing Co., Eureka, Cal., 1987.

Faubion, William, and Baker, Tom. *Best Choices in Northern California, Bay Area Edition*, Gable & Gray, Medford, Ore., 1987.

Gebhard, David, Sanweiss, Eric, and Winter, Robert. *The Guide to Architecture in San Francisco and Northern California*, revised ed., Peregrine Books, Salt Lake City, Utah, 1985.

Gebhard, David, Von Breton, Harriette, and Winter, Robert. *Samuel & Joseph Cather Newsom: Victorian Imagery in California, 1878–1908*, Schauer Printing, Santa Barbara, Cal., 1979.

Grow, Lawrence, and Von Zweck, Dina. *American Victorian: A Style & Source Book*, The Main Street Press, Harper & Row, New York, N.Y., 1985.

Historic Environment Consultants for the Vallejo City Council. *Vallejo's Architectural Heritage*, prepared by Vallejo Architectural Heritage and Landmarks Commission, City of Vallejo, Cal.

Hoover, Mildred Brooke, Rensch, Hero Eugene, and Rensch, Ethel Grace. Third edition by William N. Abeloe. *Historic Spots in California*, Stanford University Press, Stanford, Cal., 1966.

Idle, Stephen DeLacey, and Brady, Scott C. *Idle Designs: Victorian Coloring Book*, vol. I, Alameda, Cal., 1987.

Jackson, Hal, with Loring, Ted, Jr. *Eureka: A Guide to the Architecture & Landscape*, Eureka Printing Co., Eureka, Cal., 1983.

Junior League of San Francisco, Inc. *Here Today: San Francisco's Architectural Heritage*, Chronicle Books, San Francisco, Cal., 1968.

Kegan, Stephanie. *Places to Go with Children in Southern California*, Chronicle Books, San Francisco, Cal., 1989.

Killeen, Jacqueline. *Country Inns of the Far West*, 101 Productions, San Francisco, Cal., 1987.

Kirker, Harold. *California's Architectural Frontier Style and Traditions in the 19th Century*, Peregrine Books, Salt Lake City, Utah, 1986.

Knight, Diane. *Bed & Breakfast Homes Directory*, KnightTime Publications, Freedom, Cal., 1990.

Martin, Terrence O. *Santa Catalina: An Island Adventure*, KC Publications, Inc., Las Vegas, Nev., 1983.

Orlando, Joanne M., editor. *The Old-House Journal Catalog*, Old-House Journal Corp., Brooklyn, N.Y., 1990.

Paul, Ken, and Gautraud, Alexandra. *San Mateo! A Sketchbook Tour of the San Francisco Peninsula's Past*, Castle Rock Press, Palo Alto, Cal., 1989.

Pictorial Album of Historic Angelino Heights. Carroll Avenue Restoration Foundation, photos by Bruce Boehmner, Los Angeles, Cal., 1987.

Pomada, Elizabeth. *Places to Go with Children in Northern California*, Chronicle Books, San Francisco, Cal., 1989.

Prentice, Helene Kaplan, and Prentice, Blair. *Rehab Right: How to Realize the Full Value of Your Old House*, Ten Speed Press, Berkeley, Cal., 1986.

Reece, Daphne. *Historic Houses of California*, Chronicle Books, San Francisco, Cal., 1983.

River City Renovator's Guide, KnightTime Press, San Francisco, Cal., 1983.

Roberts, George, and Roberts, Jan. *Discover Historic California*, New Fortress Publications, Whittier, Cal., 1986.

Rundback, Betty, and Ackerman, Nancy. *Bed & Breakfast USA: A Guide to Tourist Homes & Guest Houses*, E. P. Dutton, New York, N.Y., 1982.

Sakach, Tim, and Sakach, Deborah. *American Historic Inns: The Official Guide*, third ed., Association of American Historic Inns, Dana Point, Cal., 1990.

Sexton, Richard. *The Cottage Book*, Chronicle Books, San Francisco, Cal., 1989.

Snider, Sandra Lee. *Elias Jackson "Lucky" Baldwin: California Visionary*, The Stairwell Group, Los Angeles, Cal., 1987.

Suetterlund, Donna. *All about Ferndale Today*, Carriage House Studio Publications, Ferndale, Cal., 1989.

Van Kirk, Susie. *Touring Arcata's Architecture*, White City Publications, Arcata, Cal., 1988.

Von Normann, Bob. *Victorian Eureka and Ferndale: The Elegant Ladies of the North Coast*, FVN, Inc., Redcrest, Cal., 1986.

Waldhorn, Judith Lynch, and Woodbridge, Sally Byrne. *Victoria's Legacy*, 101 Productions, San Francisco, Cal., 1978.

Woodbridge, Sally. *California Architecture: Historic Building Survey*, Chronicle Books, San Francisco, Cal., 1988.

Worth, Cortia, Berger, Terry, and Robert R. Reid, *Bed & Breakfast Guide, West Coast*. Prentice Hall Press, New York, N.Y., 1984.

Worthen, Evelyn Shuster. *A Castle in Fairy Land & Other Stories of the Carson Family and Their Mansions*, Eureka Printing Co., Eureka, Cal., 1984.

INDEX

RESOURCE INDEX
Architectural Planning & Preservation Services